COLOMBIA
WHAT EVERYONE NEEDS TO KNOW®

COLOMBIA
WHAT EVERYONE NEEDS TO KNOW®

RICHARD D. MAHONEY

OXFORD
UNIVERSITY PRESS

OXFORD
UNIVERSITY PRESS

Oxford University Press is a department of the University of Oxford. It furthers the University's objective of excellence in research, scholarship, and education by publishing worldwide. Oxford is a registered trade mark of Oxford University Press in the UK and certain other countries.

"What Everyone Needs to Know" is a registered trademark of Oxford University Press.

Published in the United States of America by Oxford University Press 198 Madison Avenue, New York, NY 10016, United States of America.

Library of Congress Cataloging-in-Publication Data
Names: Mahoney, Richard D., author.
Title: Colombia : what everyone needs to know / Richard D. Mahoney.
Description: New York : Oxford University Press, [2020] |
Series: What everyone needs to know |
Includes bibliographical references and index. |
Identifiers: LCCN 2019044925 (print) | LCCN 2019044926 (ebook) |
ISBN 9780190262754 (hardback) | ISBN 9780190262747 (paperback) |
ISBN 9780190262778 (epub)
Subjects: LCSH: Colombia—History. |
Colombia—Politics and government. | Colombia—Civilization.
Classification: LCC F2271 .M28 2020 (print) |
LCC F2271 (ebook) | DDC 986.1—dc23
LC record available at https://lccn.loc.gov/2019044925
LC ebook record available at https://lccn.loc.gov/2019044926

1 3 5 7 9 8 6 4 2

Paperback printed by LSC Communications, United States of America
Hardback printed by Bridgeport National Bindery, Inc., United States of America

For Darlenys Mahoney
amor de mi vida

The strong do what they have the power to do and the weak accept what they have to accept.

—Thucydides

The crux of our solitude . . . nourishes a sense of insatiable creativity, full of sorrow and beauty. . . . Poets, beggars, musicians and prophets, warriors and scoundrels, all creatures of that unbridled reality, we have had to ask but little of imagination, for our crucial problem has been a lack of conventional means to render our lives believable.

—Gabriel García Márquez

CONTENTS

3 The Liberal Revolution and the Conservative "Regeneration"   **34**

4 Conservative Peace and the Liberal Republic   **51**

A NOTE TO THE READER

Colombia is perhaps the most confounding country in the Americas. Its democratic tradition remains among the most long-standing in the hemisphere, with only 11 years of military rule marring its 200-some years of independence. Possessing Latin America's third-largest population (behind Brazil and Mexico) and fourth-largest economy (behind Brazil, Mexico, and Argentina), Colombia has achieved stellar rates of export growth since the end of World War II. It has also suffered from one of the worst levels of income distribution in the Americas, however. The richest 10 percent of Colombians earn 53 times as much as the poorest 10 percent. On paper, the country has one of the most progressive constitutions on the planet (with no fewer than 99 specifically enumerated human, social, and environmental rights). Since the enactment of that constitution in 1991, however, more than 11 million Colombians have either left the country or become internally displaced—the result of what the late Colombian Nobel laureate Gabriel García Márquez termed a "biblical holocaust" of human savagery, one in which 420,000 people have lost their lives over the past 70 years.

Today, the country seems to be bouncing back, building peace among its warring factions and investing at record levels in the health care, education, and security of its citizens whose "overall life satisfaction" level, according to the 2016

United Nations Development Report, is equal to that of French citizens. How did that happen? Given Colombia's history of savage capitalism, of serving as the supplier to the world's successive addictions to gold, rubber, coffee, and cocaine, can its present well-being possibly last? After all, the United States, the country's imperial patron and leading drug buyer, seems as dedicated as ever to fighting the so-called drug war.

In the portrait that follows, I have drawn from authoritative published accounts and delved into thousands of archival documents on everything from slave manumission and the rise of women to the complex contours of the U.S.-Colombian relationship. I have also done extensive interviews with Colombian and American diplomats, journalists, military commanders, intelligence officials, and human rights leaders as well as the occasional politician and paramilitary commander. For their generous assistance I thank María McFarland Sánchez-Moreno, Robert A. Karl, Camilo Ramírez, Malcolm Deas, Carlo Nasi, Arlene B. Tickner, Michael Shifter, Jon Stivers, Lisa Haugaard, Jonathan D. Rosen, Angelika Rettberg, Jonathan Hartlyn, Mary Roldán, Richard Green, P. Michael McKinley, Robert S. Gelbard, Daniel P. Bolger, Gene Fisher, José Antonio Ocampo, Richard P. Rust, Caroline Hartzell, and Miguel M. Benito L.

This book relies on magisterial works, the most important of which are David Bushnell, *Colombia: A Nation in Spite of Itself*; Jaime E. Rodríguez O., *La independencia de la América Española*; Frank Safford and Marco Palacios, *Colombia: Fragmented Land, Divided Society*; Herbert Tico Braun, *The Assassination of Gaitán: Public Life and Urban Violence in Colombia*; Gonzalo Sánchez G., *Colombia: violencia y democracia*; Charles Bergquist, Ricardo Peñaranda, and Gonzalo Sánchez G. (eds.), *Violence in Colombia, 1990–2000: Waging War and Negotiating Peace*; Nazih Richani, *Systems of Violence: The Political Economy of War and Peace in Colombia*; Robin Kirk, *More Terrible Than Death: Drugs, Violence, and America's War in Colombia*; and, finally, the 2016 compendium edited by Bruce M. Bagley and

Jonathan D. Rosen, *Colombia's Political Economy at the Outset of the Twenty-First Century: From Uribe to Santos and Beyond.* I am grateful to six of the foregoing, foundational scholars for either having critically read parts of this manuscript or responded to my research questions. In the case of University of Virginia professor Tico Braun, he somehow took an extra lap on my behalf, sending me lucid responses to my inquiries and then providing faceted, and often profound, interpretations of Colombian history.

A succession of gifted students here at NC State's School of Public and International Affairs—Daniel M. Farfán E., Candice Bodkin, Timothy Eggert, Alex Brown, Madison Hissom, and, most of all, Melanie Riester—provided steady assistance in my research labors. Adam Isacson, associated with the Washington Office on Latin America and sans *pareil* among American Colombianists, was especially generous in sharing his insights and critically reviewing part of the narrative.

Readers will want to thank my sisters, Eileen Mahoney and Noel Shambayati, who put their exacting editorial gifts to work in making the first draft both grammatical and comprehensible. Without the patient aplomb of my good friend Tim Bent, executive editor at Oxford University Press, and a final assist by assistant editor at OUP, Mariah White, this book would not have come about.

I first went to Colombia in March 1998 to work in a shelter for displaced children in Ciudad Bolívar, a slum in the southwestern section of Bogotá. Who could have guessed that my grueling sojourn there would lead to both a happy marriage and this hard-won book? But it did.

INTRODUCTION

In no more than 20 years during the first part of the 16th century, a few hundred Spanish *conquistadores* crushed three Indian empires, ultimately delivering 25 million new subjects from the New World to the Spanish king, along with a realm stretching from Cape Horn to Alaska.[1] What consummated Spain's conquest of the New World were not the *conquistadores* themselves, however—even with their guns, armored horses, and man-killing dogs—but the missionaries who ventured after them into the deepest reaches of the mountains, deserts, and jungles of the *imperio español* in search of human souls. It was this fusion of sword and cross that produced Spain's unique "ideology of domination."[2]

The new Spanish imperium, in the view of American historian Samuel Eliot Morrison, more closely resembled the Roman Empire than the British one.[3] If English imperial policy was "lackadaisical," as Morrison put it, allowing the colonists to fend for themselves and adapt English institutions to the New World, the Spanish centralized and monopolized every feature of their New World kingdoms. They meticulously authorized appointments and budgets, drafted more than 400,000 laws in the first 90 years of the imperium, regulated every vestige of trade by the *Casa de la Contratación*, and committed convoyed fleets of galleons to transport the purpose of it all—gold and silver to enrich the crown. But from the start, Spain's monolith of absolutist governance was hollow, "tempered, by a great deal of informal bargaining, compromising and outright corruption in everyday life."[4] So distant were Spain's possessions, so divergent in their conditions, and so underfunded in their administrations that the New World Spaniards practiced a rote fealty that disguised an embedded resistance: *"Obedezco pero no cumplo"* (I obey but do not comply).[5]

If anything, the geography of Colombia (initially named *Nuevo Reino de Granada*, or the New Kingdom of Granada) only redoubled this resistance. One-third of that imperial territory was defined by the three *cordilleras* of the Andes. Running roughly from north to south (with its easternmost branch bending toward Venezuela), these ranges produced a scattered mosaic of landscapes—snow-capped peaks, chilly intermontane basins, fog-choked valleys, forest-clad slopes where tropical showers fed torrential rivers, and sweltering lowlands deep in the river basins—that kept transportation, trade, communication, and the reach of law and order to a minimum. The other two-thirds of the territory was called *tierra caliente* (hot land), a vast and unpopulated expanse of lowlands that were either parched or flooded depending on the season. Geography became destiny.

Colombia's human terrain was soon a shattered mosaic as well, a testament to the consequences of three centuries of racial and sexual predation in the view of South American liberator Simón Bolívar:

> We are the vile offspring of the predatory Spaniards who came to America to bleed her white and then breed with their victims. Later the illegitimate offspring of these unions joined with the offspring of slaves transported from Africa. With such a racial mixture and such a moral record, can we afford to place laws above leaders and principles over men?

When Napoleon seized Spain in 1808 and locked up its Bourbon king, Spanish America stumbled toward an independence of which it had hardly even conceived, much less prepared for. After more than a decade of fratricidal warfare, the unparalleled tenacity of Bolívar, in league with other key revolutionists, finally won out. Bolívar's vision of independence was to create a republican superstate, uniting the territory of modern-day Colombia with that of Venezuela, Ecuador, and Panamá. Colombia's first constitution was a monument to the ideals of the Enlightenment—abolishing the Inquisition and many monasteries, earmarking the sale of Roman Catholic Church property for public schools, legislating free trade, giving Indians citizenship, and providing slaves the right to free birth.

But it didn't turn out as Bolívar envisioned. To understand Colombia, we must ascertain how its founding myth fell apart at the start—and why the country remains, for all of its creative dynamism, the troubled stepchild of two brutal and bungling empires.

PART I

ORIGINS, 1536–1948

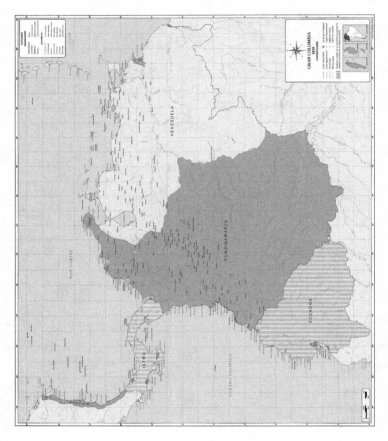

Map 1 In 1819 the newly independent state of "Gran Colombia" included the territory of Venezuela, Ecuador, and Panamá as well as modern-day Colombia.

1

CONQUEST AND COLONY

How did Spain conquer the New Kingdom of Granada?

In the wake of Christopher Columbus's discovery of the New World in 1492, Spanish explorers began traveling to the Caribbean coast of modern-day Colombia, looking for gold and slaves while continuing their quest to discover a route to the "South Sea," to India. Finding their encampments along the Colombian coast (near present-day Santa Marta and Cartagena) barely sustainable and the natives increasingly resistant, the Spanish ventured westward, eventually establishing a settlement in Darién (near the modern-day border of Colombia and Panamá). This would be the launching point for explorer Vasco Nuñez de Balboa's crossing of the isthmus to discover the Pacific Ocean in 1513. Although Balboa was put to death by Spanish rivals two years later, his compatriot, Francisco Pizarro, ventured on to Peru, where he led the conquest of the Incan Empire.[1] It was one of Pizarro's lieutenants, Sebastián de Belalcázar, who, after conquering modern-day Quito, Ecuador, launched an expedition northward into what is now Colombia.

Not long after the news of Pizarro's astounding success in Peru—in which he had lured the Incan emperor Atahualpa to a feast in his honor before seizing and ransoming him for two storerooms full of silver and gold and later killing him—Santa Marta's new governor, Pedro Fernández de Lugo, began organizing his own expeditionary force to explore the hinterland from the Caribbean. He may have done so, in part, because the Spanish takeover of Peru had caused a gold rush from Santa Marta, leaving it largely depopulated.[2] The would-be adventurers—most of whom were probably in debt as a result of outfitting themselves for plunder—had no ambition to colonize or settle in any case. They wanted *botín* (booty).[3] Sickness and food shortages in the Spanish encampment may have also impelled them forward.[4] To lead the expedition of 600 soldiers (with another 200 to serve on the ships that would provision the expedition), the governor chose Gonzalo Jiménez de Quesada, a 27-year-old lawyer from Granada. In April 1536, Jiménez de Quesada's force began threading its way through the swamps and mangrove forests toward the mouth of the river Magdalena.

The expedition was a disaster from the start. Two of the seven ships that were to sail up the Magdalena sank in a storm that blew the other five vessels farther down the coast. When their food supplies ran out, the men ate rats, lizards, bats, and their own leather to stay alive. "A great many soldiers walked barefoot," one survivor remembered, (with) "blood spilling from open wounds on their feet and many died from hunger. . . . Others were simply left behind (to die) along the way."[5] Six months into the expedition, having lost more than two-thirds of its men, the ragged force came upon a store of mined salt blocks near La Tora, indicating the possibility that a developed civilization lay somewhere ahead. Following an indigenous trade route up one of Magdalena's tributary rivers, the Opón, the Spanish expeditionaries, now only 179 strong, ultimately scaled the eastern *cordillera* of the Andes and came upon a verdant intermountain valley populated by the Muiscas, then numbering some 600,000.

The Muiscas were cultivators of corn and potatoes who wove cotton and traded for gold. They lived in scattered villages within two rival confederations, making them vulnerable to Spanish designs. Eyewitness accounts from the expedition would reveal that the Muiscas, though initially frightened by the Spaniards, soon turned hostile. But their wooden swords and lances proved no match for the guns, attack mastiffs, and horse charges of the Spaniards.[6] Still, Jiménez de Quesada, a veteran of Spain's war in northern Italy, carefully avoided any full-scale conflict with the Muiscas and kept his men under tight control. When one of them was reported to have stolen cloth from an Indian, the *conquistador* had him hanged.

Stealing gold, of course, was another matter. In the course of looting Muisca shrines and palaces, the Spaniards found finely hammered gold hanging from the eaves in billowing sheets that made "a delicious tinkling" as they rustled in the breeze.[7] But it was the rival Muisca chieftains, the Zipa (also called Bogotá) and the Zacque, whom the *conquistadores* thought held the keys to even greater troves of gold and emeralds. After killing the Zipa and searching in vain for his rumored treasure, the Spanish conquerors decided to align themselves with his successor, Sajipa, in his war against the Panches, a tribe living in the southwestern part of the country. The Spanish price in this brief alliance was all of Sajipa's gold and silver. When the new "Bogotá" declined to disclose its location, he was tortured, ultimately dying before he was forced to reveal the whereabouts of his gold.[8]

Despite its disastrous start, the expedition's three years of pillage among the Muiscas were an astounding success. The Spanish were able to stockpile 191,294 pesos of fine gold and 37,288 pesos of low-grade gold, along with 1,815 emeralds. Jiménez de Quesada's remaining troupe had also subdued one of South America's larger tribes with the loss of only six soldiers in the course of their two years in the highlands.[9] Even the aspect of sexual *botin* was deemed productive: the 300 Indian women whom Jiménez de Quesada had captured and divided up among his men for their pleasure had babies who were baptized along with their mothers.[10] In 1538, the *conquistadores* founded a Spanish encampment that Jiménez de Quesada named Santafé (to which the name "Bogotá"—the

Zipa's word for their capital city—would later be added), christening the territory the *Nuevo Reino de Granada* in honor of the city where he had once distinguished himself as a lawyer to the royal court.[11]

How did the legend of "El Dorado" arise?

In the course of their occupation of the land of the Muiscas, the Spaniards had learned about the ceremony of *El Dorado* (the Golden Man) in which the new tribal leader, covered with pine pitch, would coat his body with gold dust before plunging into the icy waters of Lake Guatavita. His plunge was "followed by a rain of devotional treasure that sank into the muddy bottom."[12] Later, after finding and draining at least part of the lake, the *conquistadores* were able to recover hundreds of pieces of gold in the muddy shallows. This only fueled a legend that had long entranced the Spanish and other European explorers—that there were places filled with gold and jewels beyond human imagining. Thus, Gonzalo Pizarro would march into the deepest Amazon in search of a lost city, reportedly one controlled by towering women called "Amazons." Another Dorado visionary was *conquistador* Francisco Vázquez de Coronado, who traversed Mexico and half the United States in his 4,000-mile expedition to find the seven cities of Cíbola.

No one was more dazzled by El Dorado, or more determined to find it, than the iconic English courtier Sir Walter Raleigh, whose first voyage to present-day Venezuela netted little more than an over-the-top account of its success in *The Discovery of Guiana* (1596). Released from the Tower of London by King James I—in whose side he was a frequent thorn—in order to find El Dorado, Raleigh headed back to the New World in 1617 with 14 ships and some 1,000 men. This time he fared even worse, losing every ship to storms or mutiny and finding nothing remotely resembling a lost city of gold. Availing himself of the ready excuse that Raleigh had invaded the territory of "our dear brother the King of Spain," King James had him beheaded. At that point, the legend of *el Dorado* lost its luster.

What happened after the conquest?

Not all the Spanish confined themselves to the targeted use of terror against native populations as Jiménez de Quesada had. Others engaged in rampant butchery. One eyewitness to those depredations was a Dominican monk, Fray Bartolomé de las Casas, who contended that in the province of Nicaragua over a 14-year period, the Spanish massacred 500,000 to 600,000 people and sold another half million into slavery. In many instances, the genocide was macabre. One day, in the presence of de las Casas, the Spanish dismembered, beheaded, or raped 3,000 people. "Such inhumanities and barbarisms were committed in my sight," wrote the monk, "as no age can parallel." The Spanish cut off the legs of children who ran from them. They poured boiling soap down people's throats. They made bets as to who, with one sweep of his sword, could cut a person in half. They loosed dogs that "devoured an Indian like a hog, at first sight, in less than a moment." They used nursing infants for dog food."[13]

To pacify the Native Americans as well as put them to work, the Spanish imposed the *encomienda*, requiring the Indians to pay a tribute (in gold, goods, or labor) to their overlords. In 1570, for example, Santafé had 600 Spanish male settlers supported by some 40,000 tribute payers. In Tunja, 200 Spanish settlers were supported by more than 50,000 indigenous tributaries.[14] Despite widespread resistance and periodic uprisings by the three to four million Indians then living in Nueva Granada, the *encomienda* permitted the colonists to sustain themselves while paying their own tribute to the Spanish crown in gold.[15]

But within a generation of the conquest, a second human cataclysm took place—the near disappearance of indigenous tribes. The combination of forced labor and the spread of European diseases such as smallpox and measles killed off large numbers of the native population, while others simply fled Spanish control. By the end of the 17th century, 70 percent of the Native American population in the highlands had disappeared; along the Caribbean coast, the factor was an estimated 95 percent.[16] Related to this demographic collapse was a phenomenon that further diminished native numbers—*mestizaje*, or Euro-Indian procreation that produced a new *casta* (caste) of people of mixed race.

The plight of the Indians in Spanish America eventually became a matter of concern for the royal court in Madrid. In November 1542, de las Casas persuaded the Spanish king to prohibit the use of Indians as slaves and to abolish the *encomienda*. Given sharp resistance to the royal order in Spanish America, the "New Laws" were never very effective. But de las Casas and his detractors, of which there were many, in Nueva Granada and elsewhere could agree, if for diametrically different reasons, about one thing—that the importation of slaves from Africa was essential to the economic salvation of the New World.

How did the importation of African slaves affect Nueva Granada?

As grotesquely inhumane as it was, slavery kickstarted capitalism in Colombia.[17] With profits estimated at 700 percent *after* having paid for the transport of slaves (553,646 of whom officially landed in Nueva Granada between 1580 and 1789*), Cartagena became the focal point of construction and merchant capital in the colony. In 1591, the port city built a paved square dedicated to slave marketing, large enough to accommodate scores of inspectors, tax collectors, and judges in courts of litigation to regulate the trade.

---

*. The official number does not include extralegal human trafficking which was extensive, or slave-running after the institution of "free trade" in 1789.

Nueva Granada's archival records in the *Archivo histórico nacional* in Bogotá detail the administrative complexity of the slave trade.[18] Since most sales were financed as loans that bore interest, the merchants, mining *empresarios*, and plantation owners as well as small-time entrepreneurs who bought the slaves needed lawyers and notaries to prepare contracts and underwrite loans as well as to enforce them. Given the importance of health in the merchandising of men, women, and children, there were also medical personnel on hand to examine the slaves in terms of their *pieza de India*, roughly translated as their unit value.[19]

Slavery also galvanized a more informal kind of capitalism: smuggling. Increased naval traffic into Cartagena brought in not just slaves but contraband. Within the holds of those same ships, smuggled cargo, such as gold, food, and tropical products like dyewood, was routed back out of Cartagena to free ports in the Caribbean. The more the Spanish crown tried to clamp down on contraband, the more illegal shipments were diverted to the other Caribbean seaports of Santa Marta, Barranquilla, Barbacoas, and Riohacha.[20]

Cartagena's sudden wealth soon made it the target of naval raids, the most destructive of which was an attack by the English privateer Francis Drake in April 1586. After landing 2,000 sailors and grenadiers from his ships, Drake put the city to the torch to exact his ransom. To protect the port from future attacks by land or sea, the Spanish crown subsequently sent one of Europe's top fortification engineers, Bautista Antonelli, to design and build defensive walls 20 meters thick. Over the next 200 years, work continued on the massive project, with Don Antonio de Arévalo (1715–1800) finally completing the walls and redoing the San Felipe Barajas fort that still towers over the city. For Spain's Bourbon kings, whose arrival from France coincided with the launching of that final phase of construction, Cartagena's walled city became a jewel in their New World crown. For the thousands of slaves who gave their lives to cut, drag, set, and finish the gigantic blocks of stone, there would be no lasting testament, however—only a series of un-marked trenches on the eastern side of Fort Felipe where their remains were disposed.[21]

With the advent of African slave labor, gold output soared in the second half of the 16th century. In Nueva Granada's three great mining zones, El Chocó, Cauca, and Antioquia, where nearly all the mining was alluvial, slave *cuadrillas* (squads) worked the rivers and streams with pans, sluices, and an assortment of other separating devices. In terms of productivity and durability, each black slave, in the racist calculus of the day, was said to be worth between three and five Indians.[22] Still, research would later indicate that African slaves, especially those working in placer mining and coastal plantations, also died off quickly. Accordingly, constant replenishment via importation was the only way Spain saw to maintain productive output throughout the colony, at least until the end of the 18th century.[23]

Slave emancipation (called manumission) was consistently greater in Spanish and Portuguese America than in North America. Sexual unions between female slaves (who were generally separated from their male counterparts) and white or mestizo men, often their masters, were one conduit to freedom. Court records reveal that sexual predation sometimes occasioned the promise of liberty for the slave mother and her children, but the *oidores de casados* (judges who heard cases involving married or common-law relations) rarely enforced such promises and much less upheld Spanish law regarding the integrity of a mother's right to her children. When Puerto Rican slave María Balbina, properly citing that law, tried to prevent her owner (and father of her children) from selling her away and separating her from the children, she lost her appeal and was sold off.[24]

Another cause of emancipation was profit. Since the price of a so-called self-purchase by a slave (who had earned money on the side to finance his or her freedom) tended to be higher than a normal sale, especially if the slave was older or infirm, there was a financial return in emancipation. The Catholic Church probably added some moral momentum to manumission by formally designating it as an act of piety. *Libertos* (freed men or women) faced a mixed fate, however. Though technically free, they still could not enter many neighborhoods, wear certain kinds of clothing, or carry weapons. In gold-mining areas like the Chocó, they were generally shunned; some became *mazamorreros* (independent prospectors), moving from placer to placer, while others homesteaded deep in the bush.[25] In the cities, *libertos* often became artisans in textiles, carpentry, and smithing, or worked as street vendors.[26] On what seems rare occasions, "honorable Spanish men, by their own free will," according to one missionary in the 18th century, found "happiness and contentment" in their marriages to black women.[27]

Procreation between races, though officially prohibited, was so abundant in its variation that new racial classifications were required to define the *castas intermediarias* (intermediary castes). The offspring of a mulatto and a white was called a *tercerón* who, when crossed with another white, produced a *cuarterón*, and then a *quinterón*. If a mulatto reentered the parental mix, the child was called *tente en el aire* (up in the air) since he or she had neither advanced nor receded on the racial scale. If a child, for whatever reason, was darker than his mixed parent, he or she was denominated a *salta atrás* (a jump backward). *Zambos* (African-Indian mixed bloods) carried their own nomenclature based on skin tones and features, as did *mestizos* (Euro-Indians).

Atop the racial pyramid were whites, who imposed a sort of affidavit that previously had been used in Spain to racially repress Moors and Jews—the *limpieza de sangre* (blood cleanliness). A foreign visitor in the 17th century observed, "Each person so esteems the status of his caste, that if by chance he is taken for a step below that which belongs to him, he blushes and takes it as an insult, though the oversight was in no way malicious."[28]

In Cartagena, the week-long festivities around *Carnaval* (a pre-Lenten celebration featuring parades and partying whose history dated back to the beginning of the colonization of the New World) reinforced that rigid racial order while infusing it with a musicalized and sexualized exuberance. The *blancas de castilla* (white Spanish women) would enter the great dance hall first followed by the *pardas* (free colored), *libertas* (free blacks), slaves (who had previously been allowed to parade in their owners' jewels and best clothes in an African regal parade), Indians, and then the poor (*gente pobre*). The dances included the African-derived *curralao* (a free-wheeling courtship dance), the erotically simulative *mapalé*, also of African origin, the stately *gaita* (a promenade to indigenous flutes and drums), the Spanish *quadrille*, and the waltz. "The dances and music tended to reinforce stereotypical notions of culture—the African perceived as more sensual, the indigenous more restrained, and the Spanish more ordered."[29]

The origin myth of the *cumbia*, a dance and music genre native to the Caribbean coast of Colombia that fuses Amerindian flutes with African drums and Spanish lyrics, is based on clandestine celebrations of courtship and sexual union between black men and Indian women. "The historiography of *cumbia*," noted anthropologist Peter Wade writes, "debating the relative weight of Amerindian, African and European heritage, sees its own reflection in the dance itself, as a dramatic replaying of an original—and in this case subversive—act of mixture."[30]

As in other parts of Spanish and Portuguese America, Nueva Granada was the site of widespread miscegenation but also violent resistance by slaves. In addition to the constant problem of fugitive slaves, the imperial administrators also faced the threat of uprisings that included armed takeovers of towns and cities or even breakaway slave settlements called *palenques*.[31] By the 18th century, there were more than 30 *palenques* in the colony, some of which remained armed and autonomous for more than a century.[32]

Why some *palenques* survived and even prospered against all odds as self-ruled enclaves remains part of Colombia's lost history. The brilliant anthropological research of Nina

S. de Friedemann suggests that by re-creating African clan and cohort-based socialization—with women playing critical roles as warriors, love-mates, and mothers—*palenques* could and did achieve a self-sustaining, communal dynamism.[33] San Basilio, for example, a *palenque* some 50 kilometers (or roughly 31 miles) south of Cartagena, was such a threat to the great port city, especially when the armed community aligned itself with English pirates and privateers plying their terror off the Colombian coast, that Spanish King Carlos II issued a decree in 1691 effectively guaranteeing the black settlement's independence. [34]

What role did the Catholic Church play in conquest and colony?

To enshrine their conquest as moral and legal, Spanish lawyers and theologians at first drafted seven *Justos Títulos* (Rightful Titles) to empower the king in the name of the Church to rule in the New World. Brandishing a document called *El Requerimiento* (The Requirement), the invaders made a formal proclamation to the conquered:

> I require you to . . . recognize the Church as the lady and mistress of the entire world; and the Supreme Pontiff, known as the Pope, in her name; and the king and queen our lords in her stead . . . you will consent and give way to what the religious fathers shall declare and preach. . . . If you do not do this, I shall move forcefully against you in all areas and forms and I will take your persons and your women and children and I shall make slaves of them. . . . The deaths and wounds will be your fault and not that of his Highness.[35]

But the ultimate pacification of the New World was not accomplished by such royal edicts as much as by the Franciscan, Dominican, Augustinian, and later Jesuit missionaries who ventured into the remotest reaches to bring the gospel to Native Americans. In the course of these missions to convert and baptize millions, the Church itself was transformed.[36]

Whether it was to infuse faith or exact tribute, the evangelists' missions faced the huge challenge of language. Within a generation of the first wave of missionaries, however, many of the priests and friars were speaking a wide variety of native languages and vernaculars. They were also publishing books and treatises on Native American culture,[37] some of which questioned the ideologized dogma of Spanish domination. Over a 30-year period ending in 1775, Fray Bernadino de Sahagún published a 12-volume history of the Aztecs in both *Nahuatl*, a native Mexican language, and Castilian Spanish. Sahagún's *General History of the Things of New Spain* laid bare conquistador treachery in the secret attack in Tenochtitlán, the Aztec capital, and, accordingly, vice-regal authorities saw fit to repress it.[38] Another monk, Fray Pedro Aguado, wrote the 17-volume *Historia de Santa Marta y Nuevo Reino de Granada* (History of Santa Marta and the New Kingdom of Granada). Composed between 1575 and 1583, Aguado's monumental treatise was blocked from publication by the royal court in Madrid until, three centuries later in 1906, the yellowing, phantom manuscript was rediscovered and put to press.[39]

The Church both rationalized and socialized the slave trade, predestining baptized slaves not just for heaven but for the mines, fields, and factories of America.[40] However, in the late 16th and early 17th centuries, two Jesuits tried to change things. Alonso de Sandoval, S.J., citing an Aristotelian passage about mutual interest across classes and races, asserted that slaves and their masters could share "reciprocal friendship." Sandoval's treatise on the ethnicities and beliefs of African slaves (published in 1627 as *De Instauranda Aethiopum Salute*) became the primer that inspired his understudy, Peter Claver, to become the "slave to the slaves."[41]

When the slave ships would anchor in Cartagena, Father Claver would board them to feed the survivors bread, lemons, and *aguardiente* (a sugar-cane spirit) as well as to care for the sick and dying. In the course of his ministry, Claver recruited a large cohort of interpreters from the ranks of the Africans and developed a multilingual means of evangelizing the *bozales* ("simpletons," as the Spanish called them, though not Claver, of course). In his 40 years among the slaves, he baptized no fewer than 300,000 of them and was later canonized as a saint.

What gave the Church such singular power in the colony, however, was not so much its social agency as its statist character. In exchange for the *patronato real de las Indias* (an agreement in which the Church formalized the rights of the king's representatives in Spanish America to oversee key clerical appointments and other kinds of church governance), the Church gained significant concessions in education and property ownership.[42] In addition to receiving income from parish fees, tithes, and mortgages, the Church served as both the colony's chief money lender and its largest landowner.[43] By founding universities like Santo Tomás de Aquino (1580), La Pontificia Universidad Javeriana (1623), and Nuestra Señora del Rosario (1653), the Church socialized the creole elite, shaped the Catholic view of Enlightenment ideas, and advanced scientific research and the arts.

The Society of Jesus remained the Church's odd man out, sourcing its legitimacy to obedience to the Pope (as opposed to the *concordat*) and administering colonies, which Church elders thought "utopian." In Nueva Granada, the Jesuits developed successful cattle ranches and sugar plantations.[44] In Paraguay, they organized more than 100,000 Indians into a single community where the native Paraguayans learned handicrafts, built their own houses, and even produced books in their native *Guaraní*, something the French *philosophe* Montesquieu termed the equivalent of the achievement of Plato's *Republic* in the New World.[45]

But for all their "great economic aptitudes and political sagacity and cunning," in the words of one account from that time, the Jesuits often found themselves in conflict with both

civil and ecclesiastical authorities. Among the accusations lev-
eled against them was that of profiteering. When the rulers of
Cartagena authorized the building of massive fortifications to
encircle the city, it was the Jesuits who cornered the market
by selling the *carolina* stone to build the walls. In 1767, Carlos
III, citing their qualities of worldly independence, ordered
the Jesuits to be expelled from the New World. In 1773, Pope
Clement XIV abolished them outright.

In concert with the Spanish king, the Church did its best
to enforce social and sexual boundaries. In 1571, for example,
Philip II specifically forbade black and mixed-race women in
the New World from wearing gold, capes, or pearls.[46] Other
mandates sought to outlaw the widespread practice of magic
and witchcraft. In *Latinoamérica; el continente de siete colores*
(1967), considered one of the classic works on the subject,
Colombian historian Germán Arciniegas describes the early
Spanish settlements in the New World as saturated by sorcery,
necromancy, and devil worship. As the Indians retreated into
their rituals and cosmologies, the Spanish, as much through
their friars as their soldiers, introduced their own witches'
Sabbaths, Moorish enchantments, secret ceremonies, love phil-
ters, and incantatory antiphrasis (talking backward in medi-
eval codes). Slaves landing in the port of Cartagena brought
not only their own oracles and secret rituals, but new forms of
black magic to rationalize or imaginatively reconfigure their
lacerated fate.

After three centuries of "heroic struggle" in the characterization of one leading historian, the Catholic Church turned
lax and corrupt, and by the end of the 18th century it was routinely breaking its vows of humility and chastity and filling its
coffers with lucre.[47] The holy office of the Inquisition (established in Cartagena in 1610 by Philip II) was already a citadel
of abuse. To protect the faithful from heresy, witchcraft, and
necromancy, Church censors in the *Palacio de la Inquisición* engaged in random terror. "As Jews and Lutherans were not always available, the jails and torture racks tended to be devoted

to unruly members of the underclass"—blasphemous slaves who had cursed out their masters, or an "insolent, dark mestizo" who had dressed "bawdily" for church.[48] Occasionally, there were more dramatic *autos-da-fé* (acts of public penance) such as occurred in 1632, when two black women from Tolú, who had reportedly flown through the air as well as danced and fornicated with goats, were burned at the stake for witchcraft.[49]

The Church's decay was part of a larger breakdown in Nueva Granada. By the beginning of the 18th century, the kingdom was an imperial basket case. Regions and cities governed in open disregard of the authority of both Bogotá and Madrid. Cartagena was under almost continual assault by the British Navy, and Nueva Granada's trade in gold, slaves, and essential foodstuffs had largely been taken over by smugglers and foreign merchants.[50] When King Fernando VI sent two emissaries, Jorge Juan and Antonio de Ulloa, to investigate conditions in the kingdom, their report (later published as *Noticias secretas de América* or *Secret News of America*) to the king in 1747 spoke of "cruel oppression, extortion . . . [and] scandalous abuses."[51]

How did Spain's change in imperial rule affect Nueva Granada?

Determined to reestablish control over Nueva Granada and the rest of Spanish America, Spain's new rulers, the Bourbons, who ascended the Spanish throne in 1700 and whose reign lasted until 1808 when they were deposed by Napoleon, first took action to reform the Church. As Jaime Rodríguez has argued, the expulsion of the Jesuits was part of a larger drive to secularize the absolutist state.[52] Carlos III appointed Spaniards to high ecclesiastical appointments and stripped the Church of its *fueros*, the term applied to the code of privileged immunity from criminal and civil liability. The lower clergy, most of whom were creoles, saw their endowments called *capellanías* (chaplaincies), often their only source of income, taken away.

In 1798, the Spanish crown went a step further and ordered Church property seized and auctioned off.[53]

Upgrading Nueva Granada to a vice-regency, the Bourbons poured on the taxes and built up the colonial military to help finance their imperial wars (no fewer than four against Great Britain and one against France during the course of the 18th century).[54] In 1741–1742, the *granadinos* (as the people of Nueva Granada were now called) were able to fight off an invasion by British admiral Edward Vernon, whose force had attacked Cartagena with 180 ships and 23,600 men—the largest amphibian invasion the world had ever seen.[55]

For the creole elite, whose power the Bourbons were determined to diminish, the new royal taxes, especially on tobacco and liquor, and the complete disruption of trade caused by the wars in Europe sent shock waves through the newly minted vice-regency. In 1778, the crown imposed free trade between Spanish America and the mother country (no longer confining it to a single Spanish port, as had been the case since the mid-1500s). This policy change increased trade overall but damaged home-grown industries in the colonies, especially textiles in Nueva Granada.

As part of its centralizing construct, Madrid ordered American-born Spanish to be excluded from high administrative appointments in favor of *peninsulares*, European-born Spaniards.[56] "The second conquest" served not only to enrage the creoles but paradoxically to empower them as well.[57] In the 1780s, San Bartolomé, the Jesuit *colegio* in Bogotá, began graduating not priests but lawyers who would prove crucial to the nascent independence movement. Jesuit academics in exile published books that celebrated the depth and complexity of what one called the "American identity."[58] Spain's buildup of the colonial armed forces put creoles and even the mixed bloods, the *pardos*, into the officer corps as well as the enlisted ranks. Many of these men would use that same training and experience to fight against Spain for independence. A *pardo* teenager by the name of José Padilla, who fought for Spain in the battle of Trafalgar against the British in 1805, would one day serve as Bolívar's most brilliant naval commander.

In May 1780, when a particularly arrogant bureaucrat sent from Spain named Juan Francisco Gutiérrez de Piñeres doubled the taxes consumers paid to government monopolies on tobacco and *aguardiente*, riots broke out. Over the next weeks and months, the so-called *comuneros* formed village militias to resist royal repression. In May 1781, when 15,000 of them were on the verge of invading Bogotá, the Spanish regent fled the capital. Ultimately, the Spanish archbishop averted an insurgent takeover by temporarily acceding to their demands to reduce or eliminate taxes.[59] Once he succeeded in reestablishing control, the archbishop arrested the *comunero* ringleaders and had them hanged and quartered; other insurgents were sent away for 200 lashes and banishment to Africa.

With the advent of rebellion in the American colonies in the 1770s and later the sacking of the Bastille and the execution of King Louis XVI of France, the Bourbons took no chances in Spanish America. In Nueva Granada, Antonio Nariño, a rich, free-thinking creole who had translated and passed out a handful of copies of Thomas Paine's *The Rights of Man*, was clapped into jail along with several other suspected antimonarchists. What transfixed most of the creole elite, however, was not so much American or French republicanism as the horror of the Haitian Revolution, which started in 1791 and went on for 13 years, in which French settlers and plantation owners were slaughtered by freed slaves and mulattoes. "God forbid that the other countries suffer the same fate as Saint-Domingue [Haiti]," Venezuelan revolutionist Francisco de Miranda wrote an English friend, "the scene of carnage and crimes, committed under the pretext of establishing liberty; better they should remain another century under the barbarous and senseless oppression of Spain."[60]

With the majority of Nueva Granada now made up of black, Indian, or mixed-blood people, the "racially pure" creoles staunchly defended their right of preeminence, something

Carlos IV undermined by legally allowing *pardos* to purchase licenses, granting them white status. These so-called *cédulas de gracias al sacar* permitted them to marry whites, attend universities, join the officer corps, hold public office, and enter holy orders.[61] In addition to these licenses, the crown's promotion of blacks and mulattoes in the militia and its new slave codes seemed to signal that Spain was seeking to neutralize creole power by constructing new alliances with racially excluded groups. Although creole elites responded to these changes with shock and incredulity, their fear of a Haiti-like slave revolt was greater than any disposition to exit from the shelter of the Crown. "A great volcano lies at our feet," Bolívar darkly predicted. "Who shall restrain the oppressed classes? Slavery will break its yoke; each shade of complexion will seek mastery."[62]

2

THE CIVIL WARS
OF LIBERATION

Why did Spain lose its grip in the New World?

In a panic because of the French Revolution, especially after the execution of his fellow Bourbon regent, French king Louis XVI in 1793, Carlos IV of Spain joined other European monarchs in declaring war on France. With Spain's defeat in 1795, however, the country became a mere satellite of French imperialism and was dragged into an extended war with Great Britain. When the British Navy destroyed the combined fleets of France and Spain in the battle of Trafalgar in 1805, trade between Spain and its American colonies was effectively severed.[1]

In Madrid, royal authority was in total disarray. The weak and ineffectual Carlos IV had permitted Manuel Godoy, a 25-year-old officer of the guard and lover of the queen, to govern Spain while the king's son, Prince Ferdinand, conspired against his father, even secretly inviting Napoleon to overthrow him. Seeing his chance, the French emperor offered Carlos IV a piece of Portugal and all of its overseas territories should he permit the Armée d'Espagne to pass through Spain en route to Portugal. Once the French Army was in place, Napoleon summoned both warring Bourbons (the father, now deposed, and the son, now King Ferdinand VII) to Bayonne in the south of France. There, Napoleon forced them both to abdicate in May

1808 and then awarded the kingship of Spain to his brother, Joseph Bonaparte.

In Madrid, popular resistance to the French takeover was savagely repressed, igniting further uprisings against the invaders across Spain. In July 1808, patriotic forces routed a French army of 21,000 in Bailén, forcing Napoleon to take direct control of the so-called Peninsular War. In Santafé, the shocked creole elite joined with royal administrators in recognizing the Supreme Junta of Seville, which had assumed patriotic control in the absence of the king, and pledged the princely sum of 500,000 pesos in the fight against the French. Despite the show of unity, however, the Spanish imperium had suffered a fatal blow."[2]

How did Nueva Granada become independent?

With Spain occupied, the question was whether royal administrators or local creole leaders would rule in America in the name of the captive king, Ferdinand VII. At first, royal administrators had the upper hand and crushed creole efforts to form locally governed *juntas* (or committees). But later, with Napoleon's armies back in control of the Iberian Peninsula and the Supreme Junta in Seville dissolved in favor of a Council of Regency that was now holed up in Cádiz, the tide shifted toward creole patriots, who wanted self-rule, albeit in the name of the king.

On July 20, 1810, in its Act of Revolution, the junta in Santafé called for the formation of an independent constitution with rights vested in the people and not in absolute monarchy.[3] Over the following weeks, patriotic juntas sprang up all over Nueva Granada, with one town, Mompós, declaring its independence from Spain. In Santafé, the rebellious creoles arrested the vice-regent and shipped him off to prison in Cartagena while his wife was cursed and spat upon by hundreds of women in Bogotá as she was being escorted to prison.[4]

It was the beginning of what would be called the *Patria Boba* (the Dumb Nation) in which the cities and towns in Nueva Granada declared independence not only from Spain but from each other as the royalists among them prepared to pick up the pieces. Eventually, creole leaders formed a national government of sorts called the United Provinces of New Granada. This loose confederation did not include the newly formed province of Cundinamarca, where Santafé (recently rechristened Santafé de Bogotá in symbolic deference to a Muisca settlement by that approximate name) was located. In other places such as Santa Marta and Pasto, royalists loyal to Spain were holding out. Part of the basis for resistance was the Church, whose 3,500 clergy members not only vastly outnumbered other elite male professions such as lawyers (150), high-level bureaucrats (100), and medical doctors (27) in the first decade of the 19th century, but had a vested interest in returning Colombia to the colonial status quo.[5]

By 1812—months into nationhood—Cundinamarca and the United Provinces were at war. The conflict remained inconclusive until Simón Bolívar, then a 29-year-old Venezuelan *independentista* escaping from his own bloody defeat back home in Venezuela, sailed to Cartagena. Once one of Venezuela's richest men, Bolívar arrived in Cartagena as little more than a refugee, his trunks full of silver bars and pesos having been confiscated at a stop in Curacao the week before. What military experience he offered Cartagena's republican leaders was largely a testament to his own self-inflicted disaster.*

---

*. Bolívar had been one of the key figures in Venezuela's brief effort at independence under the leadership of the aging, if still eminent, Francisco Miranda. Given command of a key fort at Puerto Cabello, Bolívar promptly lost it. When General Miranda decided to give up and negotiate terms of the royalist commander, General Monteverde, Bolívar first contemplated executing Miranda for cowardice before conspiring to turn him over to the Spanish royalists—this, before making his own escape.

Why did Simón Bolívar become the most important figure in the history of Spanish America and the Republic of Nueva Granada?

Much like George Washington, to whom he is often compared, Bolívar was a wealthy planter who took up the cause of independence. Unlike Washington, however, Bolívar never wanted to return to his vast plantations, instead aiming to fashion a superstate in his own image. In this endeavor, he more closely resembled a man he both detested and admired—Napoleon Bonaparte.[6] If Bolívar was, on the one hand, a tribune of the Enlightenment, studying Rousseau, quoting Montesquieu, and, later, composing republican constitutions, he was also the precursor to something he would have abhorred, the *caudillo* (military strongman). Within his volcanic contradictions—he was, in John Lynch's words, "a liberator who scorned liberalism, a soldier who disparaged militarism, a republican who admired monarchy"—Bolívar embodied the makings of Colombia's contested identity.[7]

Soon hired by Cartagena to protect the city's vulnerable southern front, Bolívar instead used his tiny force to attack Spanish emplacements on the lower Magdalena River. With each victory, he moved up the river, recruiting new partisans with his headlong bravura. In a matter of 15 days, his forces freed the lower and upper Magdalena from the royalists. In May 1813, the United Provinces, now militarily preeminent in Nueva Granada, granted Bolívar permission to attack royalist Venezuela. For Bolívar, this invasion was more than a flanking move to liberate his native country; it was the first act in fulfilling his vision of "Colombia," as set out in his *Manifiesto de Cartagena,* a country in which praetorian force would excise the "poison of factionalism," "the ethereal republics" of feckless lawyers, and the disease of clericalism, thereby restoring "natural rights" to Americans.[8]

But first came conquest. The aptly named "Admirable Campaign" began with Bolívar's extraordinary roll-up of royalist forces in the summer of 1813. It was also memorable, however, in terms of the terror practiced by both sides—the beginning of the civil wars of independence.[9] But in the *llanos* (plains), the royalists were not yet finished. Now led by a pitiless, blue-eyed Spaniard by the name of José Tomás Boves, who turned his mixed-race troops loose with the express purpose of killing whites and plundering their property, the *llanero* (cowboy) cavalry proved unstoppable. Shortly before the patriotic forces were entirely routed, Bolívar slipped back into Nueva Granada where, for a period of several weeks, he rallied the revolutionists before unsuccessfully laying siege to Cartagena. From there, facing impossible tactical odds, he fled to Jamaica in 1814.

By this time, with France having withdrawn from Spain and the Spanish king back on the throne in Madrid, the resurgent Spanish decided to reassert control over Spanish America. In July 1815, a battle-hardened Spanish army of 10,000 landed in Santa Marta and immediately put Cartagena under siege. After 100 days and widespread starvation, Cartagena surrendered and became the site of mass executions. Spanish brutality in Bogotá was, if anything, even worse—the patriotic elite, who might have provided critical support later in Colombia's later development as a nation, were systematically slaughtered or sent away in irons.

From Jamaica, Bolívar appealed to Great Britain to intercede against the Spanish, but his appeal was ignored. What the British did permit, however, was the recruitment of mercenaries from the Duke of Wellington's recently decommissioned army of 500,000 (then thought to be a danger to law and order in Britain itself).[10] Ultimately, 6,000 Irish and English volunteers, including officers of rank, hired out and set sail for the islands off the coast of Venezuela.[11] Bolívar had meanwhile befriended the president of Haiti, the mulatto Alexandre Pétion, who agreed to supply him with 6,000 rifles, supplies, naval transport, and a sizeable sum of money on condition he abolish slavery in any territory he liberated.

Back on the mainland, Bolívar regrouped in the remote plains of the headwaters of the Orinoco with *llanero* (cowboy) irregulars under the command of José Antonio Páez, a rough-and-ready *mestizo* brigand. (Bolívar was a mixed bag when it came to military strategy. His true talent lay in gaining the confidence of people.) Now nominally in command, Bolívar accused a *pardo* (mixed-race) general, Manuel Piar, of treachery and had him executed, admitting that it was necessary to stop a race war: "The death of General Piar was a political necessity which saved the country, for otherwise he would have started a war of *pardos* against whites, leading to the extermination of the latter and the triumph of the Spaniards."[12] As the Irish and English soldiers of the British Legion, as it was now called, infiltrated into the *llano* redoubt, Bolívar made a fateful decision: not to push east into Venezuela but to strike west across the *cordillera* into Nueva Granada, where Spanish forces were thought to be weaker.

Bolívar's army of some 2,000 began marching west just as the rainy season was starting. For seven days, according to one Irish volunteer, the troops marched with "water up to their waists, camping in whatever dry patches they could find." Then came the ascent. Across range after range in snow and freezing rain, with animals and men dying all around them, Bolívar led the desperate convoy, urging them on. More than 60 soldiers in the British Legion alone lost their lives.[13] After descending the *cordillera*, the survivors spent a few days taking care of their sick and dying, as Bolívar himself scrambled to reprovision his forces and find them horses. Then they attacked. In the first battle, Pantano de Vargas, the Anglo-Irish commander of the British Legion, Colonel James Rooke, was mortally wounded, but Bolívar's patriots prevailed. In the second battle in Boyacá, Bolívar's army routed the Spanish. So brave was the British Legion that Bolívar renamed it *Batallón Albión* and decorated the entire unit with the Star of the Order of Liberators. Bolívar's army reached Bogotá on August 10, 1819. The fleeing Spanish had left behind a large store of treasure and military supplies in the Casa de la Moneda. Five months later, a patriotic congress met in Angostura (modern-day Ciudad Bolívar). The delegates listened and wept as Bolívar unveiled his concept of a great new state, "Colombia," which would unite Nueva Granada with Venezuela and a yet-unliberated Ecuador.[14]

Later in Cúcuta in May 1821, a larger assembly of delegates ratified Bolívar's concept of a rigidly centralist state via a new constitution that abolished the Inquisition and all monasteries with fewer than eight members (earmarking the sale of Church property for secondary schools), made Indians citizens, eliminated the *alcabala* (the royalist sales tax of up to 14 percent), and provided slaves the right to free birth (on condition that they would serve their mothers' masters without pay until the age of 18). Bolívar was elected the first constitutional president of Colombia with Bogotá as the new capital. The selection of vice president went to a *granadino*, a 29-year-old former law student named Francisco de Paula Santander, who had been promoted to General of Division for his brilliance in the epic strike across the Andes.[15] Bolívar dubbed Santander "*el hombre de las leyes*"—the man of laws.

Before the ink on the parchment of the new constitution was even dry, Bolívar was off to Peru to make war on the final redoubt of the royalist forces. Santander meanwhile tried to manage Colombia's enormous war debt (amounting to about five times the republic's annual revenue) while raising loans to underwrite Bolívar's new army, which was now eating up three-quarters of the republic's budget.[16] In the wake of nine years of war, many of the country's 1.2 million inhabitants were malnourished, living as refugees and with no means to support themselves.[17] When Bolívar ordered Santander to round up 5,000 slaves from the goldfields of Chocó and Cauca to fill out the ranks of his depleted army in exchange for their freedom, Santander protested that gold production, the only export the new country had, would be negatively affected. Reiterating the order, Bolívar noted that in fighting to acquire their freedom, the men would also be reducing "their dangerous numbers" in the process.[18] Despite this brutal calculation, Bolívar himself was an abolitionist; having freed all of his own Venezuelan slaves, he later proposed that the million-peso bounty he was offered for freeing Peru be used to buy the emancipation of slaves.

Did the United States help Bolívar?

The Latin American revolutionists entertained high hopes that the North Americans, whose own decisive victory at Yorktown in 1781 was delivered by the French, would intervene decisively on their behalf, but the Americans never did. Having guided his country through a thorny neutrality at the beginning of the Anglo-French war, President Washington had enjoined his countrymen in his farewell address to avoid "entangling alliances" at all costs. Neutrality afforded the Americans a bonanza of cross-Atlantic trade with the warring Europeans while enabling them to purchase the Louisiana territory from Napoleon, solidifying the hands-off approach. Bolívar, who had sent his brother to Washington, D.C., to plea for help, was dismayed by U.S. neutrality and indeed the indifference of "our brothers to the north who have remained but passive spectators of our anguish.[19]

No Founding Father was as opposed to helping Bolívar in his war for independence as Thomas Jefferson, who predicted that "rivers of blood must yet flow & years of desolation pass over" before Spanish America would attain real self-government. Jefferson believed that Spanish Americans were "habituated from their infancy to passive submission of body and mind to their kings and priests" rendering them unqualified to "think and provide for themselves."[20] Jefferson's pessimism was based not only on his disdain for organized religion, especially of the "monkish," "papist," and "priest-ridden" variety, but his conviction that there was a fundamental difference in the two revolutionary uprisings: the

North American colonists, in fighting for independence, had only been trying to restore English ideals of democratic rights and the rule of law—plowing familiar ground, as it were. The Spanish Americans, on the other hand, with no organic traditions of their own to restore or revive, had no basis for self-government. They should only separate from Spain, Jefferson wrote Adams, "by degrees" and not by any declaration of immediate independence.[21]

When Washington did recognize Colombian independence in 1822, the first country in the world to do so, the Monroe administration offered the Colombians a commercial treaty on condition that it include a declaration of religious freedom. Santander readily accepted this condition and additionally proposed that by treaty the two countries abolish slavery, something the U.S. Senate righteously denounced and rejected.[22]

The long shadow of Jefferson's skepticism about Spanish America—"we have seldom seen neighborhood produce affection among nations," he had acidly observed as president—was evident yet again when Spain contemplated an attempt to retake its former colonies in 1823.[23] The 80-year-old Jefferson offered his counsel to his former understudy, President James Monroe, when the latter was contemplating joining Great Britain in warning Spain and the Holy Alliance not to militarily repossess Spanish America.[24] The Monroe Doctrine, as it was later called, was a monument to statecraft as passive aggression: in advising Europe that any future intervention in the Americas would be considered a hostile act against the United States, the Americans implicitly indicated that there would henceforth be but one enforcer in the neighborhood.[25]

Bolívar came to view the Americans with mordant ambivalence, citing his admiration for their "rational liberty" while, at other times, saying that he would rather see his fellow Spanish Americans adopt the Koran than the government of the United States. The United States, he wrote a British friend, "seems destined by Providence to unleash a plague of miseries in Latin America in the name of liberty."[26]

To fulfill his vision for the confederation of the new states of Spanish America, Bolívar organized a hemispheric conference in Panamá, hoping that Great Britain would embrace the fledgling countries in a protectorate of sorts. Bolívar decided to exclude the Americans from the conference, a decision Santander reversed by formally sending an invitation to the United States while Bolívar was away from Bogotá. President John Quincy Adams hailed the vision of hemispheric union in public while plotting its undoing in private: the United States wanted no rivals in its neighborhood.[27] In the end, the conference accomplished little. As for the two American representatives who were to attend, one died of yellow fever en route while stuck on a boat beached on a sandbar in the Magdalena and the other showed up in Panamá after the conference had already adjourned.

Why did Gran Colombia* fall apart?

Given economic destitution, fiscal bankruptcy, racial divisions, and rampant warlordism, only Bolívar's enormous talents and energy could have contained Gran Colombia's centrifugal tendencies. Instead of shouldering this burden, however, the Liberator departed Bogotá and headed off for new fields of martial glory.

In his biography of Bolívar, John Lynch argues that there were sound national security reasons for mopping up the royalist die-hards in Peru while keeping Ecuador from falling into the hands of Bolívar's rival liberator, the Argentine general José de San Martín. But the reason was intensely personal as well: "I am the *chosen son*," Bolívar emphasized to Santander.[28] It was precisely that self-adulation that kept Bolívar in the Peruvian Andes for another two years as he attended to the heroic passage of Peru and Upper Peru (to be renamed "Bolivia") into statehood. The Bolivian constitution, which Bolívar wrote himself, gave the president tenure for life and the right to choose his successor, something he soon lobbied for Colombia to adopt as well.

Vice President Santander, who was governing Colombia in Bolívar's absence, opposed any constitutional change. The new government already had its hands full battling the Catholic Church, urging it to sell off its empty monasteries and raise the age for taking religious vows to 25.[29] Priests and bishops were repeatedly directed to state from the pulpit that "the cause of Liberty has an intimate connection with the Doctrine of Jesus Christ."[30] The fact that Santander, along with several of his cabinet ministers, was a Freemason was cause enough for opposition. Additionally he had ordered all schools and universities to adopt a "plan of study" that included Jeremy Bentham's treatises on law, Antoine Destutt de Tracy's use of deductive methods in social theory, and Jean-Baptiste Say's writings about the behavior of markets. Of these, most galling to Church leaders was Bentham, the apostle of utilitarianism who argued that human nature was hedonistic, responding experientially to pleasure versus pain.[31] So furious was the clergy in Colombia about this and other perceived assaults on the Church that Secretary of the Interior José Manuel Restrepo wondered if the Church would start a civil war to stop Santander.

Gran Colombia's perilous first years as a nation were first buoyed and then dashed by a surge in speculative capital from Britain. After securing a credit line of 7.2 million pounds sterling (or $1.3 billion in today's value) from British capital firms, the government in Bogotá defaulted, along with other newly independent Latin American nations, in its interest payments.[32] In 1825–1826, the British bond market collapsed, cutting off Colombia from all external financing.[33]

The crisis in public finance coincided with a far more toxic political situation in Gran Colombia. Bogotá was occupied by several hundred Venezuelan soldiers and officers who openly disliked Santander and may even have been conspiring against him. One of Santander's ministers described the Venezuelan

military as a "cancer that is devouring the people's substance."[34] When Colonel Leonardo Infante, one of the most
decorated of Bolívar's Venezuelan officers, was arrested and
accused of murder in Bogotá, civil-military relations reached
the breaking point. Although the evidence against "*el negro
Infante*"—Infante was black—seemed circumstantial at best,
the *granadinos* forced the issue, convicted and then executed
him in Bogotá's main plaza.[35] Santander used the occasion of
the full-dress execution to lecture the assembled officers from
horseback about the sanctity of the law.

In April 1826, the Colombian Congress relieved Venezuelan
general José Antonio Páez of his command in Venezuela,
causing Páez to start a rebellion. Bolívar hastened to Venezuela,
where he got Páez to back down but at a price: total amnesty
for all the rebels and promises of constitutional reform. In an
atmosphere of extreme tension, Bolívar called for a constitutional convention, which met for three months in the small
town of Ocaña. Among Bolívar's fervent opponents was his
former admiral, José Padilla, now the leader of the *pardos* who
supported federalism as a means of furthering mixed-race
rights. In the end, the convention reached a stalemate when
Bolívar's supporters walked out and, days later, a dictatorship
was declared by the Liberator himself.

In September 1828, Bolívar survived a coup d'état that was
to have begun with his assassination. As he escaped from the
Palace of San Carlos by jumping from the balcony, his lover,
Manuela Sáenz, confronted the assassins with a drawn sword.
Although Bolívar rallied his forces and soon reestablished
power, the subsequent prosecution of the would-be assassins
proved equivocal. Admiral Padilla, who had rebelled against
Bolívar—though never conspired to kill him—was brought to
Bogotá, where he was quickly tried and shot. Santander, who
knew about the plot in advance although he had not actively
participated in it, was sent into exile. Bolívar wondered about
the fairness of it all: the blacks were readily put to death, but

not "this infamous white, whose services do not compare with those famous patriots."

With rebellion in Cauca and Antioquia, a mutiny in Peru, and stirrings of secession in Ecuador and Venezuela—all directed against Bolívar's dictatorship—the Liberator, now fatally sick with tuberculosis, resigned and withdrew to the Caribbean coast in 1830. Reflecting on the reasons for Gran Colombia's unraveling in a letter to a friend, Bolívar thought that "blood, death, and every crime were the patrimony resulting from a federation combined with the rampant appetite of a people who have broken their chains and have no understanding of the notions of duty and law and who cannot cease being slaves except to become tyrants. . . . I am ashamed to admit it, but independence is the only benefit we have gained at the cost of everything else."

American historian Jeremy Adelman puts the predicament in historical context: "Sovereignties multiplied across the former Iberian colonies. At times they coexisted in unstable hybrid models. At times they polarized and motivated decades of civil war. . . . The way in which these empires collapsed also deprived colonists of any means for reaching back to grasp doctrines of ancient rights or liberties to build something new."[36]

3

THE LIBERAL REVOLUTION AND THE CONSERVATIVE "REGENERATION"

What changes did independence bring?

Independence had torn through Spanish America like a great storm, in the telling metaphor of John Lynch, "sweeping away the lines of attachment to Spain and the fabric of colonial government, but leaving intact the deeply rooted bases of colonial society."[1] The seigniorial systems of hierarchy and patronal dependence that had formed the bedrock of social cohesion in colonial times remained—shaken, and often fractured, but still in place. The Church was battered, having lost land, churches, and monasteries, and up to half its clergy, but it slowly regrouped. Although the Vatican refused to recognize the government of Colombia until 1835, hundreds of Catholic parishes throughout the country continued to function, sanctifying birth, marriage, and death, making loans and managing agricultural tenants, resolving disputes through their good offices, and providing Catholic education. With the Bogotá government bereft of public revenue, divided over who should lead and how, and often threatened by rebellion, the Church was the sole institution that maintained a working solidarity with the masses.

The new country was scarred deeply by 12 years of civil war. As a result of conscription at gunpoint, scorched-earth tactics, and the violent requisition of food, livestock, and draft animals, agricultural production had fallen off drastically and mining had largely stopped. A substantial proportion of Nueva Granada's slaves were no longer bonded to their plantations and placer mines but were scattered around the country. The long war had also produced an abundance of military veterans, many of whom remained armed and looking for bounty—or liberty, in the case of black veterans. A good number of these fighters remained at the side of their former commanders, men like José María Obando, José Hilario López, and Tomás C. Mosquera. All of these former generals, now *caudillos* and later presidents, variously controlled conquered land, key economies, and trade routes as well as their loosely configured militias.

For all of that, there was a strange, almost picaresque, effervescence in the new citizens of the "Republic of Nueva Granada" (as the constitution legally renamed the country after the disintegration of Gran Colombia in 1830).* A travelogue from the time written by British naval captain Charles Cochrane describes a priest showing off his procreated clutch of children; "knavish" black boatmen called *bogas*, writhing, grunting, and singing in unison (and offending their white clients) as they pole a riverboat up the Magdalena; and enterprising young men at a mass in a Bogotá church charming and seducing their female "enslavers" and arranging "assignations, by no means likely to improve the country's morals."[2]

Even 30 years after Captain Cochrane's spirited travelogue about the newly independent country appeared, Bogotá still struck foreign visitors as a grimy dump—a city of 29,000 that, after more than 300 years as an urban capital, had no hotels or banks and only three covered carriages that clattered over roughly cobbled streets that doubled as open sewers. In 1856,

---

*. The country's name changed as follows: Republic of Colombia 1819–1832; Republic of Nueva Granada 1832–1858; Granadine Confederation 1858–1863; United States of Colombia 1863–1886; and Republic of Colombia, 1886–present.

visiting American botanist Isaac F. Holton described a city filled with single-storied houses made of adobe brick which had "large, ugly portals and a few small grated windows from which the female inhabitants seem to be constantly looking out like prisoners." Holton visited a "dirty" hospital and a cemetery for the poor where he observed a vulture "desiring to defile his beak with the flesh of Christians."[3]

How did independence affect the role of women?

The winds of war and freedom opened a modicum of social and economic space for women. No longer consigned to either the status of maritally conscripted madonnas by the regal Church or roving objects of carnal predation by all-powerful males, women were suddenly making their mark, even if social and economic taboos remained.[4] Many women, having lost their husbands in the war, were now heads of households. Some owned taverns or managed farms or plantations. Nuns were known to invest in property and trade slaves, and it was not impossible for the mulatto son of a slave–concubine to inherit the estate of his father, even over otherwise legitimate white offspring.[5] Archival records show that women, usually with the help of male family members, increasingly sought legal redress against rape, spousal violence, and robbery.

The fact that a handful of women had entered the annals of legend as heroines of the war of independence also had a liberating effect. Thus, the 22-year-old seamstress Policarpa Salavarrieta, known as "La Pola," who had served as a resourceful spy for Bolívar's patriotic forces during Spain's reconquest of Nueva Granada in 1817, was arrested along with another 150 women accused of being rebel supporters. Taken out to be executed by a firing squad, La Pola refused to kneel as ordered, yelling: "I have more than enough courage to suffer this death and a thousand more. Do not forget my example!" With her execution, she instantly became a rallying force for the patriots and was later sainted in song and poetry. She now adorns the 10,000-Colombian-peso banknote.[6] Another patriot was Bolívar's lover Manuela Sáenz, who could shoot and ride horses like a man and had been decorated for valor before Bolívar set his sights on her. The fact that their famous love affair was conducted in *libertinaje* (debauchery), since Sáenz was married to a wealthy English merchant *and* was also rumored to be sexually involved with a beautiful *mulata* slave as well, only added salacious allure to her enduring fame.[7]

What happened after Bolívar's demise?

The Liberator's resignation and later death in December 1830 led to a deep division between those who had stood by him in his quest for strong central government and those who had opposed him and joined Santander in the cause of a government of laws with limited powers and autonomous regions. In 1831, Santander's backers decided to write a new constitution and invited their leader to return from exile to serve as provisional president.[8] At the time, Santander was living in New York City, where he had become something of a celebrated figure sought out by a steady stream of U.S. political leaders, including President Andrew Jackson, who, Santander noted in his diary, was friendly but had "no manners whatsoever."[9]

Once elected and in office, President Santander cut the military's share of the budget by 25 percent and also took away its *fuero* (code of judicial privileges). On issues like free trade and the dissolution of Indian *resguardos* (communal properties), Santander moved cautiously, but he boldly renewed his lifelong commitment to opening up universities and *colegios* to non-Catholic thinking, something he hoped would spur European and American immigration to Nueva Granada. Given the dire lack of public revenue, the main sources of which were customs duties and state monopolies on tobacco and salt, the national government lacked the means to build order, address extreme poverty, or extend the rule of law.

After a single four-year term, Santander retired from office. Pasto, the ultra-Catholic provincial stronghold in the South, veered toward rebellion under General José María Obando, who named himself "Supreme Chief of the War in Pasto, General in Chief of the Restoring Army and Protector of the Religion of Christ Crucified." When other regional caudillos joined him as *jefes supremos* (supreme chiefs), Nueva Granada experienced the first (1840–1842) of its eight postindependence wars of the 19th century. "*La Guerra de los Supremos*" was a foreshadowing of subsequent conflicts in which the caudillos, fighting as Conservatives (in the tradition of Bolívar) or Liberals (in the tradition of Santander), engaged in a crazy quilt of armed intrigue, alliances, rivalries, and vendettas to control regional or national power.[10]

How do we make sense of all this? In the conclusion of noted Colombian historian Javier Ocampo López, the overarching reason for Colombia's civil wars—and some 60 other revolts, uprisings, coups, officer putsches, and declarations of rebellion (all during the 19th century)—was that Colombia's weak central government engendered a power vacuum.[11] With strong regional rule and a weak central government unable to command order, the power vacuum produced contending factions within the parties themselves as well as opportunistic coalitions between them. War became a key mobilizer in this winner-take-all syndrome.

What about the economy of the newly independent country?

Colombia (renamed the Republic of Nueva Granada in 1832, as noted earlier) was not only poor; it was export poor. Other than gold, there was little Colombia could export that northern Europe and the United States could not produce themselves or get more cheaply elsewhere. In the mid-1830s, the value of Colombian exports was about $2 per capita, as compared to Cuba's $19 per capita.[12] President Santander had proposed trade agreements with U.S. cities, but without any comparative advantage in primary product exports there was more potential for loss than gain. To make ends meet, the government, which depended on the tobacco and salt monopolies for half its revenue, often resorted to extreme measures, such as forced loans drawn on official salaries, levies on government opponents, or (after 1861) the expropriation of Church property. A fiscal snapshot of the treasury at mid-century reveals no fewer than 24 types of internal borrowing by the government.[13]

Transportation was another key factor in Nueva Granada's underdevelopment. By the 1850s, it was still cheaper to move freight from Liverpool across the Atlantic and up the Magdalena to the interior river port of Honda than to transport goods the final 80 or so miles over the mountains by mule or human porters to Bogotá.[14] Elsewhere Nueva Granada's forbidding geography, with arteries of trade and travel often infested with armed robbers, only accentuated an economy based on barter and a country balkanized into regions.

Toward the middle of the 19th century, however, premodern Nueva Granada began stirring from its slumber. Steam navigation was introduced on the Magdalena, stimulating trade and cutting transportation costs. Four-time president Tomás Cipriano de Mosquera invested in road and bridge construction as well as the first of Bogotá's great public buildings. From 1850 to 1859, Italian engineer-geographer Agustín Codazzi spearheaded the *Comisión Corográfica* (Chorographic Expedition) that explored the sprawling country, developing a single cartography and a multidisciplinary taxonomy put together by Colombian botanists, geologists, ethnologists, and sociologists.[15] The historic study enabled the elite as well as the rudimentarily educated (since geography then became an obligatory subject in the school system) to envision Colombia's vast and richly endowed territory.[16]

Did the Liberal revolution improve the status of Afro-Colombians?

Yes, but not much. The Liberal abolition of slavery in 1851 (which emancipated some 25,000 Afro-Colombians) touched off a Conservative revolt that was suppressed in part by the military mobilization of free blacks.[17] Though the once-feared race war never materialized in Nueva Granada (or in any of the five other Latin American countries that imposed abolition during this period), white anger was soon reinforced by new spurious scientific theories about Caucasian superiority. José María Samper, a follower of the French racial determinist Arthur de Gobineau, described the Indians of Pasto as "sedentary savages . . . with a stupid look . . . malicious, astute untrusting . . . indolent in morality." Samper attributed "prodigious breeding" by Afro-Colombians to their lack of intellectual and moral development, which he contrasted with the "very high degree of moral and intellectual refinement" of the French, who had slowed their own rates of reproduction.[18] For the racial determinists, the key imperative for improving the country—if it could be improved at all—was to cross the white race with the darker peoples to make them more "white, strong, benign and intelligent." This was called *blanqueamiento* (whitening), and, for a century after its initial articulation in the 1850s, it remained the social fixation of the ruling class.[19] Colombia, however, would never become the chosen destination for any large influx of Caucasian immigrants. Unlike Argentina, Brazil, or the United States—countries that absorbed millions of European aliens in the 19th century—Colombia's efforts to stimulate white in-migration netted no more than an estimated 100 foreigners per annum in the 1870s.

What drove frontier settlements in the Republic of Nueva Granada?

Colonization of new and largely uninhabited frontiers within the country proved to be among the most dynamic and destabilizing features of 19th-century Nueva Granada. The most dramatic expansion involved Antioquia, a major gold-producing state whose population tripled from 1825 to 1870. The national geographic survey from the 1850s indicated that the devoutly Catholic *paisas* (as the *Antioqueños* were called) married at ages 15–18 to women who were between 11 and 14 years of age, producing children in abundance.[20] In addition to population pressure, land crowding and soil depletion may also have pushed the *paisas* into what is now Risaralda, Caldas, and Quindío. Wherever they went, their qualities of hard work, honesty, and ambition were noted. In 1844, for example, Governor Jorge Juan Hoyos of Cauca, another state where the *paisas* were homesteading, reported to President Pedro Alcántara Herrán: "These men do not rest: no sooner do they finish sowing crops on their possessions than they come to contract themselves for . . . the rainy season." The *Antioqueño* peons, he later reported, "have only shown one bad quality, that of not stopping."[21]

Subsequent scholarship revealed frontier expansion to be a more complex phenomenon than originally supposed, one in which land speculators, large landowners, and lawyers often dispossessed the peasant settlers who had already cleared and begun cultivating the land. The purpose of usurpation (via partition suits, the filing of mining claims, or annexation by barbed-wire fencing) was not only to take over *colono* (settler) land but to turn those settlers into tenant farmers or wage workers.[22] Conflict over land rights also had a political dimension, since those who intervened to settle the disputes—mayors, merchants, or *gamonales* (local bosses)—were usually aligned with one of the two national parties. Frontier expansion during the 19th century may have absorbed hundreds of thousands of land-hungry *colonos*, but it also evidenced patterns of land cleansing and retaliatory violence that would shape Colombia for decades to come.[23]

How real was the Liberal revolution?

Whatever other policies President Santander may have failed to effectuate in his single term in office, his imposition of the "plan of study" to learn from Europe's leading, non-Catholic thinkers bore fruit. As the so-called Revolutions of 1848 rolled over Europe, French utopianism reverberated in Nueva Granada and throughout Latin America. "Democratic Societies" (as the Liberal clubs were called) echoed Joseph Proudhon's expostulation of anarchism and his "utopian truth" that "property is theft."[24]

In imitation of the first French Revolution of 1789, Liberals insisted on addressing each other as *ciudadano* (citizen), and the "Democratic Societies," in which the well-born sons of wealthy families fraternally embraced working artisans in the true French manner, became the order of the day. The French poet Alphonse de Lamartine had pointed the way to social perfectibility: "The instrument of this passion for bringing about a moral world is the press." Accordingly, Nueva Granada, despite a literacy rate at mid-century of less than 10 percent, boasted a full-throated urban press that insisted, inter alia, on the eradication of legal sanctions against libel.[25] In the center of this still small but growing civil society, with its clubs, newspapers, and noteworthy ideologues, were lawyers, whose number had multiplied by a factor of 10 from 1819 to 1840. The high altar of utopian ideas turned into a paper mill of constitution-writing: five were ratified between 1832 and 1863.

In his exegesis on the origins of nationalism, the late political scientist and historian Benedict Anderson argued that "the revolutionary vernacularizing thrust" of print capitalism is a critical agent producing national consciousness.[26] Colombia's Nobel-winning and most famous novelist, Gabriel García Márquez, concluded otherwise, however. Santander and his Liberal lawyer progeny, via their endless posturing in the press and passage of "paper laws and constitutions," García

Márquez believed, had instead created "a paper country," one that was not based in reality.[27]

What radical changes did the Liberals (1845–1885) enact?

The Liberal changes came in two waves: in the first, slavery was abolished (1851) as were the *resguardos* (Indians' protected rights in their communal lands); the Jesuits were expelled again in 1850 (only to be welcomed back in 1858, until they were thrown out yet again in 1861); church and state were formally separated by the 1853 constitution, which abolished compulsory tithe collections and the *fuero* and enshrined religious toleration; and universal male suffrage was enacted, making all offices subject to direct popular election and removing the power of the president to appoint governors. The elimination of the *resguardos* was supposed to bring Indians into the social and economic mainstream by making their communal lands marketable. Instead, it threw many indigenes into landless destitution.[28]

Liberal factionalism cut short the first period of reform when Liberal army men, joined by artisans furious at having lost protective tariffs, overthrew President Obando in a military coup. The civil war that followed removed the putschists from power but also opened the door to Conservative rule, beginning in 1855. Under President Mariano Ospina Rodríguez, the Conservatives wrote a new constitution, one that renamed the country the *Confederación Granadina* and expanded federalism, an apostasy best explained by President Ospina himself: "to provide refuge in some provinces for the victims of social reform in the rest."[29] But plummeting public revenues and further cuts in the army, reducing it to no more than 500 troops, created enough of a power vacuum for former president Tomás Mosquera to push the country into yet another round of civil war. Mosquera used the Liberals' standing as slave emancipators to recruit thousands of blacks and mulattos into his ranks.[30] Two years later, in July 1861, Mosquera's forces emerged victorious, with his army of *negro caucanos* (blacks from the Cauca Valley) marching into Bogotá to the terrified amazement of its residents.[31]

Although governing as a dictator, Mosquera proved a reformer as well, and his seizure of power occasioned the second wave of Liberal utopia. The "Radical Liberals," as they were known, drafted a new constitution in 1863, renaming the Republic of Nueva Granada "the United States of Colombia" and stripping the national government of most of its traditional powers. The new powers then accorded to Colombia's provincial states were breathtaking in scope: each state would have its own armed forces, voting rights, and tax laws. In terms of individual rights, there was complete license to bear and trade arms, total free speech (with complete immunity from libel), and the elimination of the death penalty.

Selling off Church lands, the *Mosqueristas* hoped, would produce a financial windfall for the perennially insolvent national government. So hastily did the government liquidate Church lands to pay off its creditors, however, that the properties garnered no more than one-tenth to one-twentieth of their market value.[32] The windfall instead went to land speculators and large landowners who were already consolidating vast tracts of government and Indian *resguardo* lands.

Historians would later cite the faction-ridden conceits, the war-mongering, and the anti-Church excesses of the Liberals as among the reasons for their eventual downfall. Noted Colombianist Charles Bergquist, however, argues that economic forces may provide a better explanation than political ones for the rise and fall of Liberal utopia: "The rise of the Liberal party in the late 1840s, its long period of hegemony in Colombia, and its decline and loss of power to the Conservatives after 1880 closely parallel the growth and decline of export agriculture, particularly tobacco, during the same period."[33] The fact that the elimination of the government monopoly on tobacco in 1850 roughly coincided with the tobacco boom on the world market underscored the virtue of laissez-faire while allowing the Liberal governments to double public revenue from 1865 to 1874.[34] As the tobacco boom receded in the 1880s, along with it went the Radical Liberal monopoly on national power.

Why was disagreement over the role of the Church in Colombia in the 19th century so fratricidal?

Before 1861, when General Mosquera forcibly took power, there was a rough consensus among the elite that religious liberty and an expansion of civil rights free of Church control were necessary in the United States of New Granada. The Liberal brief against the Church had nothing to do with its religious teachings, its liturgy, or its claim to being a revealed religion, for most Liberals were themselves practicing Catholics. Instead, as one Liberal wrote in 1878, "What we seek in this country is not the repression of the Catholic idea but the complete emancipation of human thought, and this requires liberty for Catholics and non-Catholics alike, for those who believe and those who do not."[35] Even the Conservatives in their "Plan of 1849" called for "real and effective tolerance against exclusivism and persecution, whether it be Catholic against Protestant or the deist or the atheist against the Jesuit or friar."[36]

In his showdown with the Church, President Mosquera made a tactical mistake that may have opened the door to the Conservative "regeneration," at least in the view of Colombian historian Fernando Díaz: Mosquera threatened to investigate his predecessor's scandalous distribution of Church property.[37] By alleging irregularities and threatening to sue for a more equitable distribution of land to the working class, Mosquera united both the Liberals and Conservatives, many of whom had profited from the fire sale, against him. When he dissolved the Congress, he was forcibly removed from power.

After Mosquera's fall in 1867, the Radical Liberals dusted off one of his initiatives and created the public National University, which soon acquired outstanding faculties in law and medicine as well as science and engineering. The Radicals also invested in primary education, increasing the number of students enrolled from 60,000 to 84,000 in a five-year period during the 1870s. As part of their plan to universalize public education, the Radicals passed the Organic Decree of 1870, making elementary education free and compulsory and requiring schools to be religiously neutral. They also promoted the establishment of schools for teacher training in Colombia's nine states, bringing in German teachers, some of whom were Protestant.

From the Vatican, Pius IX ordered resistance to the school reforms, warning in his last encyclical about the "great war" being waged against the Church by those gathering troops in "the synagogue of Satan."[38] When the Conservatives took up arms in 1876, their soldiers carried standards that bore the likeness of Pope Pius IX. The "war of the parish priests," as it became known, went on for 11 months, ending with a victory by the Radicals but weakening them sufficiently for "Independent Liberals" to head a new coalition of moderates. In a working alliance with the Conservatives, the Independents prevailed in the presidential elections of 1880, electing Rafael Núñez.[39] This was the start of the Conservative "regeneration."

How have historians evaluated the Liberal Era?

Modern historians, both Colombian and American, have judged the Liberal Era harshly. Among the historical briefs against the Liberals include their drastic reduction of the country's army, which encouraged regional rebellion and the privatization of violence; their radical provision of unbridled individual rights; and their inept liquidation of Church and Indian lands.[40]

On the positive side, the Liberals did push a premodern and deeply fragmented country toward the threshold of export development, individual rights (at least for a handful of the population), penal reform, and wider suffrage. They also succeeded in abolishing slavery and at least attempted to bring

Indians into the social mainstream. Colombia also became, if only for a few months in the single "sovereign" city-state of Vélez, the first country in the world to give women the right to vote.

Liberal initiatives in Colombia were part of a continent-wide effort to secularize society and reduce the power of the Church. Colombia's nine 19th-century wars, as disruptive as they were, were nothing like the bloody cataclysms of Paraguay (in which 400,000 lost their lives), or those of Mexico, much less the catastrophic U.S. Civil War, which claimed an estimated 620,000 lives. There were few democracies, if any at all, in Europe and the Americas that did not undergo a bloody gestation in search of representative government during the 19th century.

How did the Conservative "regeneration" consolidate state power?

As noted above, Rafael Núñez, first elected president in 1880, was a Liberal intellectual and diplomat who won with the support of key Conservatives. Núñez framed the country's challenge starkly as "either regeneration or catastrophe." Regeneration, in his view, meant establishing a centralized state with broad administrative power in open alliance with the Catholic Church as a guarantor of social cohesion and spiritual unity, and putting an end to laissez-faire trade policies.

In Núñez's second term, the Radical Liberals launched a rebellion that gave the president the justification, once it was crushed, to declare their constitution of 1863 null and void. In 1886, moderate forces drafted a new constitution, one that endured until 1991. It created a centralized unitary state and accorded the president a six-year term, along with the right to appoint all governors of the country's departments. The governors, in turn, appointed all the mayors in their departments. Catholicism was set forth as the official religion of Colombia, with public education administered in accord with Church teachings. The following year, 1887, Colombia and the Vatican signed a new *concordat*, compensating the Church for its land losses, providing an annual subsidy for the Church, and bringing back the Jesuits.

In many ways, the regeneration recycled the paternalism of the colonial era, institutionalizing obedience to the *patrón* as necessary to the higher ethos of the public good. Progress, for all its positivist themes about scientific organization and social order, remained as personalistic as before. The president's *hidalguía* (nobility) afforded him a reservoir of deference and respect that trumped the letter of any law. Individual rights were looked upon as vulgar and disorderly indulgences, especially when exercised by "the lower racial orders," as José María Samper called them. At the center of this seigniorial statism stood the Church, serving as both spiritual and secular guarantor for the Conservatives as well as the eventual scourge of the Liberals.

What changes took place during the regeneration?

Núñez and his cabinet implemented historic initiatives. In 1881, the government established a national bank that began issuing paper currency, a first in the country's history. The newly minted "Republic of Colombia" also doubled its total infrastructure of railroad tracks from 1885 to 1900, though its 650 kilometers (217 miles) hardly compared to Mexico's 20,000 (12,240 miles) or the U.S. grid of 362,000 (225,000 miles). The national government privatized huge portions (up to a half million hectares a year) of public lands and imposed new import tariffs to protect infant industries and fund the public purse.

In terms of economic impact, however, these statist reforms paled in comparison to the advent of the Coffee Revolution, which drove up national income and wages (at least in the coffee zone), brought in foreign capital, and enriched a new class of coffee cultivators, traders, and financiers. New York–quoted coffee prices, which increased from 10.6 cents a pound in 1887 to 18.8 cents a pound in 1893, led to a tripling of

Colombian coffee exports from 1878 to 1892, overtaking gold as Colombia's leading export earner.

For the Núñez government, the coffee boom boosted customs revenue, granting the national government more leeway in industrialization initiatives and an expansion of the armed forces, which grew to 10,000 by 1896. In 1894, the wily and pragmatic Núñez died, and his rigid and reactionary vice president, Miguel Antonio Caro, took over. To punish Liberal coffee producers and merchants, who were thought to have fomented a brief war against the government in 1895, the national government imposed an export tax on coffee, one that coincided with falling coffee prices. Within two years, coffee earnings fell precipitously, causing an economic slump that led to a severe reduction in government revenues. Although Caro suspended the export tax on coffee, the government's expansion of the money supply touched off a meteoric rise in inflation, resulting in the collapse of the peso in exchange markets. Caro was now facing a new coalition of opponents that grouped Liberals along with dissident Conservatives who called themselves the *Históricos*.

The ruthless exclusion of the Liberals, the country's foundering economy, and Caro's openly autocratic use of power pushed Colombia into war in 1899—one that would exceed all previous ones in terms of sheer destruction. Somewhere around 70,000 Colombians died in combat or from disease in the course of the war's 1,000 days (hence its name, the "Thousand-Day War"). Having lost major battles, the Liberals turned parts of the country into theaters of guerrilla warfare, foreshadowing what would happen a century later. The Conservatives responded with summary executions and the use of paramilitaries to eradicate suspected Liberal sanctuaries. By the time the Liberals sued for peace, the economy was completely devastated, with inflation reaching several thousand percent and refugees flooding into the cities.[41]

As Colombia tried to deal with the ruin of the Thousand-Day War, the U.S. administration of Theodore Roosevelt drafted a treaty proposing to build and operate a cross-isthmian canal in Panamá. Under the terms of the deal, Colombia would grant the United States a 100-year lease in exchange for both lump-sum and annual compensation. When the Colombian senate unanimously rejected the proposed treaty, Roosevelt denounced the senators as "contemptible little creatures," "jackrabbits," and "homicidal corruptionists." By the time Panamanian rebels declared their independence from Colombia in November 1903, American warships were already patrolling both of Panamá's coasts. Weeks later in Washington, the canal deal was signed between the United States and newly independent Panamá.[42]

Outraged but powerless, the Bogotá elite reeled in shock at the loss of Panamá. Colombia's disgrace, it seemed, was complete: the world map at the Paris Exhibition of 1901 depicted its national territory in yellow—the most leprous country in the world. Bogotá might have also vied as the world capital of syphilis, with an estimated 70 percent of young men infected in the city. Infant mortality reached 25 percent, with life expectancy at less than 30 years. The Thousand-Day War had taken the lives of an estimated 12 percent of males between the ages of 17 and 30—a staggering demographic blow. After the war, as epidemics such as typhoid fever, elephantiasis, and waterborne diseases continued to infest the country, one Cuban visitor described Bogotá as smelling like "an unburied cadaver."[43]

4

CONSERVATIVE PEACE AND THE LIBERAL REPUBLIC

How did Colombia recover from the Thousand-Day War?

Ruined and disgraced, Colombia somehow held a presidential election in 1904. Fortunately for the country, Conservative Rafael Reyes—a former general who had distinguished himself as Colombia's leading diplomat at the turn of the century—prevailed. He proved an extraordinarily resourceful individual. In a political culture largely inhabited by intellectual poseurs and conniving pretenders anxious to "cut a fancy figure," as David Bushnell put it, Reyes was down to earth, fearless, and determined to work with both Liberals and Conservatives in the cause of rescuing his country. He brandished a missionary's zeal about industrial progress, likening it to a "powerful locomotive, flying along the shiny rail, breathing like a volcano, that awakens people to progress, to well-being and to freedom. . . . And those who are resistant to progress are crushed under its wheels."[1]

Assuming office in August 1904 with the slogan "Less Politics, More Administration," Reyes faced pitched opposition from one faction of his own party, especially after he named two Liberals to his five-member cabinet.[2] Getting nowhere with his agenda of reform and reconciliation, he closed the Congress and called for the election of a national assembly. In the emerging showdown, Liberal leader and coffee *empresario*

Rafael Uribe Uribe backed Reyes, who, thanks to that protean figure, was able thereafter to govern by executive decree via the national assembly.[3]

Reyes's five years in office were filled with action. He launched a massive expansion of Colombia's rail and highway grid that set the stage for nearly two decades of rapid economic growth, imposed a drastic currency rationalization that brought the peso nearly back to parity with the dollar, and negotiated an agreement with foreign creditors over Colombia's external debt. Reyes also used state power to underwrite export growth and protect national industries through import tariffs. His signature legacy, however, was the guarantee of minority representation in future elections.[4]

Convinced that the United States was key to Colombia's commercial recovery, Reyes invited the Boston-based United Fruit Company to develop banana plantations in the department of Magdalena. In the final weeks of Teddy Roosevelt's presidency, he approached the Americans about settling the dispute over the Panama Canal, a proposition that was readily accepted in Washington. News of the proposed deal, however, sparked violent protests in Colombia.[5] Failing to quell the protests by imposing martial law, Reyes quietly boarded a United Fruit banana boat in Santa Marta and headed into exile.

How did Colombia become the "Republic of Coffee"?

At the turn of the century, Colombia was among the poorest of Latin America's 20 countries. From 1910 to 1913, it represented only 2 percent of total Latin American exports and received only 1.5 percent of U.S. investment in the continent. Taxes per inhabitant were one-seventh those of Argentina, half those of Peru, and two-thirds those of Venezuela.[6] Coffee conclusively changed all that, catapulting the country into the world's second-largest producer and converting Colombia into a leading destination for U.S. capital.

Americans, who consumed almost six times as much coffee as Europeans, imported nearly a third of world exports from producing countries. "Popular addiction" to coffee, as *Harper's* magazine termed it in July 1880, soon touched off a highly speculative futures market. In 1881, Wall Street created a coffee exchange to fix standards and grades, report critical information about production levels and diseases, and arbitrate disputes. If anything, the coffee exchange only added new, speculative runs to bull and bear coffee markets.[7]

Although Colombia was a latecomer to the new global coffee game (which had already resulted in a bonanza of export enrichment for Brazil, Costa Rica, Guatemala, and Mexico), the country had natural assets. Since coffee had no economies of scale, the only way to increase production was to bring more land into cultivation and hire more labor—and Colombia had ample supplies of both. Its other comparative advantage was that Brazil, the world's coffee leader, suffered from intermittent frosts and periodically withheld or destroyed its coffee inventories to stabilize coffee prices.

As Marco Palacios, the foremost historian on Colombian coffee, points out, the rebound of the global market in the early 20th century coincided with the surge in frontier colonization by small farmers who moved into western Colombia, the location of the country's most fertile coffee-growing soil.[8] The fact that smallholders mixed coffee cultivation with subsistence (and sometimes cash) crops like plantains, beans, yucca, and corn allowed them to live in situ on their own plots while selling their coffee at competitive prices. Since coffee cultivation required year-round fertilizing, pruning, and hand harvesting, the labor of women and children was also valuable.

From 1913 to 1929, Colombia experienced a 300 percent increase in the volume of coffee exports, with income gains widely shared among the producing and exporting parties. In contrast to Brazil, which continued to rely on huge plantations and captive labor, Colombia's coffee surge was proto-capitalist and produced a large class of yeoman farmers. The coffee census in 1932 counted some 150,000 farms, most of which were under 10 hectares (or 26 acres), with small farms producing 75 percent of Colombia's total crop.[9] Falling mortality rates for infants and young children, improved health care, and nutritional improvements were correlated to coffee earnings. From 1910 to 1930, Colombia's population nearly doubled (from 4 million to 7.5 million), thereby providing yet another labor multiplier.

Colombia's extraordinary conversion into the Republic of Coffee was also due to formation in 1927 of the *Federación Nacional de Cafeteros* (FEDECAFE), a trade association that became the country's most powerful quasi-public agency, eventually constituting "a sort of parallel government."[10] FEDECAFE managed the quality of Colombian coffee, fixed and stabilized internal prices, established depositories, and provided the beginnings of national agricultural extension programs for cultivators and processors. The organization may have also clipped the "claws of Yankee imperialism," in the words of coffee *empresario* Rafael Ospina Pérez, by curtailing the expanding financial power of American coffee roasters in Colombia.[11]

Even in the face of the Great Depression, which undermined political as well as economic stability all over Latin America, Colombia, by having used at least some of its coffee gains to create infrastructure, staved off mass social upheaval. Only when small farm expansion began breaking down as arable lands were used up and the global market faltered, Charles Bergquist concludes, did the stability of Colombian politics come under assault.[12]

What was the "dance of the millions," and why did the United States underwrite it?

In the course of almost two decades of negotiation over the canal question, Colombian leaders seemed to have learned how to play the Americans. In 1914, President Marco Fidel Suárez, a *paisa* (i.e., from Antioquia) intellectual and literary dilettante (who was proud of the fact that he been born illegitimate), had explicitly advised his countrymen to align Colombia with "the north star" (the United States). For memorable effect, he reduced this doctrine to a Latinate term: *respice polum* or "look to the pole."[13] Far more memorable for the Americans was the discovery of substantial deposits of oil in Colombia. As the U.S. Senate debated the treaty resolving the dispute over the Panama Canal, the Colombian government announced that it was canceling the 21 petroleum concessions the U.S. oil companies had been granted. The ensuing uproar provided Bogotá sufficient leverage to encourage Washington to conclude a speedy resolution of the canal question. The U.S. Senate—with "the smell of oil in the august chamber," as one senator put it—then ratified the Thomson-Urrutia Treaty in April 1921 and thus began one of the most intimate and historic alliances in the American hemisphere.[14]

In the wake of his election as president in May 1922, Pedro Nel Ospina Vázquez took a month-long victory lap, not in Colombia, but in the United States. The day after he arrived in New York City, the *New York Times* welcomed him in a front-page article with a lead editorial outlining his extraordinary career—a UC Berkeley graduate in mining engineering, the most decorated military officer of his generation, Colombia's former minister in Washington, and a self-made man of great wealth. "Don Pedro," as the New York press referred to him, had come with a simple message—Colombia was open for business. He impressed a dozen top bankers at India House on how to structure equity deals in Colombia and later addressed the International Chamber of Commerce about new investment schemes in mining, coffee, and cattle-growing. In an age of starchy, long-winded oration, Ospina spoke blunt, colloquial English without notes. It probably didn't hurt that he himself was an accomplished dealmaker as well as an agricultural magnate.[15]

Visiting Washington, Ospina was again given the royal treatment, just as he had been in New York. When he arrived at the Washington railway terminal, General John J. "Black Jack" Pershing—the hero of World War I—was on hand to greet him. Escorted by a defile of cavalry, Ospina and Pershing made their way to the White House where President Warren Harding hosted a glittering dinner for the Colombian president and his 16-year-old daughter, Helena.[16] Two days later, Harding invited him back to the White House "to talk shop," later joining Ospina in a press conference.[17] Back in New York City a second time, Ospina resumed his sales pitch, and the *New York Times* again indulged him with a headline: "Invest in Colombia, Gen. Ospina advises."[18]

Ospina's visit catapulted Colombia into a premier destination for U.S. capital investment in Latin America. The country was soon swarming with American entrepreneurs anxious to secure concessions in banana and sugar cultivation, as well as to purchase gold and emerald mines. Yankee *petroleros* (oilmen) began drilling in several parts of the country, while two major U.S. oil companies expanded their existing refineries. Ospina's strategy, however, was not to turn Colombia into a corporate neo-colony—except in the oil and banana belts, American investors generally had to settle for minority stakes—but rather to secure venture capital. The problem was that the country had a corrupt and shoddy banking sector, with an unstable currency and high internal rates of interest.

Ospina then pulled another rabbit out of his hat. With suitable fanfare, he invited a U.S. mission led by Edwin W. Kemmerer, a professor of finance at Princeton University, to overhaul Colombia's monetary and financial system. Kemmerer's plan was to create a central bank that engaged in open-market operations to stabilize interest rates and rationalize supply and demand of money, whose value would be fixed to the gold standard. Kemmerer also was charged with creating a banking superintendency, rewriting Colombia's organic budget law, and introducing a uniform negotiable instruments code based on comparable U.S. statutes.[19] The fact that U.S. secretary of state Charles Evan Hughes had personally

suggested Kemmerer's appointment lent an official conse-
quence to the mission.

Back at Princeton, the "money doctor," as Kemmerer was
nicknamed, remained on call or, more precisely, on retainer,
at the brokerage firm of Dillon, Read, steering tens of millions of dollars of venture capital to Colombia.[20] Ospina, in
turn, channeled much of this investment into city and departmental infrastructure and export-creation ventures. Ospina
also got Kemmerer to persuade one of New York's most prominent accountants, Thomas R. Lill, to review and radically revise Colombia's audit and accounting systems. By the end of
Ospina's term in 1926, the modern architecture of Colombia's
public finances was completely in place; Colombia was in perfect capitalist sync with its "north star." Triangulating off of
Washington and New York, Ospina had aggrandized presidential power, centralized the state, and instituted the most
advanced practices in monetary and financial management on
the continent.

"La danza de los millones" (the dance of the millions) went into
full swing. U.S. capital inflows increased by over 1,000 percent
in the 1920s, with commercial deposits in private Colombian
banks rising by more than 300 percent. Although direct investment in oil exploration, transport, and refining surged to
more than $50 million during that decade, the real bonanza
was the placement of more than $235 million of Colombian
securities in the New York financial markets. If anything, the
coffee boom (in which Colombia's earnings tripled during the
1920s), along with the country's distinction as a future oil pow-
erhouse (which, alas, later proved to be unfounded), pushed
capital flows to unrepayable amounts.

Colombia's infrastructural development was meteoric—
harbors were dredged, railway track doubled, telephone line
mileage grew from 5,095 miles in 1913 to 34,680 in 1927, and
freight volume increased by 800 percent during the 1920s.
"Public buildings seemed to spring from the ground," one
American academic later wrote, "as Colombia succumbed

to the heady wine of 'progress' poured from a cornucopia in the hands of U.S. bankers and their agents."[21] No fewer than 30,000 *campesinos* flocked to public works and highway construction projects in the first part of the 1920s, where they received wages five times as high as the day rate for agricultural laborers. Toward the end of the decade, more than 40,000 Pierce-Arrows, Cadillacs, and Stutz Bearcats—top-of-the-line automobiles—were traveling down Colombia's highways. The country had already established the first commercial airline in the Americas—the *Sociedad Colombo-Alemana de Transportes Aéreos* (or SCADTA).[22] In August 1922, President Ospina became the first chief executive in the world to ride in a commercial airliner.

Not everyone shared the Colombian elite's rapt fascination with all things American in the Roaring Twenties. "In the presence of the colossal republic," one skeptic lamented, "these people adopt the posture of a small bird before the hypnotic stare of the boa constrictor."[23]

What caused rising social unrest?

Even before the Great Depression ravaged the Western world, Colombia was experiencing the febrile economic effects of the Roaring Twenties. Inflation reached 8 percent per annum toward the middle of that decade. Real estate prices, especially in the cities, speculatively skyrocketed, while urban rents increased by 350 percent between 1918 and 1928.

Although the coffee boom had unleashed a tide of cash that had lifted tens of thousands out of absolute poverty, the drive to produce for export soon forced Colombia to begin importing food, so significant was the degree of labor displacement and land diversion. As the population of major cities crested, so did sickness and death among the urban poor who lived in filth and experienced epidemics. In 1928, only 5 percent of Bogotá's population of 224,000 had running water, and in the poorer parts of the city a single dwelling, on average, sheltered no fewer than 14 people. Outbreaks of scarlet fever, typhus, and diphtheria resulted in one in five infants dying during the first year of life—a rate that was among the highest on the continent.[24] For all the wealth created during the 1920s, life expectancy made only a marginal gain, from 32 to 34 years.

Colombia's urban crisis was accompanied by the beginnings of a social revolution in rural parts of the country as well. For the first time in its history, Colombia had a huge floating population, which variously headed to the cities, the oil and banana boomtowns, and the large encampments around railroad, highways, and bridge construction projects. Liberal politician (and future president) Alberto Lleras Camargo described Colombia as a "country in flood."[25] The lure of cash jobs over subsistence labor brought women, blacks, and the indigenous into a fluid and often desperate mix of job seekers, something tellingly portrayed in José Eustácio Rivera's *La Vorágine* (*The Vortex*, 1924). This novel depicted the grueling fate of rubber workers in the upper Amazon jungle—Colombia's heart of darkness.

Labor legislation gave some protections to workers, but in the oil towns and banana camps, such laws meant next to nothing when poised against the formidable power of the American multinational companies controlling those enclaves. If President Ospina was progressive on issues such as health care and education, he was more like a *paisa* magnate on labor rights, preferring captive company unions organized by the Catholic Church.[26] At Jersey Standard's facility (called Tropical Oil) in Barrancabermeja, when workers struck in 1924 for better wages (set at one and one-half pesos per day) as well as for some improvement in their appalling job conditions, they were fired upon by government troops. Tropical Oil then dismissed 45 percent of its workforce.

It was that event—the crushing of the Tropical Oil strike—that persuaded a diminutive, middle-aged librarian named María Cano to enter the violent fray of labor organizing. At first, the Revolutionary Socialist Party provided Cano nominal indulgence in the paternalist style of the time by naming her the "Red Flower of Labor" at their May Day celebration in Medellín in 1925. But soon, to the complete consternation of the Conservative government, she became a flame-throwing tribune not just to the brutalized and worn-out working men but to the vast legion of working women and children who labored (characteristically barefoot as a badge of their submission) for slave wages. In a succession of national tours into the oil and banana boomtowns on behalf of the Revolutionary Socialist Party, Cano linked up the miserable and isolated company enclaves into an archipelago of resistance: "Five thousand workers in Barrancabermeja," she declared in 1926, "want my heart to bring you the echo of their clamor for justice and their desire to put all their energies into this sacred hour. I am not going to ask for even a crust of bread. I am not going to ask for mercy. Only justice."[27]

The Conservative government, invoking the specter of Bolshevism and alleging that Cano and her cohorts were planning to shut down the country with a national strike, then passed the *"ley heroica"* (heroic law) stripping labor organizers of their individual rights. Cano's name in army and police circles soon became a noun—*mariacano,* or "subversive."[28] By the time Cano and her inseparable comrades, Ignacio Torres Giraldo and Raúl Eduardo Mahecha, began organizing banana workers at United Fruit's super-plantation in Magdalena, it seemed clear that violence would erupt.

What was the La Ciénaga massacre?

By contracting out hiring to local companies in the banana-growing zone, Boston's United Fruit Company (UFCO) had evaded the country's labor laws regarding the safety and health conditions of its workers. If UFCO's salaries (between $1 and $1.65 per day) were competitive in their day, the fact that they were paid, either in part or in whole, in company scrip (which could only be redeemed in company stores) was yet another means of managerial exploitation.[29] Additionally, company-provided housing was rife with violence and communicable infections. When 25,000 banana workers struck over wages and conditions in October 1928, UFCO manager Thomas Bradshaw wired President Miguel Abadía Méndez that "the situation here is extremely dangerous." The president then dispatched army units to the region of Santa Marta to stop strikers from blocking banana-laden trains heading for port. On December 6, 300 army troops began firing at the several thousand strikers near the railway station in La Ciénaga. How many workers were killed remains unknown.[30]

What branded the La Ciénaga massacre onto the nation's conscience was the wide-ranging investigation by the newly elected Liberal congressman, Jorge Eliécer Gaitán. Traveling out to La Ciénaga, Gaitán used his skills as a criminal defense attorney to reconstruct the slaughter from the testimony of eyewitnesses. When he returned to Congress in September 1929, *"el negro Gaitán"*—"Black Gaitán," as the dark-complected politician was referred to in the salons and elite clubs of Bogotá—provided gory details of the massacre. He indicted the Conservative government and its military units for wanton murder, and lambasted U.S. companies in Colombia as carriers of death and destruction. In the galleries of the Congress, Gaitán's supporters, at his encouragement, wore small black-and-white skulls on their lapels. "Today, tomorrow, or the day after," he declared in an outdoor rally, "that multitude, which suffers from injustice in silence, will know how to become desperate. On that day, oh scoundrels, there will be grinding of teeth."[31]

How did the Liberals get back into power in 1930?

Forty-five years into the Conservative ascendancy, the Church, despite social and economic upheaval, still ruled politically as if nothing had changed. The Church, in the view of Colombian historian Mary Roldán, was "a parallel arm of the government."[32] But Archbishop Ismael Perdomo bungled the Church's time-honored practice of designating a single Conservative candidate among those aspiring for the country's highest office. When two Conservatives then announced for president, the Liberals pounced, nominating Enrique Olaya Herrera, Colombia's minister in Washington, D.C., as their candidate. Even though women could not yet vote, Colombian suffragists like journalist Ofelia Uribe de Acosta played a key role in Olaya's victory, holding rallies and enjoining women to persuade their male associates to back the Liberal candidate. After winning the election, Olaya sat down with his mostly upper-class feminist backers and affirmed his commitment to their reform agenda—a pledge Ofelia Uribe and Anglo-Colombian writer Georgina Fletcher used to make Bogotá the host city for the Third International Feminine Congress in December 1930.[33]

The conference, in which the 200-odd delegates from various parts of the Western world openly discussed women's hygiene, venereal disease, prenuptial agreements, physical education for women, and female rights to property in marriage, produced "a gruesome uproar" in reactionary circles. Nonetheless, Olaya proved to be as good as his word, signing into law a measure giving married women the legal right to control property or income that they had either earned or brought into the marriage.

The advent of Liberal rule, however, coincided with Colombia's descent into economic depression, one in which public salaries fell by 50 percent, 30,000 public works laborers were laid off, and coffee, gold, and oil exports collapsed. In the rest of Latin America, the situation was even worse, with mass privation and social disorder resulting in military takeovers in seven countries in 1931 alone.[34]

Like General Ospina eight years before him, President-elect Olaya immediately headed to the United States for help. This time the mission was to delay repayment of Colombia's massive debt to the same U.S. creditors Don Pedro had once wooed. The administration of President Herbert Hoover, which itself was scrambling to stop a U.S. financial collapse, was in no mood to throw good money after bad. Olaya pressed his case with U.S. Treasury secretary and banking and steel tycoon Andrew W. Mellon, who was also a major stockholder in Gulf Oil. It worked. Colombia got a new $20 million loan from National City Bank of New York in exchange for a Colombian petroleum concession for Gulf Oil.[35] As for Kemmerer, the money doctor, he got a return invitation to Colombia and a working gratuity of 1,000 gold pesos.[36]

On the domestic front, Olaya's first steps as president were well-intentioned but unsuccessful in quelling partisan hatred. Having made peace with the Church during his brief campaign, Olaya appointed Conservatives to key ministries in his government of *concentración* (bipartisan consensus). He also appointed Conservatives to seven of Colombia's 13 departmental governorships. But violence began breaking out in multiple parts of the country anyway. There were pitched battles between Liberal and Conservative militias using French 19th-century Gras rifles in Santander, reports of atrocities in Quindío, and the burning of entire *pueblos* in Norte de Santander. Power-sharing through *convivencia*, or cooperative coexistence as it was known, might work among the ruling elite in Bogotá, where after a little cut-and-thrust in Congress, the rich men could retire to their clubs and share a drink. But in the devastated coffee towns and the abandoned public works *entrepots* of yesteryear, "the hereditary hatreds," as former president Miguel Antonio Caro had once called Colombia's two-party system, held sway.[37] There, vengeance over unrighted wrongs, as well as the Liberal assumption of electorally-derived spoils, produced a boiling cauldron of dispute.

With its rush of growth and sudden wealth, followed by speculative collapse, savage capitalism had shattered traditional modes of authority as well as the social controls on which they were based. The venality of local police, who usually sided with one party or the other, as well as the feeble reach of the state provided no sanction against the cycle of violence. By 1930, Colombia got its first look at the bloody abyss ahead.

What was the Liberal "Revolución en Marcha"?

The Liberals' reformist posture may have produced limited results, but it did keep the lid on open civil war or any take-over by the extreme right, something that was happening in many other Latin American countries. With the 1934 election of a second Liberal as president, Alfonso López Pumarejo, who soon launched his "revolution on the march," the promise of social transformation took on new momentum.

President López, a bourgeois progressive who favored Savile Row suits and expensive Scotch, was yet another Colombian leader fluent in English and even more schooled in high finance than his pro-American predecessors. Having made a fortune as, first, a broker at Baker-Kellogg in New York and, later, as the head of the Colombian branch of the American Mercantile Bank, López was a familiar figure in U.S. banking circles. Like Franklin D. Roosevelt, who was elected president of the United States in 1932, however, López was also something of a traitor to his class, determined to bend plutocratic interests to the cause of economic and social justice for the working poor. His *Revolución en Marcha* was to be Colombia's version of FDR's New Deal.

Even if the new president touted himself as a militant Liberal who would appoint no Conservatives to his cabinet or to the governorships, López quickly named the moderate and former president Olaya as his foreign minister in order to manage the all-important Americans. The Roosevelt administration soon proposed a bilateral trade agreement with Colombia, one in which the United States threatened to place an import tariff on previously untaxed Colombian coffee (75 percent of which went to the United States) unless Bogotá cut tariffs on 150 or so imported American products.[38] After two years of negotiations, this "triumph in free trade," as Secretary of State Cordell Hall grandly termed it, was signed on September 13, 1935.

President López was successful in advancing labor rights (including collective bargaining, the eight-hour day, and the 40-hour week), interceding *por su própia cuenta* (on his own account) in strikes on behalf of the unions. After facing down United Fruit in a labor action, López tried to seize the company's assets and transfer them to Colombian hands, a move set aside by Colombia's Supreme Court. As a result of López's pro-labor activism, the *Confederación de Trabajadores Colombianos* (Confederation of Colombian Workers), formed in 1936, expanded to some 100,000 members (about 2.25 percent of the total Colombian workforce by the end of the decade) under the political tutelage of the Liberal Party.[39]

In 1936, López pushed a series of constitutional amendments through the Colombian Congress that framed his social vision: "labor is a social obligation and it shall enjoy the protection of the state" and "property is a social function [that] for reasons of public utility or social interest . . . may be expropriated by judicial decree." He also proposed to end the Church's control over education and to provide what he termed "an equality of cults" in which civil and criminal laws would apply equally to priests for "acts contrary to Christian morals or subversive to the public order." His other proposed constitutional change was to institute universal male suffrage and eliminate the literacy requirement for voting. While women did not get the right to vote, they were granted the constitutionally-protected right to work as jurists and attorneys, which opened the doors to university education for females.

Although these constitutional reforms passed the Congress despite strenuous opposition, a sharp economic downturn in 1937, along with the implementation of new direct taxes on income and excess profits, brought the Revolution on the March to a full stop. When moderate Liberals revolted against López in Congress, he declared a moratorium on his own agenda until his term was finished.

Did the Revolución en Marcha *succeed?*

Historians would later debate López's supposed achieve-ments and his announced "revolution." On the positive side, he reframed the purpose of national government to serve all of its citizens and specifically made the state the partner of or-ganized labor. His administration also loosened the Church's iron grip on education. The shift away from the government's dependence on customs duties and excise taxes on tobacco and liquor to direct taxation proved historic in underwriting Colombia's perennially poor and feeble state. Revenue from direct taxes went from 8 percent of total public income in 1932 to 46 percent in 1950.[40] His reform to provide universal male suffrage was symbolically important even if it failed to include women. In short, the Revolution on the March advanced so-cial welfare and slowed some of the centrifugal pressures that would later shatter the country.

On the critical issue of land reform, however, López and his revolution fell short. In 1936, the Liberal legislative majority did pass Law 200, which, inter alia, protected long-standing land squatters from being summarily evicted by absentee es-tate owners. In the Department of Boyacá, for example, noted sociologist Orlando Fals Borda found Law 200 to have "forced many owners to subdivide their lands" and sell them off to tenants and squatters.[41] But another article in the new law pro-vided an escape hatch for large landowners, who were given 10 years to bring idle lands into cultivation before those prop-erties would escheat to the state. This window gave those landowners time to bring suits to enforce their titles against squatters or drive them off *ad interim* by using armed violence.[42]

At least in terms of perpetuating the Liberal hold on po-litical power, the Revolution on the March did succeed. In 1938, Colombians elected Liberal moderate Eduardo Santos Montejo, the wealthy owner of a major Bogotá daily, *El Tiempo*. Santos backed away from the pro-labor laws and practices of his predecessor and pushed for large-scale industrialization—a steelworks in Medellín, a shipyard in Barranquilla, and a rubber factory outside of Bogotá—while underwriting new industrial ventures by the newly formed *Instituto de Fomento Industrial* (Institute of Industrial Promotion). Santos also restored the servicing of Colombia's debt with the United States (which had been cut off in November 1932) and, in exchange, got new American loans and a steady flow of technical assistance.

5

"GOOD NEIGHBOR," THE NAZI THREAT, AND COLD WAR "ARMAGEDDON"

What was America's Good Neighbor policy?

Washington's closer ties to Bogotá were part of a broader U.S. effort throughout Latin America to be a "good neighbor," something President Franklin Delano Roosevelt had promised in his inaugural speech in March 1933.[1] FDR's "radical innovation," in the view of columnist Walter Lippmann, was to turn the Monroe Doctrine on its head by foreswearing armed intervention in the future while pulling the Marines out of their bloody occupations of Nicaragua and Haiti and demilitarizing the American presence in Cuba and the other so-called banana republics.[2] No longer would Washington serve as praetorian guard for Wall Street or Big Oil in the hemisphere, as was stunningly evident when Mexico nationalized American oil assets in 1938 and the Roosevelt administration sought a negotiated solution. Instead, the Americans pursued trade deals and an "inter-American system" anchored in "nonintervention" to settle disputes and engender cultural relations; it was, in Lippmann's opinion, "the true substitute for empire."[3] As the world headed toward war in the early 1940s, Good Neighbor would pay rich dividends in U.S.-led security in the hemisphere and dramatically transform America's alliance with Colombia.

FDR himself took the cause of nonintervention to the inter-American conference held in Buenos Aires in 1936. His reception in the Argentine capital was rapturous; two million *bonarenses*—as they called themselves—cheered wildly as FDR's motorcade wound its way through the city.

Although the Americans participating in that conference failed to exchange their nonintervention commitment for a continental collective security against the Germans, they found some measure of success at the next inter-American conference in Lima, Peru, in 1938. There, Secretary of State Cordell Hull and his gifted deputy, Sumner Welles, were able to push through a resolution asserting a united front among the American republics to "defend against any foreign intervention or activity."[4] In exchange, the Latin American governments got what they wanted as well—formal agreement by the United States not to interfere in the internal affairs of its southern neighbors.

In the late 1930s, Nazi Germany was rapidly expanding its influence in Latin America through trade deals, infiltration of provocateurs and spies trying to harness the loyalty of German immigrants (the so-called *Auslandsdeutschen*, or overseas Germans), and the deployment of cross-Atlantic "air bridges" by the German airline, Condor. In August 1940, after France had fallen to the Nazis, FDR named 32-year-old Nelson Rockefeller as head of the Office for the Coordination of Commercial and Cultural Relations between the American Republics (OCCCRBAR). Rockefeller, whose family foundation had already been at work for a decade funding health projects in Latin America, proved to be a creative whirlwind, deploying maestro Arturo Toscanini to do a concert tour in the Southern Hemisphere, organizing world-class art exhibitions there, and underwriting pro-American radio broadcasts in Latin American capitals while jamming pro-Nazi ones.[5]

Was there really ever any threat of a Nazi takeover in Colombia—or anywhere else in Latin America for that matter?

No, but it certainly didn't seem that way in 1940 and 1941. As the Nazi war machine rolled over Western Europe and then wheeled and tore through Eastern Europe and the Soviet Union the following year, Germany seemed invincible. Critical to the Nazi blitzkrieg tactic was the range and ferocity of its air power, something *Reichsmarschall* Herman Goering claimed could cripple the Panama Canal: "Two of my bombs dropped on the Culebra Pass would render the entire waterway unusable in ten minutes."[6] The other pressing fear concerned the Nazi capacity to spawn "fifth columns" to subvert countries targeted for neutralization or invasion from within.

When the Nazis began underwriting trade deals in Latin America, which doubled Germany's commerce in a single year, Roosevelt's economic adviser Bernard Baruch predicted that "German economic preparation could bring [Latin America] under her control without firing a shot."[7]

Owing to its strategic location—straddling two oceans and proximity to the Panama Canal—not to mention its export of platinum and rubber, Colombia was thought to be a key rampart in the defense of the hemisphere. Deciding to upgrade U.S. representation in Bogotá from a consulate to an embassy, the Roosevelt administration inventoried their ranks for a new ambassador. Welles's recommendation prevailed. Spruille Braden was a former All-American water polo player at Yale who had made a fortune (in addition to inheriting one) in Latin American mining and electricity mega-projects before joining Averell Harriman's securities firm as director. Married to a *chilena*, Braden spoke Spanish like a native and, shortly before his appointment to Colombia, had negotiated what many regarded as miraculous—a peace accord ending the Chaco War between Paraguay and Bolivia.

To sound the alarm about Nazi designs in the hemisphere, FDR showcased Colombia as a vulnerable front against the

Germans. On September 11, 1941, in a "fireside" radio address, Roosevelt warned the American public that "Hitler's
advance guards" were about to establish "bridgeheads in the
New World." FDR additionally claimed that the United States
had discovered "secret landing fields in Colombia, within easy
range of the Panama Canal." As tendentious as these claims
may have been, once the United States declared war on Japan
and Germany, Colombia quickly fell into line.[8] President
Eduardo Santos expelled Nazi agents and cut off diplomatic
relations with Berlin. He publicly supported the Allied buildup
around the Panama Canal, condemned Nazi persecution of the
Jews, and let American engineers build airstrips in the Amazon
so that the U.S. Rubber Reserve Corporation could harvest raw
rubber. When a Nazi U-boat sank a Colombian schooner off
the Caribbean coast with the loss of four lives in November
1942, Colombia declared war on Germany and Japan.

In addition to deploying 360 FBI agents in Latin America to
neutralize suspected Nazi subversion, the United States also
issued a "Proclaimed List of Certain Blocked Nationals" (PL),
a blacklisting operation created to take down companies with
supposed German connections. Within a year of its promulga-
tion, there were nearly 6,000 such listings for Latin America,
many based on trumped-up information or simple hearsay.
When, for example, the U.S. Embassy learned that the two
owners of a 100-year-old pharmaceutical company, *Laboratorios
Román*, had, while drunk, torn up a photo of FDR and made
pro-German remarks, it was blacklisted, causing that company
and dozens of others like it to be liquidated.[9]

Why did Colombia start to slip into the cycle of mass killing later called the Violencia?

During the 1930s, as social upheaval and military predation
engulfed most of Latin America, Colombia was able to avoid
political and societal breakdown. Thanks to its steady economic rebound during the 1930s when annual GDP growth

increased by an average of 4.7 percent, the country largely weathered the economic storm produced by World War II. Despite the collapse of trade with Europe, the Colombian economy continued to chug along at one of the highest annual growth rates on the continent—3.5 percent—between 1939 and 1946. The stock market, launched in 1932, enjoyed a tenfold increase in equity values during the same period. Colombia, it seemed, had secured a stable orbit of state-managed market capitalism tied closely to its "polar star."

During the war, the United States bolstered its southern neighbor's economy with over $100 million in portfolio investment and another $100 million in mining and oil extraction as well as funding upgrades in highways and public services.[10] The Americans also took the lead in negotiating the Inter-American Coffee Agreement in 1940, establishing import quotas and guaranteeing the sale of 80 percent of the country's crop to the American market. Coffee prices more than quadrupled within a year of the agreement.

But not all the news was good. Although national employment numbers increased slightly during this period, many sectors of the labor market experienced a moderate-to-severe loss in earning power. In 1940, for example, the majority of the families of railroad workers in Antioquia were found to be suffering from malnutrition. Mining employment declined nationally by nearly 50 percent between 1938 and 1951; 200,000 agricultural jobs were lost during the same period in Antioquia alone.[11] *Rentier* capitalism, because it tended to be speculative, accelerated boom-and-bust cycles in which the state lacked the means to stabilize increasingly large and floating labor populations.

The very success of small coffee farmers, whose highly productive freeholds had transformed Colombia into the Republic of Coffee, had sowed the seeds of dispute and the potential for land violence. "Coffee farmers," Charles Bergquist noted, "were encouraged by their situation to use their wits to take advantage of their rivals at every opportunity. Some stole from rival farmers. . . . Most tried to cheat landowners of part of their portion in sharecropping agreements. Others sought to change boundaries of property."[12]

Although the Liberal Party won the presidency again in 1942 and controlled the majority of Colombia's cities and towns, the party soon abandoned its agenda of social transformation.[13] In his second term, President Alfonso López not only refused to continue backing organized labor, he threatened to use government troops to break up strikes. The same thing happened with women's rights: in his first term, López had declared discrimination against women illegal, but in his second term he refused to consider granting women the right to vote.

Politically paralyzed by Liberal Party dissension, López abandoned the presidency, leaving it in the hands of his lieutenant Darío Echandía before flying to the United States to attend to his wife's failing health. Not long after he returned to Colombia, López was arrested by a group of rebellious army officers while touring the southern department of Pasto. In July 1945, he resigned the presidency in favor of his minister of interior, Alberto Lleras Camargo.

For all their setbacks, the Liberals were still the country's majority party by a wide margin and would have probably won the 1946 presidential election if they had run a single candidate. Instead they put up two—former Colombian ambassador to the United States Gabriel Turbay Abunader and populist firebrand Jorge Eliécer Gaitán, who had originally made his mark investigating the massacre of the United Fruit banana workers in 1928. An accomplished orator, Gaitán was also a gifted administrator who had served as minister of education and, later, mayor of Bogotá. "If he was conversant with communism and the more militant ideologies of his day, he was, at heart, a moralist reformer who saw the *petit bourgeoisie*—teachers, shop-owners, office workers, and self-supporting artisans—as those who would remake Colombia in their own hard-working image."[14]

In the three-way race for president, Gaitán came in third, with the Conservative candidate, Mariano Ospina Pérez, the nephew of former president Pedro Nel Ospina, winning with 42 percent of the total vote. Ospina immediately did what his late uncle would have done—he formed a government of national unity; but unlike Don Pedro, the new president lacked the political heft to make it work.[15] When local and regional Conservatives in Boyacá began terrorizing Liberal officeholders in order to seize political control of towns and small cities, the new president did nothing. As violence spread, with farms and businesses owned by Liberals being forcibly "cleansed," President Ospina did take action, but it only made things worse. He expanded the ranks of the national police by hiring and arming local Conservative enforcers who violently set upon Liberal leaders and party members. In Liberal strongholds, there were bloody counterattacks against Conservatives. Some 14,000 Colombians were killed during the first 12 months of Ospina's presidency. To stop the *"Violencia,"* as it was now called, Liberal and Conservative leaders initialed a formal agreement in August 1947, but it only worked for a short time.

How did the Cold War affect Colombia?

In June 1947, Secretary of State George C. Marshall announced a $25 billion plan to revive Western European economies and shield those countries from communist subversion. In September, President Harry S. Truman traveled to Rio de Janeiro, Brazil, to sign a treaty of "reciprocal assistance," establishing collective security within the hemisphere. When Colombia ratified the treaty later that year, it immediately received its first modern aircraft, three B-25 bombers and 35 P-47 fighters. Their first targets were Colombians.

As with the Nazi scare, the United States tended to interpret internal dissidence and unexpected regime change (seven Latin American governments were forced out of power in 1947–1948 alone) as the making of a new "Armageddon," to use the term Secretary of State Dean Acheson employed regarding the showdown with the Soviet Union. "We cannot be too dogmatic about the methods by which local communists are dealt with," Acheson's deputy, George F. Kennan, the State Department's preeminent architect of containment, concluded.[16] Along with the arms shipments, communications like Kennan's were enough for right-wing elites in Latin America to declare open season not just against suspected communists, but reformist Liberals as well. In Bogotá, President Ospina now had a crucial partner in his refusal to deploy the army or the police to stop the terror in the countryside, something U.S. ambassador Willard L. Beaulac blamed on "communists and left-wing liberals."[17] The Liberal Party, the CIA now charged, was in "collaboration" with the Colombian Communist Party.[18]

As refugees continued to pour into Colombia's major cities, Liberal leader Gaitán raised money to create *"casas de refugio"* (houses of refuge) and toured Santander state to discourage Liberal reprisals against the terror. But his efforts did little good. In early February, Gaitán called for nonviolent protest demonstrations to be staged across the country. In Bogotá, over 100,000 people dressed in black and silently waved white handkerchiefs. In his somber remarks that day, Gaitán could have rallied the throng to shut down the Congress or attack the presidential palace, but he didn't. Instead, as Colombian historian Herbert Tico Braun observes, "Gaitán demonstrated yet again his respect for the law and did the most powerful and disconcerting thing of all: he ordered the crowd home."[19]

As Colombia prepared to host the Ninth Inter-American Conference, one that would prospectively inaugurate the Organization of American States, even the normally alarmist U.S. mission in Bogotá believed that the Liberal-Conservative bloodletting would subside during the historic international gathering in March 1948. The Colombian government spared no expense in cleaning up and refurbishing the capital city. Foreign minister Laureano Gómez Castro, the conference organizer, ordered the import of a fleet of Mercedes-Benzes along with thousands of white porcelain cups embossed with the Colombian national emblem.[20]

As the days wound down before the opening of the conference, the Bogotá police, reinforced by Conservative thugs called *chulavitas* (who later comprised roving death squads), cleared the downtown streets of vagabonds and street people. Still, refugees from the strife-ridden countryside continued to stream into the outlying barrios of the city. On the eve of the conference, Germán Arciniegas wrote that there was "a chill wind of terror blowing in from the provinces."

Gaitán, now excluded by the government from participating in the hemispheric conference, got back to his law practice. On the morning of April 9, 1948, he was in a happy mood, having just won an acquittal for a client in a murder case. Leaving with friends for lunch before his scheduled meeting with a Cuban law student named Fidel Castro later that day, Gaitán walked out of his office building and onto the street. It was 1:05 p.m. A shabbily dressed man approached and drew out a revolver, aiming it at Gaitán. Shots rang out. Gaitán, hit in the head and back, fell to the pavement, fatally wounded. Passersby pursued the assassin and beat him to death.[21]

The news rang out in every radio and PA system in the country: *"Mataron a Gaitán"* (They killed Gaitán!). Miguel Ojeda, a teenage refugee from the Colombian municipality of Risaralda then living on the downtown streets of Bogotá, remembered that suddenly—"it was like in an instant"—there were huge numbers of people in the streets, "roaring, screaming, weeping."[22] The 21-year-old Fidel Castro saw "crazed people running . . . with an indescribable fear in their eyes . . . a state of indescribable rage was created."[23] Then there was the sound of glass shattering and the crackle of gunfire.

Catholic churches, whose steeples the angry crowd thought were being used by Conservative snipers to shoot down at them, were set aflame. Ojeda saw a priest hauled out to a street corner and beaten. "Someone raised him up; someone else ran forward and cut his throat." Colombia's bloodiest night had begun.

PART II

THE MODERN ERA, 1946–2019

Map 1 Map of modern Colombia

6

THE "*VIOLENCIA*" AND MILITARY RULE

What was the effect of Gaitán's assassination?

In the rioting that erupted after Gaitán's assassination, an estimated 1,000 people were killed and more than 100 buildings in downtown Bogotá were firebombed and completely destroyed.[1] The surging crowds first concentrated their attack on the presidential palace in an effort to seize President Ospina, but a detachment of his guard held them off until tanks arrived and turned their machine guns on the protesters. The crowds then began looting retail shops and businesses in downtown Bogotá. Holed up in the U.S. Embassy, Ambassador Beaulac watched the plundering from a window. "Amidst the sickening tragedy we were witnessing," he later wrote, "we could not help but be amused by the businesslike manner in which those people carried out their new trade. . . . Barefoot women trudged by, their arms loaded with furs and fancy lingerie. One ragged individual carried an electric stove on his back."[2] Other scenes were not as amusing. A young girl watched from a rooftop as a drunken rioter, his arm covered with stolen wristwatches, was set upon by another plunderer who hacked the arm off with a machete and made off with the watches.[3]

Elsewhere in the country, there were similar violent upheavals in the wake of the assassination, which the Liberals universally blamed on the Ospina regime. In the town of

Puerto Tejada on the Cauca River, outraged Liberals murdered Conservative leaders, decapitated them, and kicked their heads around soccer-style in the town square.[4] In other places like the Valley of Cauca, *gaitanistas* organized revolutionary juntas and raised popular militias.[5] But with the army backing the national government and the Liberal Party now in a power-sharing agreement with President Ospina's Conservative regime, the prospect of mass rebellion was quickly snuffed out.[6] As part of the cleanup, Colonel Gustavo Rojas Pinilla, the army commander in the Cali area, began using civilian assassins nicknamed *pájaros* (birds) to hunt down and murder *gaitanistas*.[7]

At first, the terror-stricken elite heaped scorn on the *chusma* (rabble) for its savagery in the *bogotazo* (as the popular uprising in the wake of Gaitán's assassination came to be known), but soon turned to the usual suspects—the communists. In the days following the mass upheaval, President Ospina broke off relations with the Soviet Union and ordered the arrest of Colombian communist leaders. Archconservative Laureano Gómez, who had fled Colombia for Falangist Spain, charged that the terrible events "were produced according to an infamous [Communist] plan carried out by the Liberal masses. The Liberals had placed themselves at the service of 'the beast.'"[8] Leading Liberals like Enrique Santos, anxious to distance his party from responsibility for the upheaval, much less any relationship with the "Reds," claimed he had proof of communist responsibility.[9]

Why was Gaitán's death a turning point in Colombian history?

Gaitán had embodied the dreams of tens of thousands of upwardly mobile Colombians and millions more who were poor and of mixed race. "Gaitán has put into circulation among us a new value," Juan Lozano Lozano wrote: "the social value of politics."[10] That social value was the articulation of a common identity, one in which the *país nacional* (the country of the people), as Gaitán had called it, would gain preeminence over the *país político* (the country of the elite). The moral reason for this transformation, Gaitán had said, was that "the people are superior to their leaders." With his assassination, the obliteration of popular hope touched off fratricidal mayhem.

In the wake of the *bogotazo*, the leaders of the two parties tried to go back to their collusive ways, but now there was an insuperable problem: Gaitán had exposed and undercut them. Increasingly adrift in the rising tide of rural violence, they could neither impose order nor share power. In May 1949, the Liberals withdrew from their coalition government with the Conservatives for the fourth and final time. Without that indispensable element for *convivencia* (coexistence), Ospina was stuck. He could not govern in coalition as president, and he was being undermined by the growing ranks of Conservative diehards.[11] The following September, armed Liberal and Conservative representatives opened fire on each other on the floor of the Congress, leaving two dead. Thereafter, the Liberals, still enjoying a large majority in the Congress, announced that they would impeach Ospina, who responded to this threat by closing the Congress and declaring an *estado de sitio* (state of siege).

At that point, Conservative Laureano Gómez flew back from Spain to assume the presidential candidacy of his party. Addressing a large crowd in Medellín shortly after his arrival, Gómez offered a strange and chilling portrait of why liberalism and communism were both embodied in the deadly lizard of European folk legend—"*el basilisco*" (basilisk). "The basilisk was a monster with the head of one animal, the face of another, the arms of yet another and the feet of a deformed creature. . . . Our *basilisco* walks with feet of confusion and naivete; with legs of blows and violence, the stomach of the oligarchy; its breast is fury, its arms Masonic and it has a small, diminutive Communist head, yet it is the head."[12] Leading members of the Church echoed similar sentiments.

By the time Gómez won the presidency in an uncontested election, Liberals were regrouping in the countryside, forming death squads. As the dirty war spiraled out of control, the Church began to reconsider its Conservative partisanship. The archbishop of Bogotá, Ismael Perdomo, chose "Thou Shalt Not Kill" as the subject of his pastoral letter in 1950. The following year Colombian bishops declared their partisan neutrality, saying that responsibility for violence should be made by the "judgment of history."[13] In Washington, there were also second thoughts about sending military aid to a government engaged in mass repression, but this ultimately amounted to handwringing. Even the idea of a U.S.-led hemispheric *demarche* to stop mass violence in Colombia was brushed aside as too "pro-liberal."[14]

For all of that, there was a strange and surreal quality to Colombian fratricide: because the vast majority of the victims of the *Violencia* were unarmed peasants in the countryside, the terror hardly touched the cities. The term "*Violencia*" itself objectified something sourceless precisely because the butchery occurred out of sight. By the mid-1950s, however, Colombians began raising questions about the deeper causes of the *Violencia*—and above all, why nothing could stop it.

Was it really partisan mayhem? Or was that the symptom of a deeper disorder? Perhaps it was no disorder at all but rather the system, savage and extractive as it always had been, operating at a new and devastating efficiency. After all, in the midst of the terror, Latin America's oldest democracy trudged ever on, electing a new president and a new congress (admittedly in a state of siege) and presiding over the country's record-level economic growth; this, while tens of thousands were dying violently—50,000 in 1950 alone. How could that be?

What explains the Violencia?

In 1958, shortly after becoming the first president in the Liberal-Conservative power-sharing pact called the "National Front," Alberto Lleras toured one of the worst of Colombia's massacre sites in the northern part of the state of Tolima. In the town of El Líbano, he met a beleaguered parish priest, Father Germán Guzmán, who had witnessed and survived the terror. President Lleras asked Guzmán to prepare an in-depth report.[15] Joined by two other academics in the National University's new sociology department, Father Camilo Torres and Orlando Fals Borda, Guzmán (and later jurist Eduardo Umaña) pieced together a two-volume, 430-page account. Its release in 1962 touched off an outpouring of shock and disgust as well as furious recrimination against the three authors for setting forth the unspeakable. "The book pierced the lives of urban Colombians, especially those active in public life, within the government, the Church, and the universities," remembered Herbert Tico Braun, who was 13 years old at the time and growing up in a middle-class family in Bogotá. "There was something deep in the heart of the nation that was hardly controllable."[16]

In one section of the book entitled *Tanatomanía* (roughly, "maniacal love of death"), Guzmán detailed the "profaning of corpses."[17] In the *"corte de corbata"* (tie cut), for example, the victim's throat was cut open and the tongue pulled out to resemble a tie. In the *"corte de franela,"* the entire throat was cut away so that the victim's head could be pulled back in a smiling rictus. In the *corte de mica* (the monkey cut), the decapi-tated head was placed on the victim's chest. Even rape gained a new *"dantesco"* (Dante-esque) profanity.[18] Being raped before fathers, brothers, and children was common and often pre-ceded live dismemberment. Rape of pregnant women was re-portedly followed by cutting out the child and displaying it on the mother or placing one of its dismembered limbs in her mouth. *"No dejar ni la semilla"* (Don't leave even the seed).[19]

Guzmán's account detailed not only such homicidal dep-redations but a deeply compromised country in which the custodians of law and public authority themselves—the po-lice, judges, and local party chieftains—were often either the instigators or the beneficiaries (or both) of the terror. If the *Violencia* had started as partisan mayhem between Liberals and Conservatives from 1946 until the early 1950s, later in that decade it morphed into terror sprees by criminal bands, especially in the *llanos* (plains) and the central *cordillera* (mountain chain). Until Guzmán's book, Liberal guerrilla leaders like *Desquite* (Revenge), *Chispas* (Sparks), and *Sangrenegra* (Black Blood) had enjoyed a Robin Hood–like cachet in certain Liberal circles. With its publication, however, they too were exposed as nothing more than psychopaths and bandits.

By the time Guzmán's book came out, the *Violencia* had morphed yet again. Peasant defense leagues, formed in the course of the terror, had established armed, autonomous enclaves, some with communist members.[20] Initially, the government had largely ignored these self-styled "independent republics," but under U.S. pressure to eliminate any vestige of insurgent communism, the Colombian government put into operation a counterinsurgency plan devised jointly by the U.S. and Colombian military to destroy those enclaves.

The furor over Guzmán's book was followed by a mute silence for some 15 years after its publication; the subject, Colombian scholar Tico Braun contends, became taboo.[21]

The "rediscovery" of the *Violencia* began with Paul Oquist's grand interpretative effort in *Violencia, conflicto y política en Colombia* (1978), which argued that the *Violencia*, although it varied from region to region, fed off the partial collapse of the national state, whose growing power during the 20th century had been subverted by the savage events of the late 1940s.[22]

French sociologist Daniel Pécaut's monumental *Orden y Violencia en Colombia: Evolución socio-política entre 1930 y 1954* (1987, 2 vols.) set forth an even more ambitious theory. The state, in Pécaut's argument, had never been regarded as the legitimate agent of social unification, but rather as a purveyor of material advantage via political contest. Thus, the fact that Colombia's restricted democracy had coexisted with high levels of violence was not paradoxical but mechanical. "Violence is consistent with the exercise of democracy which, far from being based on the homogeneity of its citizens, rests

on the preservation of the natural differences, collective loy-
alties and private networks of social control. . . . Colombian
democracy makes them into a mechanism of its continuity."[23]
In short, the system worked even if some 200,000 people were
murdered in the process. Robert A. Karl captures a further and
far-reaching paradox: "Even if it established a black legend for
Colombia, *La Violencia* still succeeded in binding the local and
regional into a national narrative."[24]

How did the economy fare during LaViolencia?

Surprisingly well. Between 1945 and 1953, it grew by an average of 6 percent annually, while industrial production increased at a rate of more than 9 percent. The commodity boom
at the conclusion of World War II pushed the price of coffee
from 20 cents a pound in 1945 to 50 cents a pound in 1950—
and then all the way up to a historic high of 86.3 cents in 1954.
Economic growth, however, hardly trickled down. Real wages,
depleted by outbreaks of inflation driven by internal speculative bubbles, remained flat. The *Banco de la República*, having
built up large dollar reserves during the war, was meanwhile
investing the country's savings into capital-starved domestic
industries for the purpose of industrialization.

Import substitution industrialization (ISI, as it is known)
may have had a mixed record elsewhere in Latin America, but
in capitalist Colombia it seemed to work well.[25] First, ISI was
bolstered by income from the coffee bonanza as well as by the
inflow of public and private capital from an indulgent United
States. Second, the business elite was in intimate consonance
with its businessman-president, who appointed prominent
financiers, industrial magnates, and lawyers for foreign oil
companies as his government ministers.[26] This seamless collaboration permitted President Ospina to establish a national
petroleum company, ECOPETROL, and to build a steel mill at
Paz del Río while overseeing the expansion of FEDECAFE, the
powerful coffee producers' association that Ospina himself had

once run. FEDECAFE established its own merchant fleet and opened a bank, the *Banco Cafetero*. Unlike Mexico, Argentina, and Brazil, Colombian ISI was neither populist nor union-driven, but paternalist and union-neutralizing. *Gremios* (employer associations) rapidly expanded and served as a conduit for a wide range of regional business groups in spurring business activity.[27] By the end of the 1950s, not only had industrial production doubled in the course of that decade, but capital goods (as a percentage of total industrial output) had doubled as well.[28]

In terms of land tenure, the *Violencia* seemed to fortify a plutocratic takeover in certain rural parts of the country. In the coffee-rich Quindío, for example, the *nouveaux riches* of the *Violencia* were local storekeepers, coffee buyers, estate foremen, and local political bosses who had extorted, assassinated, or defrauded their way into absconding with millions of acres of productive land.[29] *Violentólogo* (violentologist, as such analysts were later named) Gonzalo Sánchez would subsequently map the *Violencia*'s five different impacts in property tenure—all resulting in the retention or reinforcement of the power of the *hacendados* (estate owners).[30]

Why did Colombia join the United States in the Korean War?

Laureano Gómez, who had clawed his way to power in 1950, faced an untenable situation. Even with his de facto dictatorship, the Conservatives remained a minority party, unable either to put a stop to the bloodshed or to defeat the armed Liberal counteroffensive in the countryside. The Catholic Church, the age-old ally of the Conservatives, was increasingly reluctant to endorse or otherwise countenance government repression. The loyalty of the Colombian Army was also in doubt.[31] But fortune struck for Gómez when communist North Korea attacked American-supported South Korea in June 1950. As Washington tried to clear a multinational path for military intervention, first successfully persuading the UN

Security Council to declare North Korea the aggressor in the crisis, the Truman administration turned to the Organization of American States (OAS) for military backing. Most Latin American governments either rejected or ignored the appeal, but not Colombia. President Gómez pledged a frigate, the *Almirante Padilla*, as well as an army battalion to the American-led UN expeditionary force. The Truman administration, desperate for allies in the conflict, fairly jumped on the offer.

At a time when Colombia badly needed to deploy its 21,000-man army (of whom some 7,000 were combat-ready) to quell its own civil war, the country was instead sending a substantial number of its forces to fight in a faraway conflict irrelevant to its national interest. But Gómez had a more pressing priority: he sought to get the United States to back up his own war against the Liberals. To do that, he committed Colombia to America's widening conflict against communism.

In Korea, the 1,080-strong Colombian battalion, after first being embedded in the U.S. Eighth Army, joined the U.S. Army's 7th Infantry Division to fight against Chinese communist forces in a bloody campaign to secure a series of ridgelines and mountaintops near the 38th parallel. In the battle of Old Baldy, the Colombians, though outnumbered and outgunned, fought the Chinese to a stalemate, killing 750 of them while losing 20 percent of their own forces.[32] In total, 4,300 Colombians served in Korea and, given the scores of battle-field decorations and commendations awarded them by their American commanders, acquitted themselves capably.[33] From the standpoint of the U.S. military, the fact that the Colombians had fought bravely in a bitter war against communism won them a generation of respect and material affirmation.[34]

After Korea, as Washington sped up the supply of a wide array of modern weaponry to Colombia, senior U.S. national security officials groomed General Gustavo Rojas Pinilla (then serving as vice chairman of the powerful Inter-American Defense Board in Washington) in the cause of anticommunism. The American military flew Rojas to the Korean front for a victory lap, and President Truman awarded him the Legion of Merit.[35] Anti-Gómez followers of former president Ospina, with the connivance of General Rojas, were actively plotting to overthrow the isolated and widely detested incumbent. In June 1953, with the support of the Church, Liberal and Conservative newspapers, the *gremios*, the intelligentsia, and now the Americans, General Rojas bloodlessly removed Gómez from office. "No more blood, no more depredations in the name of any political party, no more rancor between the sons of the same immortal Colombia. Peace, law, justice for all, without distinction," Rojas eloquently promised.[36] Exhausted and spiritually eviscerated by six years of butchery, the whole country seemed to utter a sigh of relief.[37]

Why didn't military rule (1953–1958) stop the mayhem?

Initially, it did. General Rojas offered a complete and unconditional amnesty to the belligerents, provided they would lay down their arms. In the first six months of the amnesty, an estimated 10,000 fighters turned over their weapons, many walking miles to exchange surrender for a blanket pardon. General Rojas traveled throughout the country, presiding over the disarmament and demobilization ceremonies, preaching reconciliation and promising to rebuild at least some of the hundreds of sacked towns and tens of thousands of abandoned farms left behind in the wake of the *Violencia*.[38] The results were extraordinary. Homicides declined from 22,000 in 1953 to 1,900 by the end of the following year.

Rojas's first year in office was stellar in every respect.[39] When a catastrophic frost decimated the Brazilian coffee crop, the international price of coffee soared to 99 cents a pound, allowing Rojas to impose an export tax on coffee that filled government coffers. Along with generous aid from the U.S. government, Rojas was able to build hospitals and airports, pave roads, dedicate a state steel mill, and inaugurate television in Colombia. Using the constituent assembly (known by its acronym, ANAC) convened by his predecessor, Rojas banned the Communist Party and awarded himself the title of "president" along with a term of four years.[40] Crucially, the Church gave its blessing to Rojas's apparently benign dictatorship.

President Rojas then moved aggressively to build up the Colombian Army, expanding its forces by one-third, tripling its yearly budget, and, after institutionally embedding the national police into army ranks, renaming it the "Combined People and Military Forces." The United States actively supported this buildup, providing 25 fighter jet trainers and 16 light bombers, along with training for hundreds of Colombian officers at American bases in the Canal Zone. Sixty of those officers went on to complete the elite Ranger course at Fort Benning before inaugurating their own Ranger unit, the *Lanceros*, back home.

Rojas "the deliverer," as the CIA now called him, had totalitarian pretentions, however. He referred to himself as the "custodian of the most authentic wishes of Bolívar," while expressing his open admiration for the Argentine populist strongman, General Juan Domingo Perón.[41]

As Rojas's political stock began to slip, the leader of the Union of Colombian Women, Esmeralda Arboleda, sensed a historic opportunity, publicly calling for the president to grant women the right to vote.[42] When Rojas did so on August 25, 1954, Colombia, Latin America's oldest democracy, achieved through dictatorship what it had conspicuously failed to do through democracy—give women suffrage.

In 1954, amid growing national protest, Rojas declared a state of siege. In June, a student demonstration at the National University was fired upon by units from the recently returned *Batallón Colombia*, leaving 13 students dead and scores wounded. Later, General Rojas ordered the Liberal daily, *El Tiempo*, to be shut down, something that caused President Dwight Eisenhower to instruct U.S. ambassador Philip W. Bonsal to intercede with Rojas to express U.S. "concern."[43] Ambassador Bonsal, a former Sumner Welles aide during the Good Neighbor era, persuaded the Eisenhower administration to forbid the Colombian military from using American-provided aircraft and napalm in the brutal pacification of eastern Tolima and the Sumapaz region of the state of Cundinamarca.[44] Faced with peasant groups that had refused to give up their weapons, the government sealed off the entire Villarica area and mercilessly routed the civilian population.[45] In Cauca, government pacification was, if anything, even more draconian. Rojas's new secret police force, the *Servicio de Inteligencia Colombiana* (*SIC*) began deploying Conservative assassins, the *pájaros*, to execute known Liberals. By 1956, the *Violencia* had reignited in many parts of the country, resulting in 11,000 politically-related homicides that year.

With U.S. support still secure, however, the Rojas regime announced that the president would not step down in 1958 but rather continue in office until 1962, something that only quickened a historic rapprochement between the Liberal and Conservative Parties. The two parties signed a pact, promulgated by former presidents Alberto Lleras and Laureano Gómez, formalizing their opposition to military rule as well as their dedication to return to democracy in a bipartisan coalition government. As anti-Rojas protests spread throughout the country, Catholic archbishop Cristiano Cardinal Luque, who had once blessed the Rojas dictatorship, now damned it as "illegal," a position endorsed by ANDI, the national association of industrialists. On May 6, 1957, in a nationwide strike, banks refused to open, factories shut their gates, transport workers stayed home on paid vacations, and even sidewalk vendors, normally teeming on the downtown streets of Colombian cities and towns, were nowhere in sight. When Rojas supporters turned to thugs and assassins to break up the national work stoppage, the army moved against the dictator, forcing him into exile and publicly promising to return the country to bipartisan civilian rule.

7

THE NATIONAL FRONT

1958–1974

What was the National Front?

In the course of Colombian history, Liberals and Conservatives had, on critical occasions, put aside their partisan hatreds in order to save their country—and themselves—but the most durable constitutional construct of them all was the National Front (NF). Approved by 95 percent of the country's voters in a 1957 plebiscite, it anchored the civilian government in Liberal-Conservative power-sharing. All elective and appointive positions, local, regional, and national, would be apportioned 50-50, and presidential terms would alternate between the two parties. The "consociational regime," as it was later called, was scheduled to continue for 16 years until 1974.[1]

Not unlike Francisco Santander's dramatic return from exile in New York in 1832 after the fall of Bolívar or Enrique Olaya's coalition regime at the start of the 1930s, the National Front took the shards of a broken system and fused them into a working whole. Elections ceased to be causes for war but rather became rubber stamps for power-sharing and nonviolent succession. Colombia's historically weak state was notably strengthened, especially given the imprimatur of the military, which took over the national police and assumed responsibility for public order. The Church, having been buffeted and excoriated for its role in the *Violencia*, embraced its new status as a neutral partner in the emerging political culture. With more than 1.8 million women having voted in the plebiscite creating the NF, the bipartisan regime added a large new constituency to its voter rolls.

As part of the constitutional change, the Congress could only pass legislation with a two-thirds majority vote, something that over time strengthened the presidency even more. The national bureaucracy, which had numbered 100,000 in 1950, grew exponentially during the NF. (By 1990, almost one million people would be in the government's employ.) The age-old fault line between regional and national power was progressively bridged, and party warfare over election spoils in the wake of changes in regime was terminated. In many ways, Colombia's political elite had crafted a peaceful way of restoring its former hegemony through the National Front without having to resolve the democratic deficit that Gaitán had so vividly dramatized. If popular allegiance did wane vis-à-vis the recycled oligarchy, the institution of a professional civil service in the early 1960s helped to reinforce the state's reach as a merits-based arbiter.

In the NF's first presidential election, Liberal Alberto Lleras Camargo, the former acting president and foreign minister in the 1940s who had also served as Colombia's ambassador in Washington, received 80 percent of the vote. In the election, no less than 73 percent of those over the age of 21 cast ballots. Lleras was a man of diminutive stature who hardly seemed like the titan he would prove to be.* A journalist by training, he had served as the editor of *El Tiempo* and later as rector of one of Colombia's new universities—Los Andes. He had long been a peacemaker in Colombia's warring political culture and was the epitome of Colombia's new "modernizing

---

*. Alberto Lleras served as acting president of Colombia from 1945 to 1946. His elected presidential term was from 1958 to 1962. His cousin, Carlos Lleras Restrepo, later served as president from 1966 to 1970.

elite."[2] In a briefing book for President John F. Kennedy, the State Department described Lleras's "unselfish idealism, sincere but non-chauvinistic patriotism and personal courage."[3] Sworn in by his erstwhile enemy, former president Laureano Gómez, the new president asked his country to forgive both Liberals and Conservatives for "any of our words or acts [that] might have contributed to the overflowing of the madness" in the *Violencia*.[4]

The NF's "pragmatic, though conservative response, to the country's deep crisis" had drawbacks, however.[5] By exerting a rigid duopoly over political power, Colombian governance soon amounted to "inclusionary authoritarianism."[6] Over time, popular support for the NF plummeted, and dissident groups, unable to find a voice or a place in the two-party state, resorted to extralegal and sometimes violent means to advance themselves.[7]

Critical to the NF's ability to coopt, or, if necessary, to repress this growing opposition was the targeted inflow of U.S. aid, which propped up the deficient finances of the consociational regime while investing a substantial portion of it in counterinsurgent warfare in the countryside. For the next generation, from the Cold War to the drug war to the war on terror, Washington's national security state would remain the Colombian oligarchy's indispensable guarantor.

For all of that, the National Front did make modest headway in serving the Colombian people. Faced with a staggering increase in the urban population and the resulting need for housing, health care, jobs, and nutrition programs, Lleras's government, in the face of severe balance-of-payments deficits owing to the rock-bottom price of coffee, scrambled to deliver social goods and economic betterment under dire conditions. The NF's initial aura of hope, however, dulled rapidly. Real wage losses caused by rising inflation led to strikes and work stoppages, and the government frequently resorted to force and declared states of siege to quell labor, campus, and rural unrest.

What was the National Front's development agenda?

The National Front's 10-year (1961–1970) development plan called for annual GDP growth of 5.6 percent, 2.5 percent per capita growth, and $10 billion in public and private investment over the course of the decade. But social spending combined with shaky external balances and weak creditworthiness immediately constricted the volume of capital investment necessary to achieve such ambitious rates of growth.[8] With steadily increasing life expectancy, rapidly declining infant mortality rates along with one of the continent's highest birthrates of 3.5 percent per annum, Colombia was facing a demographic explosion: four in 10 Colombians were younger than 15 years old in 1960. As President Lleras sardonically noted, in order to succeed, he would have to be "a magician, prophet, redeemer, savior, and pacifier who can transform a ruined republic into a prosperous one."[9]

At the start of the 1960s, half of Colombia's 15 million citizens were living in cities, many residing in vast shantytowns on the edges of Bogotá, Medellín, Cali, Barranquilla, and a dozen other smaller cities.[10] The great majority of the rural-urban migrants had no jobs, and with inflation rates rising by over 10 percent every year (and by 20 percent in the 1970s), those who did find work experienced a rapid decline in the purchasing power of their wages. During these years, the poorest 20 percent of Colombians earned only 2.6 percent of GDP, while the richest 10 percent enjoyed 45 percent of total income. U.S. economist Lauchlin Currie, having adopted Colombian citizenship at the personal invitation of President Lleras in 1958, produced a crash plan called *Operation Colombia* to build 300,000 new urban housing units and put 500,000 workers to work constructing them over a two-year period. Even if the construction of urban housing never reached such stellar projections (it averaged some 23,000 new units per year during the 1960s), Currie proved to be an indefatigable resource in arguing the case for Colombian modernization in the Kennedy White House, as well as in the executive offices of the World Bank and the Inter-American Development Bank in Washington.[11]

The American-led influx of external financing (averaging some $148 million per year in the 1960s) would ultimately underwrite nearly every aspect of the National Front's development agenda, from the import of high-cost capital equipment to produce petrochemicals and plastics to the construction of schools and clinics and the funding of agricultural extension projects. The resulting stimulus, nearly all of it realized in nontraditional sectors of the economy, however, produced income gains for those who needed them the least.

In the area of education, the National Front did make critical headway, however. With the government constitutionally required to spend at least 10 percent of the national government's budget on education, key indicators shot up. By 1975, enrollment among 7- to 13-year-old children grew to 77 percent of the total population. By 1981, adult literacy, which was at 63 percent in 1960, increased to 85 percent.[12] University enrollment also rose from 19,000 in 1958 to more than 29,000 ten years later. With new buildings and facilities underwritten by the World Bank and leading U.S. foundations, Colombia boasted among the largest number of universities in Latin America—201, by one account—and some of the best.[13] Between 1949 and 1986, more than a thousand Colombian students received scholarships for advanced study in the United States, and 686 Americans studied, lectured, and did research at Colombian universities during that same period.[14]

During the 1960s and 1970s, the Peace Corps sent a total of 4,324 volunteers to Colombia to teach in schools, dig wells, dispense and repair farm equipment, advise small businesses, serve in clinics and health extension programs, develop educational programs on television, and, in the case of Ivonne Rivenbark, rally a poor neighborhood in Cartagena to crown a local girl as beauty queen.[15] Sent abroad in the cause of change, the volunteers themselves were changed and brought back an enduring appreciation of Colombia's complex struggle for nationhood. Peace Corps veterans such as Bruce Bagley, Charles Bergquist, James Henderson, and William Sharp would later produce outstanding scholarship on Colombia.

Central to the NF's modernization plan was the effort to grow the middle class and politically coopt it as a partner in the bipartisan oligarchy's electoral coalition. The slogan of *casa, carro y beca* (house, car, and scholarship) enshrined the government's promise of material betterment, even if most of that went to the upper end of the so-called middle sector—the clergy, military officers, journalists, doctors and lawyers, family farm owners and operators, and medium-sized business owners.[16] At the lower end of the middle class, hovering uncertainly above the proletariat, were small shopkeepers, white-collar government employees, teachers, and sales, clerical, and managerial personnel in private firms. Expanding unions (whose numbers increased from 250,000 to 700,000 between 1959 and 1965) helped stabilize the material prospects of the lower middle class but only at the margin.

Colombian universities, long the domain of the well-born, became a wellspring for the emerging middle class but also a breeding ground for revolutionary resistance. In a 1961 survey of university students, 80 percent of the respondents identified themselves as middle class—a gratifying, if somewhat problematic, indicator given the limited absorptive capacity of the job market.[17] Many Colombian universities became hotbeds of Marxist scholarship, anti-American protest, and recruiting grounds for left-wing revolution, especially after the United States began arming and training the Colombian military for counterinsurgent warfare in the countryside.[18]

By the early 1960s, Colombia, via its continuing strategy of import substitution, had achieved self-sufficiency in food processing, beverages, tobacco, clothing, and footwear. The next wave of import barriers, designed to nurture national producers of petrochemicals, plastics, and fertilizers, however, proved far more expensive in terms of financing import substitution. On the export front, the signing of the International Coffee Agreement in 1962, which assigned export quotas to producing countries, helped stabilize the world coffee price. Later in the 1960s, President Carlos Lleras aggressively promoted new non-traditional exports, such as meat and cut flowers, the latter of which resulted in a breakthrough: by the mid-1980s, Colombia became the world's second-largest flower exporter.[19]

President Carlos Lleras's most enduring executive achievement, however, was his 1968 reform of the constitution, expanding presidential power in public spending, taxation, state services, and public works and giving the president the unilateral authority to decree a state of "economic emergency" for up to 90 days. The 1968 reform also set forth the initial terms for the *desmonte* (dismantling) of the National Front after its term would expire in 1974: the presidency and the Congress would be competitively contested, but cabinet positions would retain the 50-50 split as they had during the NF.[20]

What was Law 135?

From 1959 to 1961, the Alberto Lleras administration pressed its draft law for agrarian reform in the Colombian Congress. With Conservatives comprising 50 percent of that body and the agribusiness and cattle lobbies contriving ways to weaken the proposed law, however, the act that passed in December 1961 was more a land modernization bill to stimulate agricultural productivity than a wholesale reform of landholding inequity in Colombia. Expropriation of land by the state was set forth only as a last resort.

Law 135 created an institute called INCORA (*Instituto Colombiano de Reforma Agraria*) that set about to grant some 100,000 titled farm parcels to settlers, the large majority of which were on public lands.[21] A total of 45,000 families received credits averaging $2,000 for seed, mechanized improvements, storage sheds, transportation, and the like. Small landholders, whose plots accounted for 86 percent of total holdings (if only 15 percent of total agricultural property in the country) were granted assistance to purchase new lands if their farms were deemed to be economically unsustainable, or because of erosion and soil depletion.[22] An estimated 40 percent of INCORA's annual budget, which averaged more than $200 million annually, was spent on road building, irrigation, and drainage projects, improvements that largely benefited large landholders and agribusiness interests.[23] Led by the United States, which deployed more than 1,000 Peace Corps volunteers in land recovery, agricultural extension, and road and irrigation development, international public lenders put more than a billion dollars into INCORA projects.

The real purpose of the agrarian reform was political—to cut losses in peasant support for the NF and to allay any violent radicalization of land-hungry *colonos* that could ignite a Cuba-like regime change in Colombia.[24] The latter contingency may seem far-fetched, though it was readily cited by the likes of Law 135's chief advocate, Carlos Lleras.[25] Even if peasant seizures of lands were often marked by violence—either by the landholder or the land invader—guerrilla groups made little headway in recruiting cadres among dispossessed *campesinos*, at least until the drug boom of the 1970s and afterward.

Beginning in the 1960s, Colombian agriculture achieved high productivity gains in its capitalist sector. Having been infused with subsidized credit, new irrigation systems, and other modalities of agricultural extension as well as controlling the vast majority of high-quality land in the country, agribusinesses generated impressive surpluses in exportable products. Small landowners' production of domestic foodstuffs, on the other hand, languished. As before, large floating populations of agricultural workers displaced by such losses in food cultivation surged into areas with capitalized production.[26]

How did the status and mobility of women change during the period of the National Front?

Perhaps the most far-reaching change during the 1960s and 1970s never showed up in the National Front's ample planning documents: the historic surge in the status of women.[27] After his election in 1958, President Lleras appointed Colombia's preeminent feminist, Esmeralda Arboleda, as minister of communication. Two years later, Arboleda was elected as Colombia's first female senator and spearheaded a law that gave women equal authority over minor children and enacted gender parity in civil law. But the real revolution in feminine power was not taking place in the polished corridors of the Casa de Nariño (Colombia's White House) as much as in the teeming Bogotá slums of Lucero Bajo, San Francisco, and La María. There, tens of thousands of recently arrived refugees fleeing from the *Violencia* in Tolima, Boyacá, Cauca, and elsewhere—the majority of them women and children—were scraping out their survival. Many of the female migrants brought skills as bricklayers, carpenters, wielders of machetes (called *macheteras*), and coffee pickers (called *chapoleras*) that aided them in their efforts to homestead in the burgeoning shantytowns. Thousands joined government-funded sweat equity squads called *juntas de acción comunal* (JACs) that built two-story block housing, laid water pipes and sewer lines, and constructed clinics and schools.[28] By 1966, 9,000 JACs had sub-municipal governing boards, many led by women. By the mid-1970s, women would make up one-third of Colombia's urban workforce.

During this period, the whole notion of women's second-class role in Colombia's patriarchy received a corrective jolt due to the pathbreaking research of Berkeley-trained anthropologist Virginia Gutiérrez de Pineda.[29] Behind the vaunted model of the provident, all-powerful male and his stainless helpmate, sanctified by Holy Mother Church, Gutiérrez's research revealed a truer model driven by region, race, and class. Gutiérrez argued in her book that the Colombian family and its culture had to be newly understood given social realities about real gender roles, sexual practices, and "multilayered families."

By the time *Familia y Cultura en Colombia* was published in 1968, yet another unanticipated breakthrough in gender status had taken place—birth control. Among the greatest barriers to economic security for women and children in the country remained the birth rate of over six live births per every fertile woman. The Catholic Church's position on family planning, reiterated in Pope Paul VI's encyclical *Humanae vitae* (1965) which designated "artificial birth control" as a sin, gave political leaders little room for action, but former president Alberto Lleras found a rationale nonetheless. Addressing an international assembly on population in Cali in August 1965, Lleras declared that "family planning should be a matter of family choice." Church fathers did not respond to that declaration and later silently acquiesced when Alberto Lleras's successor once removed (and cousin), President Carlos Lleras, signed the UN Declaration on Population (which set forth access to birth control) on Human Rights Day in December 1966—the only Latin American head of state to do so.[30]

In subsequent years, foreign funders, such as the U.S. Agency for International Development, the Rockefeller and Ford Foundations, the Population Council, and Planned Parenthood began to underwrite family planning via a broad network of Colombian medical societies, local clinics, and maternal health groups (a total of 573 health facilities by 1972) that provided counseling and birth control products throughout the country.[31] Not surprisingly, Colombian women embraced birth control.[32] Births per woman in Colombia plummeted by 50 percent between 1955 and 1995, and overall population growth declined from 3.3 percent in 1951 to 2.1 percent in 1973, among the lowest in Latin America.

Outside of the cities, where the Church and the patriarchy continued to hold sway, family planning remained out of reach but not the proven power of a single mother. Zulma Moreno de

Asprilla,* for example, a 40-year-old black mother of five with a husband long gone, continued to work with a pick and shovel a mile below the surface in a gold mine called *La Barrigona* in the Chocó. Six months pregnant, the *chocoana* earned 40 cents a day to put plantain and rice on the family table.

In what ways did Colombian culture and society change during the years of the National Front?

In the 1960s, the tide of globalized mass media swept through Colombia, bringing with it American pop culture, the British rock invasion, miniskirts and Beatle hairdos, sexual liberation, and urban counterculture. It also coincided with historic stirrings of racial and gender liberation. Manuel and Delia Zapata Olivella, brother and sister and *Afro-Colombianos* of extraordinary artistic and literary talent, were among those at the forefront of that change. Manuel, who began his career as a medical doctor in the Chocó, turned to writing after befriending American novelist Langston Hughes on a trip to the United States in 1946. He eventually wrote 27 books, mixing fiction with Afro-Colombian history and extended travelogues about race, drawn from his trips through Mexico, Central America, and the United States.[33] Delia, initially an award-winning artist and a sometime movie actress, turned to ethnomusicology, ultimately composing and choreographing an Afro-Colombian ballet featuring *seserese* (a dance genre inspired by the slave resistance settlements called *palenques*) that toured Europe, the Soviet Union, China, and the United States during the 1960s and 1970s.

Among the dancers whom Delia Zapata recruited for her first company was Leonor González Mina, an 18-year-old *negra* who had fled home after her brother had been shot dead in Robles (Cauca) during the *Violencia*. Returning to Colombia in 1965 from a European dance tour, Leonor turned to recording traditional Colombian music arranged by her husband, composer Esteban Cabezas. One such arrangement was based on an old slave song from Iscaundé (Nariño) about not wanting to die in a mine shaft. Leonor rendered the song, "A la mina," into a soaring *bolero* that quickly rose to the top of the charts, as did the album, *Canciones de mi tierra y de mi raza* (Songs from my land and my race). More than 30 other albums followed as she plumbed the extraordinary musical range of Colombia's African, Amerindian, and creole genres, giving each a fresh, often arresting interpretation.

Key to the national and international success of *la negra grande*, as Leonor billed herself, was not just her vocal talent but the expanding reach of radio and television and the advent of new recording technologies. By the early 1960s, Colombian record companies like Disco Fuentes, Sonolux, and Codiscos were using multitrack recordings and a home-grown synthe-sizer called the "Solovox" (that electronically replicated piano and wind instruments) to produce Colombian rock, religious, folk, and a new genre of sorts—"tropical music."[34] For four centuries, Colombia's richness in music had been geographi-cally confined, a phenomenon of region reinforced by race.[35] But the new generation of artists and bands began mixing and recording a syncretic musical melting pot, largely drawn from Afro-Caribbean traditions, that "tropicalized" the entire country. By the end of the 1960s, the tropical tide of *cumbia* and *vallenato* as well as Barranquilla- and Cali-based salsa had engulfed the entire continent.

At the core of dance and music transition was the "sexu-alization of racial identifications."[36] What once had been for-bidden was now inviting. Whether in the huge *discotecas* in Juanchito on the outskirts of Cali, the devotional merriment of the *fiestas patronales* (patron-saint celebrations) in thousands of small towns, or the all-night revelry during beauty pageants, the time-honored indices of social separation—race, class, and region—tended to dissolve into a kind of erotic communion of dancing, drinking, and celebration. When another killing spree swept the country in the 1980s, as we'll see, Colombians came up with a sardonic saying about joy-making in their failing state: *"Colombia se derrumba y nosotros de rumba"* (Colombia's falling down and we're partying down).

How did the novel Cien Años de Soledad (One Hundred Years of Solitude) *gain such iconic global status?*

No single artistic event so illuminated Colombia's hooded and unsettled encounter with itself as the 1967 publication of *Cien Años de Soledad*, a picaresque 1967 novel by a struggling novelist turned advertising hack named Gabriel García Márquez. In addition to critical acclaim—the *New York Times* review by American novelist William Kennedy described it as "the first piece of literature since the Book of Genesis that should be required reading for the entire human race"—the sales of *Cien Años de Soledad* reached 28 million copies (with translations into 37 languages) 10 years after its initial publication.

The novel's surreal storyline chronicles seven generations of the fictional Buendía family, whose founder and his tiny band makes a Jiménez Quesada–like trek through "pools of steaming oil as their machetes destroyed bloody lilies and golden salamanders" to establish their town of mirrors— Macondo. Although inbred from incest and consigned to an idiosyncratic solitude in their lost town, the Buendías are enchanted by magical events and otherworldly forces. Death sometimes arrives in a shower of dead birds, as a lady in blue, or in billowing clouds of tiny yellow flowers that bury everything. For the nubile temptress, Remedios the Beautiful, who has already killed four men with the odor of her perfect body, there is no death (much less defloration), but rather an ascension into heaven as she hangs out the family sheets. If the men in *Cien Años* were wastrels given to egotistical fancy, sexual depredation, and bloodletting, the women were stoic, resourceful, and long-suffering. "My women," García Márquez explained, "are strong." He would later comment that "the only new idea that could save humanity in the twenty-first century is that women assume the direction of the world because masculine hegemony has squandered the opportunity for ten thousand years."[37]

The book's climax takes place when an American banana company, whose massive plantation has magically put Macondo to work, turns on its striking workers. Three thousand people are gunned down by the armed forces, which then load the dead and dying on railcars for burial at sea. The gringos decamp (much as United Fruit historically did after the 1928 massacre), but not before conjuring up a four-year flood to erase both memory and evidence of the atrocity.

In 1982, García Márquez, by that time the author of more than a dozen books, was awarded the Nobel Prize for Literature. Bringing along 60 Colombian musicians with him to Stockholm for three days of nonstop celebration, the author spoke at the conclusion of the award ceremony about

> the crux of our solitude . . . that lives within us and determines each instant of our countless daily deaths, and that nourishes a sense of insatiable creativity, full of sorrow and beauty. . . . Poets, beggars, musicians and prophets, warriors and scoundrels, all creatures of that unbridled reality, we have had to ask but little of imagination, for our crucial problem has been a lack of conventional means to render our lives believable.

How did the Church change in the 1960s and afterward?

In the same year that the National Front took office—1958—the ultramontane Pope Pius XII died. His replacement was the 76-year-old Angelo Giuseppe Roncalli, who at his advanced age most observers thought would serve as a benign caretaker. Instead, Roman Catholic power passed into the hands of a pastoral revolutionary. Pope John XXIII called for the Church to embrace the social apostolate of peace and justice for the poor, though his appointment of Monsignor Luis Concha Córdoba

as Colombian primate in 1959 suggested the opposite—a continuation of Pius's statist authoritarianism.

The pastoral constitution entitled *Gaudium et Spes* (Joy and
Hope) that was adopted by Vatican II enjoined all Catholics
to embrace the "anguish and hope of the poor and afflicted"
and openly spoke of the need to understand secularization
and pluralism. It was an extraordinary document. If anything,
the conclave of Latin American bishops known as CELAM
(*Consejo Episcopal Latinoamericano* or Latin American Episcopal
Conference), which met in Medellín in 1968 and was chaired
by John XXIII's successor, Paul VI, went even further. "The task
of re-evangelization is urgent among us," the Colombian hierarchy pronounced at the conclusion of the conclave.[38] But what
this meant was already a matter of pitched division within the
Church.

The Jesuits took the lead in the developmentalist tendency
within the changing Church. Having formed their own social
science research center in 1962, the Society of Jesus took over
the Institute of Doctrine and Social Studies (IDES) formed
by Colombia's bishops in 1967. IDES organized hundreds of
workshops for clergy and laity as well as students and peasant
leaders on the challenge of *concientización* (consciousness-
raising), a term that called for the poor and oppressed to
develop self-worth. In the cause of raising such liberating
awareness, authentic Catholic faith required action. This was
the essence of what has become known as liberation theology.

To advance the rights of land-hungry *colonos*, the Jesuit-
led national agrarian federation, *Federación Agraria Nacional*
(FANAL), organized peasant invasions of uncultivated estate
properties in the departments of Magdalena and Atlántico
during the 1960s. After President Misael Pastrana Borrego
(1970–74) declared the national agrarian reform law 135 a dead
letter, the Colombian Army began intervening to stop land invasions and even arrest priests for "subversion."[39]

Beyond the fissures and disputes, the Church's greatest set-
back by far was the progressive loss of its core constituency,

women, for whom education, urbanization, birth control, and professionalization undermined the submissive and procreative ideal of Marianism. Church fathers nonetheless continued to do their best to warn women about the dire results of sexual decadence. One article, for example, published in a university journal argued that the pursuit of erotic pleasure would lead not only to social breakdown but to the loss of the Cold War and the triumph of international communism.[40]

How did the Cuban Revolution influence Colombia's turn to counterinsurgency?

The National Front, Colombia's experiment in bipartisan, reformist government, coincided with the most dramatic historic event of that era—Fidel Castro's seizure of power in Cuba in 1959.

Angry about Castro's drumhead trials and summary executions (some of which appeared on U.S. TV) of the accused thugs of overthrown dictator Fulgencio Batista, President Dwight Eisenhower refused to see the new Cuban premier on Castro's trip to Washington in April 1959. More troubling news followed Castro's visit—massive land expropriations by the populist dictator, the exodus of thousands of Cubans seeking shelter in the United States, and the conclusion of a trade agreement with the Soviet Union in February 1960.

It was under these circumstances that President Alberto Lleras visited Washington in April 1960. In what proved to be a reckoning of historic importance in Colombia's relationship to its "polar star," Lleras leveraged American fear of communism into a calculated overture for a military alliance with Colombia. "You must purchase a decisive stake in the material civilization of the West before Latin America turns into a retreat, a rout, a historical disaster," he told a wildly cheering joint session of the U.S. Congress, one of whose attendees was Senator John F. Kennedy, the front-running Democratic candidate for president.[41] In conversations in the White House, Lleras pressed

President Eisenhower to provide Colombia with a "counter-insurgency battle group"—an American-trained rapid deployment force of 1,500 Colombian Rangers equipped with 23 helicopters and the most advanced U.S. firearms.[42]

What was the Alliance for Progress?

JFK's victory in November 1960 made Colombia, along with Chile, the template of the New Frontier's *Alianza Para el Progreso*—the Alliance for Progress, an ambitious, continent-wide plan that Kennedy unveiled at a glittering dinner at the White House in March 1961. The Alliance's enumerated goals—economic growth, elimination of illiteracy, commodity price stabilization, and comprehensive agrarian distribution, among 90 others—were premised on broad internal reform and the combination of Latin American financing underwritten by U.S. long-term funding. The conviction was that economic growth, social betterment, and popular mobilization could produce a transformative legitimacy in representative government that would forestall violent communist revolution. "Within a decade," U.S. Alliance coordinator Teodoro Moscoso grandly promised, "the direction and results of centuries of Latin American history are to be changed."[43]

In retrospect, the goals of the Alliance were undoubtedly overblown. Why would Latin America's entrenched oligarchies cede wealth and power to those whose dispossession they had perfected over four centuries? How could Latin American governments, nearly all of which were struggling to feed, educate, and at least marginally employ their surging populations, possibly harness the internal savings and foreign funding necessary to capitalize "self-sustaining growth"? A further canard was the one President Kennedy held dearest: that the revolutionary transformation wrought by the Alliance would somehow immunize the countries of the southern continent from communist Cuba. The Latin American perspective was a little different. As one Mexican diplomat put it, "If we publicly declare that Cuba is a threat to our security, forty million Mexicans will die laughing."[44]

President Alberto Lleras, however, sensed a golden opportunity, urging the White House to make "a really major economic commitment" at the upcoming Punta del Este conference to inaugurate the Alliance. When the Americans did make this commitment (pledging $20 billion over a 10-year period), Lleras did his part in a secret quid pro quo by leading the effort to expel Cuba from the Organization of American States.[45]

Not everyone was as sold on the Alliance as were Lleras and JFK. Economist Albert O. Hirschman, then writing a book on Latin American economic development, thought the Alliance was a testament to "simplistic optimism," one that could well contain within its grand design a praetorian fallback of *machtpolitik* that was so brutally evident in the Bay of Pigs invasion. "We may well have to choose between *alianza* and *progreso*," he predicted.[46] JFK's preferred approach, in fact, was to have it both ways, a policy he called "two-track": the United States would back peaceful change—the first track—but switch to the second (covert action and counterinsurgency) to contain the communist threat should the first falter.[47] Lleras cleverly played on that duality. In October 1961, he made an urgent appeal to Washington for aircraft and small arms to neutralize military plotting against him as well as to contain the "subversive activities of communists." The Kennedy administration hurried to the rescue.[48]

President Kennedy visited Bogotá in December 1961. Just days before he and the First Lady arrived in the Colombian capital, Lleras wrested a modest agrarian reform bill from the Colombian congress and severed diplomatic relations with Cuba. Although the Americans were worried about protests during the visit, they shouldn't have been: over a million people lined the streets of Bogotá to cheer the presidential motorcade, the press showered praise on the American visitors, and JFK performed with all his charismatic flair. After dedicating a new low-income neighborhood called *Techo* (roof) on the southern outskirts of the capital city, he spent an hour chatting with a crowd of Peace Corps volunteers and later spoke with addressed Colombian leaders at a state banquet given in his honor.

For all the fanfare and speechmaking, however, the Alliance remained a symbolic showcase. The very primary school, the *Escuela Alianza para le progreso*, whose first blocks President Kennedy had put in place during his visit, remained an empty, garbage-strewn field seven months after its dedication. With confusion reigning in Washington about the core purpose of Alliance aid, let alone the methods for its effective investment, and with Colombia's inexperienced planners vulnerable to the designs of the country's practiced kleptocrats, the Alliance ultimately succumbed to Cold War clientelism.[49]

Behind the scenes, the Kennedy administration was laying the groundwork for "track two"—counterinsurgency. Two months after the president's visit to Bogotá, General William P. Yarborough, the officer Kennedy had appointed commander of Fort Bragg's Special Warfare School, flew into the Colombian capital for an in-depth assessment of combined operations with Colombia's elite forces, something that would be later christened *Plan Lazo* (lasso or snare).

Did Plan Lazo *end the* Violencia*?*

Partially, yes.

General Yarborough made two critical recommendations in a secret supplement to his report to Kennedy: first, that American officers be inserted in-country under direct U.S. command to manage the counterinsurgency campaign; and second, that they form "hunter-killer units" to "perform counter-agent and counter-propaganda functions and as necessary execute paramilitary, sabotage and/or terrorist activities against known communist proponents." President Guillermo León Valencia (1962–66) later signed a decree giving the military much broader authority to arm and deploy civilians as well as to arrest and strip suspected insurgents of due process and arraign them before secret military tribunals. The path to Colombia's next killing field had been cleared.

The first Colombian-American counterinsurgent push (called "Operation Sovereignty") took place in May 1964. The mission was to eradicate the "communist" enclave of Marquetalia.[50] The military campaign began with "civic action" initiatives—leaflet drops, parachuted food, and even the deployment of small medical teams into areas near the focus of the assault. As 2,000 Colombian troops were readied for the search-and-destroy sweep, American Special Forces commanders from a nearby base guided the helicopter-borne strike force into a clearing close to the main camp of the peasant irregulars. Almost immediately, however, the army unit encountered fierce resistance and made no headway for the better part of a day. By the time the operation's full troop force was airlifted into the battle area, the rebels had disappeared into the mountainous jungle.[51] The Colombian military went on to declare victory, but one of its chief targets, peasant commander Pedro Antonio Marín (alias Manuel Marulanda), who would go on to lead the *Fuerzas Armadas Revolucionarias de Colombia* (FARC) for another 44 years, had slipped out of its grasp.

By the late 1960s, in the wake of the secret war against Fidel Castro and the successful "search-and-kill" operation against Che Guevara in Bolivia, national security leaders in Washington abandoned any pretense regarding "civic action" in favor of the expanded militarization of counterinsurgency.[52] Hundreds of Colombian police and military officers went through the U.S. Army School of the Americas at Fort Gulick in the Canal Zone and the so-called Bomb School in Los Fresnos, Texas (run by CIA officers at a Border Patrol academy), where they learned the best techniques in interrogation, torture, assassination, and bomb-making.[53] Even if U.S. intelligence could find no credible Soviet communist threat anywhere on the continent (except, of course, for Cuba), Washington's penchant for "worst-case contingency planning" required an all-out search for enemies. Latin America's corrupt and rickety regimes had plenty of them.

Colonel Edward M. Lansdale, Kennedy's counterinsurgent chieftain, believed that a 20th-century update of Machiavelli's *The Prince* might be in order. As Michael McClintock explains it, "He [Lansdale] did so in the belief that Americans could perpetrate small evils, and indeed must shoulder a burden of such evil, while remaining pure of heart."[54] The national security state's next crusade would be the drug war. The scale of its collateral damage in Colombia would make the crimes of the Cold War seem like child's play.

8

THE DRUG WAR I

How did the United States become the world's leading drug consumer?

Around the time America's "addiction to coffee" propelled Colombia to become the world's second-leading producer of that stimulant in the late 19th century, the United States was already consuming record amounts of a more "medicinal" drug—opium. The great majority of those eating or imbibing opium were middle- and upper-class women, a substantial number of these under the care of doctors for whom opium (and also laudanum and morphine) had become the remedy for nearly everything from menstrual pains, syphilis, lockjaw, hemorrhoids, or, as one physician put it, "our mad race for speedy wealth . . . which finds rest in the repeated use of opium or morphine."* Whether happily or otherwise, the country was hooked.[1] "We have an army of women in America dying from the opium habit," Dr. Joseph Pierce wrote in 1894.

Fortunately, the United States found a cure for opium addiction—a new wonder drug from Europe called cocaine,

---

*. The United States remained the world leader in the first decade of the 21st century in the per capita use of heroin, opioids, and amphetamine; was tied with Spain for the lead in cocaine consumption; and was second to Iceland in cannabis use, according to the United Nations Office on Drugs and Crime, https://data.unodc.org/2003-2014.

which the Parke-Davis pharmaceutical company marketed as "the most important discovery of the age, the benefits of which to humanity would be incalculable." Dr. Sigmund Freud offered his august endorsement: "The psychic effect of cocaine consists of exhilaration and lasting euphoria. . . . One senses an increase in self-control and feels more vigorous and capable of work." Prominent neurologist and former army surgeon general Dr. William Hammond noted in 1886 that cocaine could also treat sciatica, painful intercourse, eye infections, if not "the relief of masturbation."[2] Ironically enough, the rising force of the Women's Christian Temperance Union (1874) and the Anti-Saloon League (1895), which sought to eliminate alcohol, made cocaine a more socially correct stimulant, at least for a while. One doctor reported that "fashionable ladies" in great numbers were coming "to get hypodermic injections of cocaine to make them lively and talkative." As long as cocaine stayed within the corridors of privilege, Madame de Stael's dictum prevailed: "The only good we discover in life is something that produces an oblivion of existence." Outside those corridors, however, the WASP majority was intolerant, even fearful, when the lower orders trafficked in drug-induced oblivion.

As newly arrived immigrants and impoverished people of color flooded into America's already-teeming cities during the first decade of the 20th century, the nation experienced its first race-based panic over drugs. "10 Killed, 35 Hurt in a Race Riot Born of a Cocaine 'Jag': Drug Crazed Negroes Fire at Every One in Sight," a Hearst newspaper reported in 1913.[3] A *New York Times* headline the following year warned, "Negro Cocaine Fiends Are a New Southern Menace."[4] Press reports tended to fixate on how opium enabled Chinese, black, and immigrant "predators" to ply white women sexually. Cocaine supposedly was being used to drug young girls to force them into the "white slave traffic."[5] Hollywood seized on these images and produced scores of silent films such as *Morphia the Death Drug* (1914), and *The Devil's Needle* (1916), which fixated on the degenerative horrors of drug use.[6]

As the price of opium and cocaine spiked and police began shutting down sanitariums for addicts, drug users flooded into the streets. They soon found a replacement narcotic, originally developed for respiratory ailments, one that could be sniffed for a mind-numbing high—heroin. What might have remained, for most users anyway, a pleasurable palliative was soon pushed by law enforcement into something far more lethal. When supplies of heroin powder shrank on the street due to police interdiction, dealers began to adulterate the drug to maintain sales. Users then made up for the depleted high by injecting the drug directly into their veins. The result was a health catastrophe—"sepsis of every imaginable variety, hepatitis, endocarditis, emboli, tetanus, overdose and early death."[7]

The public furor over drugs and alcohol was part of a broader search for enemies within the United States. The temperance movement, in addition to inveighing elected leaders to ban the sale of alcohol, called for the "racial purification" of America, a cause shared by the resurgent Ku Klux Klan.[8] For temperance leaders, World War I brought a windfall—the German scare for which Congress passed the Espionage Act (1917), the Sedition Act (1918), and the Alien Deportation Act (1918), empowering six federal agencies to hunt down spies while shutting down German-American beer breweries and liquor distributorships. The end of World War I produced yet another panic, the Red Scare, which led to mass arrests of unionists and prosecution of suspected immigrant anarchists such as Nicola Sacco and Bartolomeo Vanzetti. In a state of declared national emergency, in 1920 the U.S. Congress passed the Volstead Act banning the sale and manufacture of alcohol.

America's 13-year experience with alcohol prohibition proved to be a disaster of historic proportions. It corrupted government at every level, criminalized millions of Americans, and awarded an enormous industry to the Mafia. The repeal of Prohibition in 1933, however, did nothing to slow the rise of drug control. Federal Bureau of Narcotics director

Harry Anslinger demanded that Congress take action against "marihuana-crazed Mexicans" before they committed violent acts on "loco weed."[9] The American Medical Association contested this claim, testifying to a House committee that there was no evidence that cannabis was harmful. Hollywood, however, again sought to capitalize on the new drug panic, releasing a popular motion picture entitled *Reefer Madness* (1936), in which a partly smoked joint occasions rape, reckless driving, murder, and suicide. The Marihuana Tax Act passed in 1937 and was quickly used to justify criminal arrests. Law enforcement provided a new and compelling measure of success in fighting drugs: race-based incarceration.[10]

In white America, pharmaceutical companies were soon moving on to new "medicinal" pastures, pushing a new wonder drug—amphetamine. The target market was once again women. A 1950 Dexedrine ad urged doctors to prescribe the drug for "housewives [who] are crushed under a load of dull, routine duties that leave them in a state of mental and emotional fatigue. Dexedrine will give them a feeling of energy and well-being, renewing their interest in life and living." It did indeed. In 1958, Americans swallowed an estimated 3.5 billion amphetamine tablets; by 1967, the number was 8 billion.[11]

Faced with the country's dynamic condition of drug dependence, President Kennedy hosted a national conference on drug abuse in 1962. It did no good, Kennedy said at the opening of the White House conference, to reduce one form of addiction only to have new ones replace it. If the Kennedy administration succeeded in requiring that amphetamines be regulated more restrictively, the president himself was not quite ready to kick his own habit of taking them and getting "cocktail" injections of speed on the side. Confronted by his younger brother, Attorney General Robert Kennedy, with proof that the substances he was ingesting were illegal, the president was forthright: "I don't care if it's horse piss. It works."[12]

Why did Washington first declare a "war on drugs"?

The tumultuous upheavals of the late 1960s—black riots, violent student protest against the war in Vietnam, political assassinations, the ruined presidency of Lyndon B. Johnson, and the rise of female militancy—threatened traditional values and social cohesion. Drug prohibition again provided an instrument of social order and racial repression. President Richard M. Nixon admitted as much privately to his chief of staff H. R. Haldeman: "The whole problem is really the blacks," the president said. "The key is to devise a system that recognizes this while not appearing so."[13]

President Nixon can be credited with another first—taking the drug war international. Nine months after his inauguration, the president launched "Operation Intercept," militarizing the U.S.-Mexico border and subjecting all air, road, and foot traffic across the border to blanket searches for drugs. A week into "Intercept," although there was little to show in terms of confiscated drugs, 90 percent of cross-border commerce had been cut off. Nixon's own Bureau of the Budget sent a scathing critique to the White House about the *"high risk of making the Administration appear inept by playing into the hands of organized crime and creating more hard drug addicts"* (emphasis in original).[14] "Operation Intercept" might have been better named "Operation Relocation," because by the early 1970s up to 70 percent of America's massive marijuana habit was being supplied by Colombia.

How did Colombia become the global epicenter of the illegal drug business?

Geography proved to be destiny in the drug trade. Colombia has two oceans from which to smuggle drugs northward and across the Atlantic as well as enormous expanses of empty, fertile lands for mass cultivation. For 400 years, high-value commerce in Colombia—whether gold, slaves, coffee, or guns—had been successfully diverted into robust channels of contraband. The country's embrace of savage capitalism in the 20th century added a critical ingredient to Colombia's comparative advantage in drugs: with agro-industrial developers having cleansed peasants and small land-tillers from productive properties, the country was replete with a large, floating labor population, quick to surge into the two new hubs of the exploding marijuana trade—the Caribbean ports of Riohacha on the Guajira Peninsula and the Gulf of Urabá, near Panamá.

The quality of Colombian pot was another factor. The fact that "Colombian gold" (a blond-colored cannabis bud grown on the slopes of the Sierra Nevada massif famous for its lemony smell and euphoric effect) and Colombian red (whose buds displayed reddish fuzz when ripe) contained more tetrahydrocannibinol (THC) than Mexican weed made for a bigger and better high.[15]

The hub of seaborne smuggling became the Atrato River delta where, in hundreds of inlets, destroyer-sized banana boats were loaded up with cannabis for transit to the Florida Keys and the Louisiana coast. On the return trip, the banana boats smuggled automatic rifles and Japanese electronic products as well as sacks of cash for the drug traffickers. The hub of airborne trafficking was high in the desert mountains of the La Guajira Peninsula, where dozens of dirt airstrips permitted small aircraft, piloted mostly by Americans, to land.[16]

The Colombian marijuana bonanza started tailing off by the mid-1970s when Americans increasingly grew their own cannabis in closets and basements, in northern California's "green triangle," or anywhere law enforcement, they hoped, would not find it. The Drug Enforcement Agency (DEA) responded by deputizing the state national guard units and local law enforcement to launch large ground and air operations such as California's Campaign Against Marijuana Production (CAMP) to wipe out cannabis fields and to jail growers. Like Prohibition, such spectacle warfare didn't do much to curtail supply, but it did expand antidrug budgets and enable elected officials to follow in Nixon's footsteps by pitting Americans against each other.

By the mid-1970s, Americans were imbibing a new "club drug"—cocaine—and Colombian drug traffickers were quick to capitalize on skyrocketing demand in the United States. In Medellín, Pablo Escobar, a former car thief, began building labs in the Magdalena River Valley to convert Bolivian *paco* (coca-leaf paste) into cocaine.[17] To further consolidate control over the market, Escobar also sold risk insurance, charging his fellow cocaine traffickers a 10 percent premium on the U.S. wholesale price that would cover them for loss or seizure of shipments to the United States payable at the Colombian purchase price.[18] In addition to earning an enormous return for his growing cartel, Escobar's risk insurance scheme attracted a flood of equity investors who purchased *apuntadas* (stakes) in the business. On Norman's Cay, a 165-acre island in the Bahamas, fellow Colombian trafficker Carlos Lehder built a 3,000-foot concrete airstrip and a yacht harbor to transport tons of cocaine into the United States. After returning from a successful delivery flight to the United States, pilots and their crews were richly compensated in both cash and kind. "I have a vivid picture of being picked up in a Land Rover with the top down and naked women driving to come and welcome me from my airplane," Carlos Toro, a Lehder lieutenant in charge of bribing airport personnel, remembered. "And we had a house that we called the 'the Volcano' because it had that shape. And there we partied. We partied. And it was a Sodom and Gomorrah."[19]

What was the Bourne Memorandum, and what part did it play in the drug war in Colombia?

Jimmy Carter's inauguration as president in January 1977 seemed like a breath of fresh air for the drug war.[20] In an early message to Congress, the newly elected president recommended that "penalties against possession of a drug should not be more damaging to an individual than the use of the drug itself."[21] With the Democrats in charge of both houses, the passage of a marijuana decriminalization bill seemed likely, especially since five states had already reduced penalties for marijuana possession, with another six states following suit during the next two years. Carter's new drug czar, a 38-year-old British psychiatrist named Peter G. Bourne, also seemed ideal in the cause of shifting drug policy toward what he called "harm reduction." As an aide to Governor Carter in Georgia, Bourne was credited with getting nearly all of the state's 6,000 heroin addicts on methadone (a synthetic form of heroin).

But instead, Carter, ever the Sunday school moralist, abandoned "harm reduction" and embraced the drug war. In his long-awaited drug reform message to Congress in August 1977, he promised to cut narcotics off at the source—namely, in the countries cultivating, processing, and trafficking drugs. He proposed to convert drug-corrupted governments into drug-fighting partners and sent his wife, Rosalynn, to Bogotá to confront President Alfonso López Michelsen (1974–78) personally about his government's ties to the drug trade. When that didn't work, Carter dispatched Dr. Bourne to the Colombian capital to hand-deliver a sharply worded presidential letter along with an 11-page list of ministers, generals, and police commanders supposedly in the pay of the traffickers.[22] Back in Washington, Bourne reported to the president that they could expect a breakthrough: "the interest you and Rosalynn have taken in him has lighted a fire under him and given him the energy . . . to redeem himself."[23]

That was enough for Carter to formally alert the U.S. Congress the following month that "the problem of drug trafficking is his [López Michelsen's] highest priority."[24] To sweeten this apparent breakthrough, Carter then gave the go-ahead to provide three antidrug helicopters to the Colombian military, an authorization Carter had delayed pending Lopez's response to the U.S. initiative.[25] Attending the helicopter transfer in August 1977 was Colombian defense minister

Abraham Varón Valencia, a ranking general whose name could be found near the top of the Bourne Memorandum's list of drug-infested malefactors.[26] Over the following weeks, when President López took no action to dismiss, fire, or prosecute either his accused ministers or the legion of drug-corrupted police commanders named in the Bourne Memorandum, the Americans were galled; López was refusing to be reborn.

Someone in the Carter administration then leaked the Bourne Memorandum to the CBS News program *60 Minutes*.[27] Among those named in the news report for ties to drug traffickers was Colombia's ambassador in Washington, Julio César Turbay, now running for president. The story touched off a storm of protest in Colombia.[28] "We are not corrupting the Americans," President López angrily told the press. "The Americans are corrupting us."[29]

The U.S. Drug Enforcement Agency (DEA) was meanwhile fighting the war in the only place where it knew how to—the press. A *TIME* cover story, "The Colombian Connection—How a Billion-Dollar Network Smuggles Pot and Coke into the US," in January 1979 showed DEA agents in their boom-and-bust mode pushing back the forces of darkness in Colombia.[30] In reality, the opposite was happening. In Medellín, all six of the DEA's informants were murdered within a year of their recruitment. Another man, who had spoken with the DEA's lead agent in an airport, was found dead the next day with his eyes gouged out. When the wife of a trafficker was arrested in Miami, the contents of her handbag included the transcription of a cable from the DEA director in Medellín.[31]

Another drug war casualty—this one, political—was Dr. Bourne himself. Exposed for having filled out a Quaalude prescription for a female staffer (and using an alias to conceal her identity), Bourne was also accused in the press of snorting cocaine at the Christmas party of the National Organization for the Reform of Marijuana Laws (NORML).[32] He was forced to resign. "Our present cocaine policy," Bourne had bluntly concluded in a message to the president, "is a complete failure."[33]

Why didn't supply-side militarization work during the 1970s?

Supply-side militarization of the kind being advocated by Carter and the presidents who were to succeed him faced insuperable obstacles. Coca and marijuana could be grown (and eventually were) in an area over half the size of the continental United States. Eradication in one area would only result in cultivation elsewhere, as Bourne specifically had warned President Carter. Another faith-based tactic in the drug war was the theory that by reducing supply, you could raise the street price of cocaine in the United States, thereby pushing down consumption. Ten years into the interdiction campaign, however, the U.S. street price for Colombian cocaine had actually *decreased* by more than half.[34] Even if 90 percent of the drug contraband were seized, one veteran DEA agent wearily concluded, the drug dealers would still make a profit.[35] Later, court testimony from arrested traffickers suggested another feature in the so-called war: that many of the drug "busts" by U.S. law enforcement were set up by the criminals themselves.[36]

In Bogotá, the Americans were also getting played. López's successor as president, Julio César Turbay Ayala, found that the best way to keep the details of the infamous Bourne Memorandum (in which he had been named for his ties to drug trafficking) under wraps while neutralizing his rebellious military was to conduct war against his own people. A month after being sworn in as president in September 1978, President Turbay launched *Operación Fulminante*, an American-inspired mass bombardment of the herbicide Paraquat on six million acres (or so they claimed) of cannabis in northern Colombia. Ten thousand Colombian troops then swept through marijuana-growing areas on the ground, arresting hundreds of mostly small farmers.[37] In total, 18,000 families were displaced and most were rendered destitute.[38] American military officers in Colombia then recommended that Turbay take this "military option" nationwide, but the Colombian military rejected the proposal.[39] On Capitol Hill, there was consternation about the massive spraying operation in northern Colombia. Senator Edward M. Kennedy, with support from two liberal Republican senators (Charles Percy and Jacob Javits), passed an amendment to the U.S. Foreign Military Assistance Act of 1978, prohibiting the use of defense money for antidrug herbicidal spraying.[40]

To address rising insecurity and armed rebellion by the drug cartels, the Turbay government in June 1982 enacted the "Security Statute," which authorized military tribunals to try civilian suspects in secret and gave the government wide leeway in press censorship. The Carter White House said nothing. "Although nominally directed toward all forms of organized crime," Marco Palacios notes, "the statute was employed only against the left—and not just the guerrilla left— rather than against drug traffickers or kidnapping networks."[41] By 1979, there were 60,000 Colombians being held in prisons and army detention centers. Amnesty International reported that detainees were being subjected to torture.

How did the flood of narco-dollars in the 1980s affect the Colombian economy?

By the late 1980s, the export of marijuana and cocaine was earning from $2 to $4 billion per annum—somewhere between 5 and 10 percent of Colombia's total GDP, depending on the estimate.[42] In dollar terms, income from illegal exports was roughly the same as that for legal exports of coffee, oil, cut flowers, and manufactured products combined.[43] One positive effect of the inflow of narco-dollars was in capitalizing new and existing industries and underwriting the country's perilous balance-of-payments situation.[44] The flood of cheap dollars also led to a building boom (especially in Medellín), as well as to a dizzying rise in multilevel banking and front companies to launder narco-dollars, and exponential increases in imports of all kinds.[45]

The drug lords spent lavish amounts of money on fleets of cars, antiques and art treasures, gold bullion, stables full of race-horses, shopping centers, hotels, skyscrapers, soccer clubs, and luxury apartments. They also bought up huge *fincas* (ranches) mostly in the north of the country or in its eastern plains to raise cattle. The Federation of Colombian Cattle Farmers estimated that, by 1991, the drug traffickers owned 30 percent of the best farming and ranching land in the country. As they bought and consolidated huge tracts of productive land, the traffickers financed paramilitary units to protect their properties and murderously cleanse the countryside of peasant groups and cooperatives—along with anyone suspected of ties to the leftist guerrillas. CIA analyst Sidney Zabludoff analyzed the employment dimension of the cocaine trafficking industry, estimating that by 1987 it comprised a total of 160,000 people, or about 1.3 percent of the national workforce.[46] (The coffee industry, by contrast, employed at least 740,000 workers, or 6.1 percent of the total workforce.)

Overall, the drug industry hurt Colombia far more than it helped it. In addition to undermining some of the country's productive industries, touching off unsustainable speculative booms, and financially poisoning most of the country's banks, it stalled Colombia's recovery from a severe financial crisis in 1982. In the pre-cocaine period (1960–1980), Colombia's economy had grown by an average of 6 percent per annum, increasing its per capita income from $245 in 1960 to $1,700 in 1979. From 1981 to 1991, however, legal (i.e., nondrug) per capita income fell by 36 percent, from $2,000 in 1981 to $1,280 in 1991.[47] Substantial amounts of narco-cash went into so-called superconglomerates like *Grupo Grancolombiano*, which alone bought up 168 firms, some of them respected companies but most recently erected fronts for laundering drug money. Eventually, the *auge turbolista* (the Turbayist boom) burst with *Grancolombiano*'s CEO, Jaime Michelsen Uribe, the former president's cousin, escaping to Panamá before he could be arrested in Colombia. The scandal widened the breach within the Liberal Party (which put up two candidates for president in the 1982 elections), paving the way for the electoral triumph of Conservative Belisario Betancur Cuartas as president in May 1982.[48]

Betancur, a former attorney from a small town in Antioquia, was no blue blood; his father had worked as a mule-driver before getting a job in a textile mill. Betancur believed deeply in the social and political transformation of his country. On assuming the presidency, he threw open the doors of Turbay's military stockades, declaring an amnesty without conditions for insurgents of all denominations. He also began lobbying other Latin American presidents, whom he had hosted at a peace conference on a Panamanian island called Contadora in January 1983, to join Colombia in peacefully resolving the bitter civil wars in Central America. When U.S. president Ronald Reagan made a five-hour visit to Bogotá in the first week of December 1982, Betancur bluntly enjoined him during their meeting to stop exporting terrorism into Central America. In the course of their formal lunch, Betancur went even further, inviting Reagan to "not to be impassive before the mass graves—300,000 dead in El Salvador alone."[49]

9

THE DRUG WAR II

Why did threat of extradition to the United States cause the drug lords to engage in mass bloodshed in the 1980s?

In the mid-1980s, the Medellín drug lords were at the peak of their power. By this time, Escobar's million-dollar payoffs to politicians and church leaders as well as his building of football pitches and housing for the poor in Medellín had won him a seat to the national Congress as an alternate affiliated with the New Liberals. The drug lord's affectation as a man of the people, however, was cut short when the leader of the New Liberals, Luis Carlos Galán, threw him out of their caucus in April 1983.

Betancur's attorney general, Rodrigo Lara Bonilla, followed suit, seizing narco-owned soccer clubs, revoking the licenses of drug pilots, and pushing a judge in Medellín to prefer murder charges against Escobar for having conspired to assassinate two DAS (*Directorio Administrativo de Seguridad*, State Security Agency) agents in 1976. Then came the final straw for the drug cartel: Lara persuaded the Colombian supreme court to extradite Carlos Lehder to the United States for trial, a decision that coincided with lifting Escobar's parliamentary immunity from prosecution. After quitting the Congress, Escobar then gave out a contract worth 50 million pesos ($521,000) to one of his assassination squads, *Los Quesitos*, to murder Lara.

On April 30, 1984, two of Escobar's *sicarios* (hit men) riding a Yamaha motorcycle pulled up behind Lara's white Mercedes and shot him to death. The assassination stunned the country. President Betancur arranged for Lara's body to lie in state in the rotunda of the capitol building.[1] Later, in his eulogy at the National Cathedral, the president declared, "Stop, enemies of humanity. Colombia will hand over criminals wanted in other countries so they may be punished as an example." Six days later, he signed the extradition order to send Lehder, then in hiding, to the United States for prosecution. The *Extraditables* (as the drug lords now called themselves) then went on a murder spree, killing 32 judges and magistrates in less than six weeks.

What effect did Iran-Contra have on Colombia?

In order to bypass the U.S. Congress, which had outlawed U.S. weapons shipments to the *contra* rebels in their war against the Sandinista regime in Nicaragua, the Reagan administration began making secret weapon sales to Iran to free American hostages held in Lebanon. The proceeds from those sales were used to illegally fund the *contras*. A far more lucrative subterfuge followed, allowing the *contras* to ship cocaine into the United States in order to fund weapon purchases. Lieutenant Colonel Oliver North, the anti-Sandinista point man in the White House, made 15 notations in his logbook regarding his authorization of drug smuggling as a means of funding the *contras*, according to a subsequent congressional investigation.[2] The CIA Directorate of Operations was also in the loop about the drug shipments. A cable in October 22, 1982, for example, described a prospective meeting between *contra* leaders in Costa Rica for "an exchange in [the United States] of narcotics for arms" which would then be shipped to Nicaragua.[3]

At the center of this cocaine-for-guns operation was American pilot Barry Seal, the Medellín cartel's leading

U.S.-based drug smuggler who had retained his long-standing ties to the CIA while airlifting hundreds of tons of cocaine into the United States. Seal deployed a veritable squadron of aircraft specially equipped with the most advanced avionics, fuel bladders, and customized bays (to drop the 300-pound satchels of block cocaine in precise locations in the southeastern United States). In 1982, after relocating his operation to an airport in Mena, Arkansas, Seal began ferrying weapons to the *contras* in exchange for the CIA clearance to bring in loads of cocaine in his retrofitted C-123K Vietnam-era transport plane, nicknamed "Fat Lady." In congressional investigation a decade later, a Seal associate alleged that the CIA had not just excused the drug shipments but had given the pilot an encoding device to evade U.S. air defenses as he reentered American skies.[4]

As bizarre and heinous as the foregoing may seem, it represented a new twist in low-intensity warfighting—what one-time U.S. ambassador to Colombia Lewis A. Tambs called "criminal counterforce." U.S.-backed proxies like the *contras* or the anti-Soviet mujahedeen in Afghanistan required criminal enterprises—drug-smuggling, gun-running, extortion rackets, or murder-for-hire—to sustain the costs of irregular warfare. U.S. strategy had to facilitate this criminality.[5] No less a *contra* enthusiast than Ronald Reagan took to calling them "vandals" in National Security Council meetings.[6]

In Colombia, the emerging criminal counterforce was the paramilitaries. President Betancur's *apertura democrática* (democratic opening), which offered a blanket amnesty to all insurgent groups, convinced the FARC to accept a cease-fire and enter the political mainstream. Along with the Colombian Communist Party, the FARC formed a political party in 1985, *Unión Patriótica* (UP), which won five seats in the Senate and nine in the Chamber of Representatives in the national election the following year. The UP's candidate for president, Jaime Pardo Leal, received over 328,000 votes, or 4.5 percent of the total. At that point, paramilitary death squads, working with the Colombian military and self-defense units linked to the

Medellín cartel, gunned down Pardo and his successor in the 1990 presidential election, Bernardo Jaramillo Ossa, along with 2,000 to 3,000 mayors, congressmen, professors, and suspected supporters.[7] American ambassador Charles A. Gillespie Jr. cabled Washington, "If enough UP leaders are murdered (how many would be enough can only be speculative), the UP will be driven to depart the Congress and the FARC from what remains of the peace process."[8] That was precisely what happened. But then there was blowback.

What happened in the sacking of the Palace of Justice in 1985, and how did it change Colombia?

When M-19 (an urban-based guerrilla group with some 2,000 fighters) entered into democratic dialogue with the government in 1985, paramilitary death squads, using Colombian Army intelligence lists, began another assassination spree, gunning down scores of M-19 leaders and their followers. Pablo Escobar then saw an opportunity. He offered M-19 one million dollars to seize the Palace of Justice and put President Betancur on "trial" for his alleged knowledge about the targeting of M-19 leaders. On the Supreme Court docket at the time was a debate about whether to issue a judicial order to extradite Escobar to the United States for criminal prosecution.[9]

On the morning of November 6, 1985, 35 M-19 operatives stormed the Palace of Justice in downtown Bogotá, taking more than 300 hostages, including 25 justices. Betancur initially called for a negotiated settlement but then turned the situation over to the army, which succeeded in taking back the lower floors of the building. When the chief justice himself attempted to make an appeal directly to the president the following day, Betancur refused to take his telephone call, confining himself to the role of a "spectator," as the 2006 Truth Commission later termed it.[10] The army then made an all-out assault, shelling the palace for several hours and blasting its interior with tank fire. More than 100 people, including 12 of the 25 justices, were killed in the battle to retake the Palace of Justice, which was engulfed by a fire that destroyed 6,000 case files, including, conveniently enough, the one involving the extradition of Escobar to the United States. After the building was finally secured, the army took 11 people into custody, 10 of whom were members of the palace's service staff. All were thereafter murdered and their remains "disappeared" in a sinister reflection of cover-up and impunity.[11]

For the next 20 years, the country wallowed in confusion over who did what and why in the Palace of Justice siege. Was it, as some alleged, a "24-hour coup" by the Colombian military against President Betancur? And what of the rumored conspiracy between the left (M-19) and the right (the drug cartel) in the massacre? One thing was sure: Betancur's peace initiative, along with his presidency, had been liquidated, along with nearly the totality of M-19's cadre of leaders, 350 of whom were murdered in the first four months of 1986. Henceforth, the armed forces (whose budget doubled between 1984 and 1990) would, at will, sabotage presidential peace overtures with rebel groups and not-so-surreptitiously align themselves with paramilitary forces.[12]

It was under these dire circumstances that Virgilio Barco Vargas, a distinguished 65-year-old Liberal with an engineering degree from MIT, was elected president in 1986. Barco had previously worked in Washington as a director of the World Bank and then as Colombia's ambassador to the United States. In a mood of national gloom over the soaring murder rate and violent impunity by the drug lords, Barco promised to continue Betancur's peacemaking in Central America, relaunch the drug war, and make an all-out attack on poverty in Colombia. At least on the diplomatic front, the new president scored impressive victories, getting M-19 to publicly surrender its weapons and persuading the states of

Central America to reinvigorate the Contadora process, one that ultimately brought about a peaceful solution to those wars.[13]

In the drug war, however, Barco made little headway against the cartels. Brazenly issuing edicts under their nom de guerre, "the *Extraditables*," the Medellín drug lords offered *plata o plomo*—silver or lead (i.e., bribery or death)—to prosecutors, judges, and journalists like Guillermo Cano Isaza, the pro-extradition editor-in-chief of the daily *El Espectador* who was murdered in December 1986, two days after President Barco reinstated the extradition treaty through executive order. After 30 more judges were killed, extradition was declared unconstitutional by Colombia's highest court in June 1987.

At that point, President Barco probably had no choice but to open a channel of negotiations with Escobar through the latter's godfather, Joaquin Vallejo, Colombia's former ambassador to the UN. Escobar's terms were the same as the ones he had made in Panamá four years earlier: an end to extradition, a judicial pardon, and a tax amnesty.[14] What chances the draft agreement might have had were torpedoed by the Reagan administration, which, despite its role in cocaine smuggling on behalf of the *contras*, had formally declared the flow of drugs across U.S. borders to be a "national security threat" and had won congressional passage of a draconian new drug law. In terms of racial cleansing, the effects were devastating. Within three years of the passage of the Anti–Drug Abuse Act, 35 percent of all African American males between the ages of 16 and 35 years of age were detained or arrested in a single year (1989). A year after that, more African American young men were in prison than in college, with 1.6 million blacks having lost their right to vote due to felony convictions. Blacks, although they accounted for 12 percent of the population and an estimated 14 percent of total drug use in the United States, now comprised 73 percent of those incarcerated for drug charges.[15]

In what ways was the assassination of Liberal presidential candidate Luis Carlos Galán a turning point?

If the drug war provided a political reprieve of sorts for President Reagan from the disgrace of Iran-Contra, it resulted in dire tragedy for Colombia. No politician had attacked the cartels more fervently than Luis Carlos Galán Sarmiento, the front-running, 46-year-old presidential candidate who had once expelled Escobar from the New Liberal movement. Galán combined the austere, no-nonsense virtues of his mentor, former president Carlos Lleras, along with the towering rhetorical style of Gaitán. In August 1989, despite the fact that he had narrowly escaped an assassination attempt only a few weeks before in Medellín, Galán decided to attend a political rally in Soacha, a large slum in southwest Bogotá. This time, the Medellín cartel had 18 assassins seeded among Galan's cheering supporters. The corrupted general Miguel Maza Márquez, the head of DAS, the government's security and intelligence bureau, provided a lethal assist by reducing by half the security detail surrounding Galán, who toppled over on the stage after an Uzi submachinegun burst tore into his throat.[16]

Galán's assassination touched off a national outpouring of grief and indignation. Declaring a state of emergency, President Barco unleashed the military and police, arresting over 10,000 suspected (mostly low-level) drug traffickers and *testaferros*, men who fronted for the drug lords. The *Extraditables* responded by recruiting hundreds of Medellín gang members and putting bounties on the heads of city policemen, 300 of whom were murdered by the *sicarios* in a matter of weeks. In Galán's place, the Liberals ran 43-year-old César Gaviria Trujillo, who braved a succession of attempts on his life and won the 1990 presidential election by a margin of 24 percent.

Colombia's narco-war coincided with a sea-change in world power—the fall of the communist bloc and the dissolution of the Soviet Union in 1991. President George H. W. Bush was quick to articulate the prospect of a "new world order."[17] Beyond the question of grand strategy, there was the imperative of redeploying the vast array of forces within the national security state. Among the units seconded to the drug war were the U.S. Special Forces, whose new mission permitted targeted killings provided they were approved by the president himself.[18] Escobar's next outrage—downing an Avianca airliner and killing 111 aboard, including two Americans—got him on that list a few weeks later. The intended target of the assassination attempt was César Gaviria, the Liberal candidate for president. In the wake of the terrorist act, the Bush administration gave the go-ahead to eliminate Escobar. As a U.S. Navy task force of Delta Force operators and SEALs aboard the USS *America* positioned itself off Colombia's Caribbean coast, a top-secret U.S. Army "Intelligence Support Activity" (ISA) group, was deployed in Bogotá. The ISA team, whose specialty was tracking human targets via intercept of phone or radio signals and then pinpointing their exact location via the overflight of a small plane, was codenamed "Centra Spike."[19] U.S. covert operatives technologically guided the death squad (made up of a government strike force known as *Bloque de Búsqueda*— Search Bloc—and a criminal counterforce of assassins called *Los Pepes**) toward its target. In the shadows of that operation was the Cali cartel, Escobar's major competitor, which had provided an estimated $50 million to get the job done.[20]

How did the United States and Colombia hunt down Pablo Escobar?

For the better part of the next two years, Escobar was able to outfox his pursuers.[21] When the Search Bloc eliminated some of the drug lord's best assassins as well as his most trusted partner in crime, Gustavo Gaviria, Escobar turned to kidnapping members of the Colombian elite.[22] The Colombian government finally persuaded Escobar to surrender for the "gift of imprisonment," as García Márquez termed it. Escobar, his

*. *Perseguidos por Pablo Escobar* (People persecuted by Pablo Escobar).

brother, and 13 of his henchmen took up residence in a 30,000-square-foot compound on the outskirts of Medellín that, over time, was converted into something resembling a Club Med, replete with elegant dining, the latest game and video electronics, a soccer field, and, rather usefully, a small subterranean dungeon. Hundreds of visitors came and went from *"La Catedral"* (the Cathedral), as it was nicknamed, and Escobar was able to restore command over parts of his illicit empire and arrange murders at will. When the Colombian police moved in to arrest Escobar at the Cathedral for these and other crimes, he managed to escape on foot. It was then that *Los Pepes,* made up of Escobar's disaffected former traffickers and killers, began their campaign of counterterror in earnest.

In February 1993, *Los Pepes,* working hand in glove with the American-supported Search Bloc, began a murder campaign against Escobar's lawyers, bankers, money launderers, drivers, couriers, and relatives, using "the very charts that Centra Spike (the secret U.S. tracking team) and the CIA had painfully assembled over the previous six months."[23] Of particular concern to Washington was whether or not the Delta Force team was directly participating in the assassinations. Ultimately, the Clinton administration performed a series of bureaucratic arabesques in the cause of plausible deniability: U.S. ambassador Morris Busby righteously informed the Colombian government that the United States wanted *Los Pepes* and Search Bloc investigated as murderous vigilantes, while the Pentagon debated pulling Delta Force out of Colombia.[24] Neither initiative made much headway; Delta Force stayed on, and the death squad kept on killing

By November 1993, Escobar, deprived of his battery of handlers, snitches, and killers, was practically alone, spending his final weeks desperately trying to arrange safe passage for his family to a foreign country. Meanwhile, Centra Spike was monitoring his multiple phones and changing frequencies with increasing precision. On Thursday, December 2, Escobar's lengthy phone conversation with his son, Juan

Pablo, was picked up on the Centra Spike monitor and relayed to a Search Bloc detail, patrolling a neighborhood in Medellín. Suddenly, the detail leader spotted Escobar looking out of a second-floor window and hastily assembled an assault force that broke down a heavy metal door to the apartment where Escobar was hiding. As the fugitive, who had put on considerable weight, made a run for it across a tiled roof, he was shot dead. The Search Bloc team was able to pose thereafter, grinning triumphantly, over the riddled remains of the once-notorious drug lord.

What was the constitution of 1991, and how did it reform both state and society?

Newly-elected President Gaviria, within weeks of taking office in August 1990, struck deals with guerrilla groups, agreeing to create a constitutional assembly as a concession to get M-19, three small splinter guerrilla fronts to demobilize their forces. In a special election held three months later, M-19 won the largest number of delegates to the constitutional assembly and then fashioned a coalition agreement with a right-of-center grouping called the National Salvation Movement, the second largest vote-getter. The Liberals, though still by far the majority party in Colombia, were content to fight it out among each other and proved no match for the oddball coalition of electoral newcomers.

Elected to merely revise the 1886 constitution, the assembly instead wrote an entirely new one with 380 articles (and 60 provisional ones) that radically decentralized the state, enshrined 99 specific human and civil rights (including self-determination for indigenous peoples and a national electoral district for Afro-Colombians), substantially empowered the courts and criminal justice system, and provided for direct citizen redress (*acción de tutela*) against administrative and judicial decisions.[25] The document also prohibited the extradition of any Colombian-born citizen.

If the new constitution was, as critics charged, a patchwork of lofty ideals and implausible mandates that openly targeted the two-party ruling class, it did succeed in creating a breathing space for a frightened and besieged citizenry.[26] With the absence, however, of representatives from the paramilitary fronts, the FARC, and the Colombian military, the constitution brought about no buy-in for disarmament and demobilization by powerful armed groups, much less any codification of civil versus military powers. If political power in the country was democratized by the 1991 constitution, the democratization of property never even made it to the agenda for debate.[27]

The 1991 constitution did, however, mandate public spending for the poor, providing them direct subsidies to sustain their households. There was also pension reform, which allowed private capitalization to compete with the existing public-sector system. The decade-long result of democratized public spending resulted in notable gains in health-care access and secondary school attendance as well as in the reduction in poverty as measured by unsatisfied basic needs.[28] Colombia's chasm in income distribution, however, remained unchanged. Part of the reason for this disparity was Gaviria's other reform track: the privatization and liberalization of trade to stimulate GDP growth. Tariffs were slashed from an average of 44 percent in 1990 to 12 percent in 1992. Quantitative import restrictions were eliminated, as were export incentives. The government aggressively sold off state enterprises, either wholly or partially, and eliminated exchange controls. The result of these measures was a three-year spurt in growth (the high was 6 percent in 1993) in which Colombia outperformed the rest of Latin America while achieving record inflows of foreign direct investment. The poor, however, languished.

How did Escobar's death affect the drug war?

The drug war drove drug criminalization into new places. The criminal counterforce with which the U.S. and the Colombian governments had partnered in order to hunt down Escobar seized the remnants of his business and forcibly consolidated control of the cartel's smuggling routes. Escobar's death also touched off a paramilitary surge that took over the spreading infrastructure of coca and poppy (heroin) cultivation and production, a surge in which the newly-trained and now armed self-defense forces cleansed the FARC and, especially, peasants and local leaders rumored to have associated with the left-wing insurgency. During this period, the Colombian government authorized the creation of armed private groups called *CONVIVIR* (live together) whose number increased to 414 private security units, ultimately accounting for an estimated 120,000 armed counterinsurgent irregulars. The degree to which *CONVIVIR* coordinated its "defensive" operations with the army and paramilitary units would remain in dispute, but later analysis would attribute at least two-thirds of Colombia's politically-motivated homicides during the 1990s to the combined operations of those groups.[29]

In Bogotá, the Americans settled on a new drug war champion in 1994, Liberal president-elect Ernesto Samper Pizano, only to find out—what else?—that he, too, was "dirty." Samper's narrow win in the 1994 election had been underwritten, according to surreptitious phone tappings by the Colombian police, by a $3.75 million donation from the Cali cartel.[30] At first, U.S. officials secretly threatened Samper with public exposure if he did not take action against the Cali cartel. Then, the DEA agent in charge in Bogotá, embittered because "we had sold our soul" to get Escobar, took matters into his own hands, passing out "narco-cassettes" to the Colombian press, recordings that supposedly proved that Samper (or, more precisely, his campaign team) had been on the take.[31]

President Samper, however, would prove a nimble mouse to the lumbering American cat, ultimately escaping from any formal censure by the Colombian Congress in the drug probe, while currying favor with the United States by hunting down and arresting the Cali cartel's Rodríguez Orejuela brothers in June 1995.[32] Among the fish caught up in the anti-Cali dragnet were leading drug warriors from the Reagan administration. The Justice Department announced, to its evident embarrassment, the indictment of Justice's former director of international affairs, Michael Abbell, for his own ties to the Cali cartel. Two other former federal prosecutors, Donald Ferguson and Joel Rosenthal, along with 56 others, were indicted on similar charges.[33]

With the Republican sweep of both the House and the Senate in the 1994 election, the drug war returned to the furor reminiscent of the mid-1980s. Congressional drug hawks blistered the Clinton administration for having failed to fight the drug war in Colombia, demanding the delivery of attack helicopters armed with mini-guns to aid the new chief of the Colombian police, General José Serrano.

The drug war was once again the health of the national security state, padding military, intelligence, and drug enforcement budgets and sending trainers and advisers to the South American front. The U.S. Special Forces began launching an estimated 175 antidrug sorties per day throughout the Andean region while training the Colombian Army's first anti-narcotics battalion at the Larandia military base 40 miles from Bogotá.[34] U.S. Navy Seabees began building a base on Barracón Island in the Guaviare River (Meta) for counternarcotics training by the Green Berets. An additional 200 U.S. officers were flown in to provide crash training for regular Colombian Army units, a deployment rendered problematic when its commander was implicated in trafficking cocaine himself via the embassy's diplomatic pouch.[35]

As the dirty war spiraled out of control (with almost daily reports of massacres by the paramilitaries and, to a lesser extent, the FARC), the United States launched a massive chemical fumigation campaign to eradicate coca and poppy cultivation. Working out of three bases and two regional airports in the southern part of Colombia, U.S. Turbo Thrushes and OV-10

Broncos began blanketing Caquetá, Putumayo, Guaviare, and parts of Nariño with glysophate (commercially sold in the United States as Roundup).[36] Forced to fly at full speed well above the treetops to evade gunfire from the ground, the aerial bombardment destroyed not just coca and poppy fields but food crops as well, contaminating streams and rivers, killing thousands of livestock, and causing widespread sickness among subsistence farmers.[37] The cataclysm touched off mass protests by peasants, 150,000 of whom marched on Puerto Asís in Putumayo in 1996.[38] In Miraflores, the FARC attacked and wiped out an antinarcotics base and fumigation supply dump operated by the Colombian police.

The State Department stuck to its story that the glysophate fumigation was "highly accurate," claiming that aerial spraying of the herbicide was "less toxic than common salt, aspirin, caffeine, nicotine and even Vitamin A."[39] Subsequent investigation by international agencies and nonprofit organizations, however, indicated otherwise—that chemical additives (Cosmo Flux-411F and Cosmo-InD) mixed in with the glysophate caused a wide range of sicknesses, especially among children and the elderly.[40]

What was the Leahy Amendment, and what effect did it have?

In July 1997, AUC paramilitaries, with the support of the Colombian Army's 2nd Brigade, seized control of a coca-producing town called Mapiripán (Meta) and went on a murder spree. Because the massacre had occurred with the assistance of a Colombian Army unit that had just been trained by the Green Berets on Barracón Island, Senator Patrick Leahy (D-Vermont) demanded that the Pentagon give an accounting of the Special Forces' relationship with the complicit military officers. Leahy used the investigation to successfully amend the Foreign Assistance Act, "prohibiting assistance to any unit of the security forces of a foreign country if the Secretary of State has credible information that the unit had committed a gross violation of human rights" (defined as torture, extrajudicial killing, enforced disappearance, and rape).

Like a flare fired over a darkened landscape, the Leahy Amendment illuminated the Colombian military's role in paramilitary massacres and drug running, forcing U.S. diplomats and military officers to incorporate audits of the human rights records of all Colombian units earmarked for U.S. military aid.[41] When the Colombian military tried to fudge its reporting or to cover up its crimes, the U.S. Departments of State and Defense were required to mothball everything from Black Hawk helicopters, armored personnel carriers, automatic weapons, and night-vision goggles pending compliance. U.S. ambassador Curtis W. Kamman went even further by attempting to block promotions and new command appointments for Colombian generals tainted with paramilitary ties.[42]

Despite angry resistance by senior Colombian Army officers, the Leahy Amendment brought hope and measurable change. Human rights groups gained a more influential voice during this period. Organizations such as the Jesuit Center for Research and Popular Education (CINEP), the National Network of Initiatives for Peace and against War (REDEPAZ) and the United Nations Development Programme (UNDP) developed human rights databases. Their work, in a sense, gave the dead back their names. In 1996, 2.7 million children cast ballots supporting the "Children's Mandate for Peace," and the following year 10 million Colombians voted in favor of a nonbinding resolution to affirm their support for a peaceful end to the fighting. On a single day in October 1999, 8 million people marched for peace chanting "No Más!" (No more!) in 180 municipalities across the country.[43]

For Americans (like myself) working in human relief programs in Colombia, it was an invigorating but still frightening time. In addition to having the highest murder rate in the world, Colombia also had the highest rate of kidnapping— and American and European NGO workers were prize quarry. The FARC's seizure and execution of three Americans working

with the U'wa indigenous people in March 1999 put everyone on additional edge.[44] When some of us learned that a
key Leahy ally in the U.S. Senate, Minnesota's Paul Wellstone,
was going to visit Colombia in November 2000, we tried to get
a meeting with him, bypassing the "war department," as we
called the American embassy in Bogotá, and going straight to
the senator's Washington office to see if we could be put on his
schedule. To our surprise, it happened.

On the appointed Thursday (November 30), eight of us
were herded by a detail of State Department security officers
to the corner of the Airport Holiday Inn lobby where we were
told to sit and wait. Around 10:15 a.m., a squad of Marine
guards entered the lobby, two with drawn 9mm pistols, and
walked quickly toward us. Someone in our group said, "Oh,
great. They're going to arrest us." About that time, we spotted
the bald, diminutive man in the middle of the Marines—the
senator himself—who then greeted us and sat down on a
couch. He asked us to tell him about our work in Colombia.
I remember one middle-aged man, a Maryknoll lay worker,
saying that he didn't know "if the senator wants to hear this"
when Wellstone interjected, "Yes. I do want to hear it. I am here
in Colombia to listen to you." The senator sat there for more
than an hour, occasionally looking up and asking questions
but otherwise taking notes on a small flip-pad.

When it was my turn to introduce myself, instead of telling
Wellstone about my work at a temporary shelter for displaced
children in Ciudad Bolívar, Bogotá's largest slum, I described
how I had hitched a ride on a C-23 Sherpa cargo plane flying
a ton and a half of herbicide to a fumigation base in Puerto
Asís in the coca-growing region of Putumayo. Venturing off
the heavily guarded base on foot, I had come upon hundreds
of refugees, walking along the highway and dirt roads. Many
were clearly ill. Here and there were the swollen carcasses of
dead livestock. Seeing a large shed where people had gathered,
many seated on the ground near the building, I went inside
where I encountered what looked like a makeshift clinic with

maybe two dozen people lying on cots being attended by a few health-care workers. When one of them asked me what I was doing there, I told him I had come to see if coca spraying was causing any health problems. "Here's one," he said, turning around and walking over to a cardboard box on the floor. He picked up an infant, a little girl perhaps six months old, emaciated and sweating. "Blind," he said in English, handing her to me.

10

PLAN COLOMBIA

How did Plan Colombia come about?

Writing in 2000, Stephen M. Walt identified the "central paradox" of America's unchallenged global power as one in which the United States "enjoys enormous influence but has little idea what to do with its power or even how much effort it should expend."[1] If Plan Colombia would demonstrate the vast reach of American imperial power, the $10 billion project also underscored Washington's continuing confusion about how to apply that power, at least until the war on terror came along. Then, with enemies personified, the new crusade took on a compelling narrative reminiscent of the hunt for Pablo Escobar 10 years earlier. President George W. Bush would even draw on an executive order issued by his father at the start of the hunt for Escobar; only this time it would be used to authorize targeted killings in "decapitating" the leadership of the FARC.

In June 1998, the Pentagon began sounding the alarm about the potential to "lose Colombia." "The Colombian Armed Forces could be defeated within five years," the Defense Intelligence Agency (DIA) predicted, "unless the country's government regains political legitimacy and its armed forces are drastically restructured."[2] This statement was issued first as a classified intelligence finding before being released to the press. Then, another influential franchise in the national security state issued a warning reminiscent of the old 1930s drug panic about rampaging Mexicans high on "loco weed": the CIA reported in January 1999 that the FARC was launching a seeding campaign in Putumayo with a high-yield variety of the plant cannabis, one that would supposedly net the insurgency an extra $200 million to $500 million in drug revenue.

The tipping point that Washington was looking for came in the spring and summer of 1999. In the wake of the FARC's refusal to turn over those responsible for executing the three American activists assisting the U'wa Indians in northeastern Colombia, the State Department, which had been engaging in secret, direct talks with the FARC in Costa Rica, severed all channels of communication with the insurgency. The FARC attacks on government security forces on the outskirts of Bogotá in late June and early July seemed to sustain the Defense Intelligence Agency's prognostication that the FARC would eventually topple the government.[3] The economy meanwhile was cratering, contracting by 8 percent in two quarters.

In late June 1999, the new Republican Speaker of the House, Dennis Hastert, took matters regarding Colombia into his own hands, informing Clinton administration officials that he was tripling military aid to the beleaguered country.[4] Determined not to be upstaged, the administration immediately formed a National Security Council Executive Committee (or "ExCom") and tasked it to make "emergency recommendations." (The mere name "ExCom" resurrected the memory of President Kennedy's deliberative group during the Cuban missile crisis.) The man chosen to head the new ExCom was the Clinton administration's reigning foreign policy heavyweight—Under Secretary of State Thomas R. Pickering, the former ambassador to Russia, India, Israel, Jordan, El Salvador, and the United Nations. The question was, Pickering told his star-weighted committee, "What is Colombia prepared to do?"[5]

The obvious answer, of course, was anything the Americans wanted, but the factor—as well as the price tag—of partnership was critical. If Colombia was to pick up more than half of the cost of Plan Colombia, Colombian president Andrés Pastrana Arango (1998–2002) would need to take the lead, especially since his military, restless to the point of rebellion about the president's peace talks with the FARC, didn't like to fight in general and, most especially, against drugs. The Colombians had to get their act together. Beyond Colombian buy-in, however, there was also the conundrum of the U.S. Congress, riven with bitter disagreement, most recently over Clinton's impeachment trial. Even in the most bipartisan of times, supplemental requests of the multibillion-dollar variety tended to touch off partisan shelling before extended states of siege.

But if the Americans were divided, the Colombians were not, and as had happened so many times in the past, they seemed almost effortlessly to fall in step with the strange dance of U.S. statecraft. In advance of Plan Colombia's unveiling, Colombia's ambassador in Washington, Luis Alberto Moreno, after retaining a Washington lobbying firm for $100,000 per month, began lobbying key committee chairs on Capitol Hill. In September, President Pastrana announced Plan Colombia as his own, committing $4 billion to the project.[6] Of the $3.5 billion the international community would provide, the United States would primarily fund military assistance and the European Union humanitarian aid. Plan Colombia, it seemed, had something for everyone—drug warriors, counterinsurgency gurus, humanitarian champions, and energy and mining moguls looking to corner the market on Colombia's newly-discovered fossil fuel deposits.

How did American politics shape Plan Colombia?

The Clinton administration's legislative strategy seemed astute: to use the anti-drug thunder of the Republican majorities on Capitol Hill to neutralize any opposition from the president's own party—triangulation at its best.[7] The very Republicans who had tried to impeach Bill Clinton a year earlier would now be carrying his historic bill to "save Colombia." For the Democrats, the president's comeback could mean an electoral shot at returning to majority power in the House and Senate in the upcoming elections and even get another Democrat into the White House again in 2001. But some liberal House Democrats, especially those who had cut their legislative teeth fighting Reagan's sanguinary mayhem in Central America in the 1980s, wanted no part of Clinton's rehabilitative gamesmanship.

California congresswoman Nancy Pelosi, showing parliamentary skills that would later take her to the House Speakership, very nearly succeeded in moving all of Plan Colombia's proposed funding into domestic drug treatment.[8] Supported by Michigan congressman David Obey, she distributed a RAND study to the Democratic caucus which concluded that domestic drug treatment was 23 times more effective than "source country control," 11 times more effective than interdiction, and 7 times more effective than domestic law enforcement.[9] Although her drug treatment amendment failed narrowly in the House debate on Plan Colombia, the liberals did succeed in embedding human rights conditions into the bill.[10]

Joining forces with the Republican majority in the U.S. Senate, the Clinton administration delayed the floor debate in that chamber for two months until the end of June, giving the powerful defense and energy lobbyists time to work their pecuniary magic on undecided members. By that time, the Colombian government, under "structural adjustment conditions" imposed by the International Monetary Fund (IMF) in exchange for a $2.7 billion standby loan, was drafting a law to ease restrictions on foreign investments. No sector was more enticing to U.S. investors than oil, gas, and coal extraction, as Energy Secretary Bill Richardson made clear during a visit to Cartagena. "The United States and its allies will invest millions of dollars in two areas of the Colombian economy, in the areas of mining and energy," Richardson said, "and to secure these investments we are tripling military aid to Colombia."[11]

In the end, Plan Colombia breezed through the Senate by a vote of 95 to 4 and was approved in the House-Senate conference committee, where the conferees granted the president the discretion to waive human rights conditions, if necessary.[12] On July 13, 2000, President Clinton hosted President Pastrana at the White House for the signing of Plan Colombia. The following month, when the State Department informed the White House that the Colombian military was in full violation of the human rights conditions in the law, Clinton immediately waived them.

After everything that went into making it happen, did Plan Colombia work?

Not at first. As the administration of President George W. Bush took office in January 2001, the disarray was such that a *New York Times* editorialist advised that the fundamental strategy of Plan Colombia had to be completely rethought.[13] From January to April 2001, the new administration addressed that confusion in at least one sense. Bush's energy task force inventoried global energy sources, including those of Colombia, with a view to bring them into active extraction and production, if necessary by military force.[14] In May 2001, Los Angeles–based Occidental Petroleum approached senior U.S. officials, warning that it would close down its Caño Limón-Covenas pipeline in Colombia unless the oil conduit could be protected from FARC and the Ejército de Liberación Nacional (ELN) attacks. [15] By the time the Bush administration announced its decision to deploy U.S. Special Forces to equip and train a "Critical Infrastructure Brigade" to protect that pipeline, Al-Qaeda's attacks on the World Trade Towers and the Pentagon on September 11, 2001, had ushered in the U.S.-led "war on terror."

Colombia meanwhile was speeding toward open war. When government forces retook Caquetania (the enclave previously awarded to the FARC) after the suspension of peace talks in 2002, the FARC struck back with unprecedented violence, blowing up pipelines and electrical grids, and engaging in a terror campaign that forced half of the country's 1,050 mayors to abandon their posts. In a May 2002 battle with paramilitaries in the Chocó, FARC fighters launched a crude gas-canister mortar into a church where villagers were sheltering themselves, killing 119 of them. The FARC also stepped up its kidnapping of leaders of national peacemaking initiatives and seized a popular candidate for president, Ingrid Betancourt. In April, Álvaro Uribe Vélez, a long-shot independent candidate for president who was advocating a full-scale assault against the leftist insurgencies, himself narrowly escaped assassination when a remote-controlled bomb blew up his armored vehicle on a street in Barranquilla. The Bush administration publicly accused the FARC of being "the most dangerous international terrorist group in this hemisphere" and won approval from Congress to make Colombia a front in the war on terrorism.

In May 2002, Uribe swept to victory in the first round of the presidential balloting, beating the runner-up, Liberal Horacio Serpa, by more than 20 points. Colombians no longer wanted a man of peace as they had in 1998, but rather a man on horseback, one whose candidacy had activated a powerful new political force in the country—the paramilitaries, who boasted openly about their role in electing Uribe and a new congress.[16] During the election, Uribe had fended off credible press reports of his ties to the paramilitaries and, a decade earlier, to the Medellín drug lords.[17]

At another time, Uribe might have been designated persona non grata by Washington, if not extradited to the United States or simply eradicated by *Los Pepes*. But in 2002, the war on terror eclipsed all other strategic considerations. America, Vice President Dick Cheney said, had to operate "on the dark side." Torture, "extraordinary rendition" (spiriting terrorist suspects into the bowels of Second and Third World prisons), and leadership decapitation became operational staples in the war on terror. Uribe was accordingly embraced as a counterterrorist champion with a bold plan.

How did the paramilitary forces play into Uribe's strategy of "democratic security"?

By the late 1990s, the paramilitary forces, which had operated for a generation in scattered units called *bloques* (blocks), had begun to coalesce into their own parastate. The paramilitary fronts from Córdoba and Urabá, along with those from Middle Magdalena and Eastern Plains, formed the *Autodefensas Unidas de Colombia* (AUC, United Self-Defense Forces of Colombia) in 1997. From a base of controlling about 5 percent of all the nation's municipalities in the early 1990s, the "paras" predominance grew to an estimated 23 percent of all municipalities by the end of that decade.[18] In the course of their metamorphosis from armed defenders of agricultural estates to guns-for-hire for the narcotraffickers and later death squads joint-venturing with the Colombian military, the *paras* became the country's most dynamic criminal counterforce.

One U.S. think-tank analyst and longtime expert on Colombia, Adam Isacson, who was then working at the Center for International Policy in Washington, flew down to Medellín in July 2006 for a firsthand look at the improving security situation. Isacson found that the Antioquian capital, long engulfed by criminal and political violence, was undoubtedly more secure but not for the reasons the American embassy was telling everyone. Leftist forces had indeed been routed, but whole neighborhoods were now subject to paramilitary control and enforcement.[19]

Paramilitary peace, if anything, was even more draconian in Barrancabermeja, an oil-refining center (population 300,000) in the Middle Magdalena. There, the local paramilitary front, *Bloque Central Bolívar,* had, with the support of local Colombian armed forces, eviscerated the once-powerful oil workers union by murdering scores of its members and driving an estimated 18,000 people out of the city from 1998 to 2001. Coca-Cola, which operated a large bottling plant in the city, had also been coopted by the paramilitaries, who imposed *vacunas* (extortion payments) on the company after destroying its union.[20]

The achievement of public order via gangster capitalism and vigilante justice was linked, ironically enough, to Uribe's most dramatic peacemaking achievement during this period: negotiated disarmament and demobilization of the paramilitary armies under the *Ley de Justicia y Paz* (Justice and Peace Law) signed in 2005. The *New York Times* had called the initial draft legislation, "Impunity for Mass Murderers, Terrorists, and Major Cocaine Traffickers Law."[21] After blistering international criticism and the intercession of the Constitutional Court (established in 1991 to review constitutional questions), the law, however, was improved, giving victims the right to truth, justice, and reparations in conformity with international law.[22] In the course of the demobilization, an estimated 32,000 AUC fighters handed over their weapons to the army and police in televised ceremonies punctuated by grandiose speeches from their paramilitary commanders.

In terms of political theater, the Justice and Peace Law was undoubtedly a success. On the ground, however, the reality was otherwise: warlords like Salvatore Mancuso, Ernesto Báez, and Hernán Giraldo retained control over massive tracts of land, drug-trafficking routes, and hundreds of cities and towns in the country. At least 4,000 paramilitary fighters soon regrouped to form new criminal bands.[23]

Paramilitary vengeance, it turned out, was part of a national conspiracy that came to be known as the *parapolítica* (parapolitics). Up to one-third of Colombian congresspersons and senators, including the president's cousin, Senator Mario Uribe, were in the pay of the warlords and secretly advancing their criminal agendas.[24] President Uribe himself was deeply implicated and did everything in his power to stop the Supreme Court's criminal chamber from investigating the *parapolítica*.[25]

Although Uribe easily won a second presidential term in May 2006, polling over 62 percent in the first round, he had come to embody the very word he routinely used to describe the FARC—*impunidad* (impunity). Representatives of one of the most feared warlords in the country, Diego Murillo Bejarano (known as "Don Berna"), visited the presidential palace for talks with Uribe's aides. Within that entourage was an assassin known by his nom de guerre, "Job." At issue was Don Berna's agreement to give sworn testimony in the Supreme Court investigation of the government's ties to the paramilitaries. After the meeting, Job made a call to Don Berna to say that everything had gone very well in "*Casa de Nari*" (the presidential palace). At that point, Don Berna told the court that thereafter he would no longer cooperate with its investigation. Job was then assassinated.[26]

What happened in the May 2008 overnight extradition of Colombia's paramilitary warlords to the United States?

Three weeks after Uribe's aides had met with Don Berna's attorney, the U.S. embassy got an urgent appeal from *Casa de Nariño*: President Uribe wanted the Americans to extradite 13 paramilitary warlords, including Don Berna, and to do so in the dead of night before the Supreme Court began work the next morning, May 14, 2008. The United States complied, scrambling all available airplanes to get the men out of Colombia that same night. The country woke up to police photos showing shackled paramilitary leaders being escorted onto American planes.[27] None of the warlords would ever implicate Álvaro Uribe in their crimes.

Human rights activists cried foul, likening the airlift to removing "14 Pinochets" (the Chilean military strongman Augusto Pinochet) from criminal prosecution. Duly arraigned in U.S. federal district courts, the warlords generally pled guilty, getting an average of seven-and-one-half-year prison sentences for their drug-trafficking crimes. Other criminals who had worked directly for President Uribe were even luckier. General Mauricio Santoyo, Uribe's former chief of security, after pleading guilty in U.S. District Court in Virginia to drug trafficking (but not, of course, to his other crimes), got a 13-year sentence that was reduced to 18 months for "good behavior."[28]

The "rule of law," sanctified by the absurd ideal of stopping drugs, thus rationalized asylum for murderers. Twenty years earlier in the hunt for Escobar, the Americans had deemed slaughter of judges, journalists, and honest cops as necessary for the achievement of a handful of drug extraditions. Further expedients in the imperial dream world followed.[29] After news of the role of the State Security Agency (*Directorio Administrativo de Seguridad*) in mass surveillance and paramilitary collusion went public, U.S. ambassador William R. Brownfield asked his country team how many U.S. agencies had working relationships with the corrupted agency. No fewer than eight hands went up.[30]

The U.S.-led drug war made about as much sense as the idiotic search for "El Dorado" had 400 years earlier. Even seasoned diplomat Myles R. R. Frechette, who had served as U.S. ambassador in the mid-1990s, wondered, "What is the endgame?" as he titled his candid monograph about U.S. policy in Colombia. There wasn't any.[31]

How did Plan Colombia impact the drug trade?

Hardly at all. The U.S. Congress had mandated, as a condition of its passage of Plan Colombia, that the Colombian supply of illegal narcotics would be reduced by 50 percent within six years. If drug war officials could point to Colombian cocaine production dropping in at least one year by more than half (from 700 metric tons in the early 2000s to an estimated 345 metric tons in 2011), coca cultivation, by that time, was already migrating to new places in the country and surging in neighboring Andean countries. Even when aerial spraying of coca fields reached an all-time high of 170,000 hectares in 2006, the street price of cocaine in the United States hardly even changed.[32]

Nearly everywhere, the collateral effect of spraying was enormous, poisoning food and other legal crops while pushing desperate subsistence tillers into the indenture of guerrillas and armed criminal gangs. Despite the evidence, U.S. agencies like the DEA and Southcom (the U.S. armed forces Southern Command) stuck to their cops-and-robbers narrative, showcasing dramatic drug busts, unveiling new numbers supposedly denoting success, and wrapping it all in fatuous warfighting motifs.[33]

When the World Health Organization declared in May 2015 that the aerial spraying of glysophate probably caused cancer in humans, the Colombian government ordered the Americans to stop. It was probably just as well. The previous year's massive chemical bombardment had actually netted a 39 percent *increase* in coca cultivation.[34]

Did the American-supported "war on terror" in Colombia succeed by anyone's standard?

Uribe, who was president from 2002 to 2010, proved to be a formidable commander in chief, reversing Colombia's long tradition of weak presidential control over the country's armed forces. The president micromanaged every feature of military command-and-control, appointing and removing generals and admirals at will, personally directing complex military operations, poring over intelligence assessments provided by the Americans, and ramming through a 1.2 percent tax on liquid assets—a so-called security tax on wealthy Colombians—that netted $800 million for the police and armed forces.

By continuing their terror attacks and kidnapping operations, the FARC played perfectly into Uribe's martial narrative about *la guerra contra los terroristas* (the war against the terrorists). The FARC launched mortars at Uribe's inauguration ceremony in downtown Bogotá, killing 19 people, including three children in a poor neighborhood near the presidential palace. On February 7, 2003, FARC operatives planted 350 pounds of high explosives in the basement parking lot of the Club El Nogal, an exclusive athletic and social club in northern Bogotá. At 8:15 p.m., the bomb went off, ripping through at least half of the building's 10 floors, killing 33 persons (six of whom were children), and wounding 160. Among those killed was my former student and NGO partner Luisa Fernanda Solarte, then only 30 years of age, who had just arranged a corporate gift of $385,000 to improve nutrition and security at a temporary shelter in a Bogotá slum where I was working.[35] Uribe seized on the bombing to appeal to the country to join the fight against the FARC. The day after the attack, thousands of *bogotanos* took to the streets, chanting, "*Bogotá llora, pero no se rinde*" (Bogotá weeps but won't surrender). Over the exploded façade of the Club El Nogal building, they draped an enormous national flag.

By the end of 2005, Washington was trumpeting the results of Plan Colombia's signal success in stabilizing the country—"back from the brink," as one Washington think-tank put it.[36] Between 2002 and 2006, kidnappings had fallen by 80 percent, and homicides, both criminal and political, had decreased by a little over 40 percent. Economic growth, which had flatlined in 2000–2001, had rebounded to 6.9 percent in 2007 with foreign investment having quadrupled in Uribe's first four-year term. Polls showed the president's approval ratings to be above 70 percent, enough for Uribe to have the 1991 constitution amended to enable him to run for a second term. The human cost of "democratic security," however, was also coming into focus. In 2002 alone, warfare displaced 412,000 Colombians. By 2005, the total number of internal refugees in the country rose to over 2 million.

In 2010, with Plan Colombia's funding now cresting annually to over $600 million (with some 80 percent devoted to military and police purposes), the Uribe government began building and qualitatively improving Colombian security forces. The national police force more than doubled, reaching a total force of 170,000. The Colombian armed forces grew to 275,000 members during the same period. In terms of advanced weaponry, operational intelligence, and mobility of forces (with the world's fourth-largest fleet of Apache helicopters), it became Latin America's biggest and best-armed military with the exception of continental giant Brazil. Long derided for corruption and combat unreadiness, the new Colombian armed forces enjoyed high public approval ratings.[37] As for the police, two-thirds of Colombian citizens reported their positive impression, in striking contrast to popular disaffection about police in most other Latin American countries.[38]

Why was the FARC targeted for "leadership decapitation" by the United States?

After 9/11, the Bush administration had confined targeted killings to war zones such as Afghanistan and Iraq or to specific places where key Al-Qaeda terrorists were operating. Why then did FARC leaders, with no history or intention of attacking the U.S. homeland, much less exporting terrorism outside of Colombia, become targeted for assassination?

The short answer is because they could be targeted. In the words of one of the SEAL Team 6 veterans interviewed for this account, targeted killings represented "an operational opportunity."[39] Late in 2005, the CIA and Special Forces recommended executive action against FARC leaders, a proposal that Colombian defense minister Juan Manuel Santos sent forward (in a one-page memo drafted by the U.S. Air Force mission chief in Bogotá) to U.S. defense secretary Donald Rumsfeld. President Bush formally approved the request in his June 2006 meeting with President Uribe in Washington. Couched in the exigencies of counterterrorist warfare, the fraternity of risk developed over 50 years between Colombia and the United States secretly culminated in targeted violence as statecraft.

The technical problems proved more difficult to surmount than the legal ones.[40] There were no drones, F-16s, or Stealth Bombers—the normal delivery vehicles of smart bombs and antipersonnel missiles—in Colombia at the time, and the Americans, with major military operations in Iraq and Afghanistan, were loath to redeploy those aircraft. Enter a newly arrived U.S. Air Force attaché in Bogotá with an idea: Why not jerry-rig a 500-pound bomb (with a Raytheon GPS kit as its brain) onto a Cessna A-37, a Vietnam-era light attack aircraft? As U.S. technicians went to work on that one, there was a further problem: What if the Colombian military began using the weapon to assassinate its political enemies? The CIA solved that problem by inserting an encryption key that only the Americans could unscramble. Once in place, the GPS kit could communicate with the satellites that would laser-guide the bomb to its target.[41] In terms of the risk of blowback (i.e., violent retaliation by the FARC against the United States), one CIA officer observed, "Targeted killings by clandestine proxy are a whole lot better than doing it yourself."[42]

The first hit on September 1, 2007, took out Tomás Medina Caracas (aka *el Negro Acacio*), commander of the FARC's 16th front; the second killed Gustavo Rueda Díaz (aka Martín Caballero), commander of the 37th front. The targeted attacks soon employed a technique to conceal the use of smart bombs by following up the first strike with conventional bombing runs and machine-gun strafing by AC-47 gunships. On March 1, 2008, Raúl Reyes, the second-ranking member of the FARC secretariat, was killed at his hideout a mile inside Ecuador on that country's border with Colombia. The Reyes killing sparked a regional furor when both Venezuela and Ecuador, after denouncing the hit in angry terms, moved troops to their borders with Colombia. To placate his neighbors, Uribe issued an apology.

As the targeted killings continued, FARC forces suffered nearly 4,000 desertions. After the death from natural causes of long-time FARC leader Manuel "Tirofijo" Marulanda in late March 2008, the FARC received another blow in July when the Colombian military, having located 15 high-value hostages, including the three captured U.S. contractors and former presidential candidate Ingrid Betancourt, painstakingly put together a high-risk ruse called *Operación Jaque* (Operation Checkmate) to rescue them. Posing as an international humanitarian team that was supposedly going to supervise the transfer of the hostages to a new location by helicopter, the faux NGO group spirited them away to freedom without a shot being fired. Amid global rejoicing, Uribe's approval ratings soared to over 90 percent.

Why did Washington have second thoughts about Plan Colombia?

When the Democrats took control of the House and Senate after the 2006 midterm elections, incoming House Speaker Nancy Pelosi and Senator Pat Leahy, the new chairman of the Senate Appropriations Subcommittee on Foreign Operations, put Plan Colombia on the chopping block. Before Secretary of State Condoleezza Rice could certify Colombia's human rights progress, the Democratic leadership in the House opened hearings on the murder of 72 Colombian trade unionists the previous year, and the alleged connivance of Uribe's government in those assassinations.[43] Leahy's subcommittee blocked approval of $55 million in military aid for Plan Colombia, citing a CIA report leaked to the *Los Angeles Times* linking the Army chief of staff, General Mario Montoya, to a paramilitary massacre of civilians in Medellín.[44] Around that time, there were the first confirmed "false-positive" reports that the Colombian military had rounded up hundreds of young men who had been dressed up and executed to build up body counts. These reports, which the U.S. mission had known about for a period of years, refuted Southcom's sworn assurances that, for example,

the Colombian military was responsible for "less than two percent" of all human rights violations in the country.[45]

In his final year in office, President Bush was determined
to bring about a bilateral free trade agreement between the
United States and Colombia. But when the president called
House Speaker Nancy Pelosi on Monday, April 7, 2008, in
order to invoke presidential "fast-track authority" (in which
the House would be required to vote within 60 days of the submission of the treaty draft), Pelosi curtly reminded him, "You
don't have the votes." Bush was furious.[46]

On the presidential campaign trail, Senators Barack
Obama and Hillary Clinton joined the Democratic chorus
of resistance to the proposed trade deal. But not everyone
in the Clinton household shared that opinion. In what
might be called triangulation *en famille*, former president
Bill Clinton, having picked up $800,000 for four speeches
from a Colombian development group called Gold Service
International in 2005, began promoting not just the proposed
free-trade agreement but multimillion-dollar investment
deals in Colombian mines, ports, and oil fields. His two partners were billionaire Canadian oil magnate Frank Giustra,
who had pledged $100 million to the Clinton Foundation,
and Álvaro Uribe. The three men met multiple times in
Bogotá, New York City, and the Clinton family home in
Chappaqua, New York.[47]

Just who got what out of that gilded confederacy is not clear,
but it underscored the fact that Colombia's historic trajectory
into the "natural orbit" of U.S. market capitalism had long been
pushed forward by speculative deal-making on the inside.[48]
Eighty years earlier, as we might remember, the American
"money doctor," Edwin Kemmerer, after establishing a central bank and a U.S.-like financial infrastructure in Bogotá, had
steered hundreds of millions of dollars in U.S. equity invest-
ments into the construction of roads, railroads, ports, public
buildings, and coffee roasteries. When the Depression hit,
Colombia had first tried to shoulder its massive debt before

trading away sovereignty over its energy, mines, and roads for a new loan from Washington. The Cold War, the drug war, and the war on terror had further tightened the sinews of Colombian-American strategic interdependence and had set the stage for corporate integration of the two economies.

11

NEOLIBERALISM AND COUNTERINSURGENCY

How did the U.S.-Colombia free trade agreement come about?

The officially named "U.S.-Colombia Trade Promotion Agreement" was the stepchild of a rancorous hemispheric divorce between the United States and five Latin American governments over the proposal to extend the North American Free Trade Agreement (NAFTA) to the entire hemisphere minus Cuba.[1] It was to be called the Free Trade Area of the Americas (FTAA), but Washington encountered pitched opposition to the proposed deal at the November 2005 summit meeting that brought together 34 heads of state in the Argentine coastal resort of Mar del Plata. Having anticipated the standoff, President Uribe cleverly proposed to President Bush that in the event the FTAA failed that their two countries begin negotiating a bilateral free trade agreement instead. Bush enthusiastically agreed.[2]

As President Obama would later discover, the cause of free trade was inextricably entangled with the larger challenge of continued U.S. hegemony in Latin America. With the rise of Venezuelan strongman Hugo Chávez in 1999 and that of other leftist heads of state in Bolivia, Ecuador, Uruguay, Argentina, and Paraguay, strategic anxiety in Washington fueled fear about a new bogeyman at the gates of the Monroe Doctrine—China—which was stalking the southern continent in search of long-term resource deals. "Is Washington Losing Latin America?," asked one *Foreign Affairs* article.[3] Not really, of course, but the politically battered Bush administration couldn't be sure enough. In the course of his meeting with Uribe in August 2005, President Bush not only gave the go-ahead for the free trade agreement but also promised the Colombian president that the United States would consider the use of targeted killings of the FARC's leadership. This proved to be what Plan Colombia largely wasn't—a game-changer.

Was the U.S.-led counterinsurgency in Colombia successful?

Everybody at least said so. As the Obama administration debated the case for a "surge" of up to 30,000 U.S. troops in Afghanistan in its first year in office, the White House looked to the "Colombian model" as illustrative of the right formula for "stability operations." U.S. Central Command (commonly known as "Centcom") even began flying senior Colombian officers to Kabul to lead briefings and consultations on the finer points of counterinsurgency.

By that time, the U.S. Southern Command and the Colombian government had identified 12 "consolidation zones" where military occupation could give way to civilian governance and economic development.[4] The U.S. mission had earmarked up to $1 billion to finance "Plan Consolidation."[5] The largest such targeted zone was La Macarena, a former FARC stronghold 220 miles south of Bogotá, where the Colombian Army had succeeded in clearing out insurgents from six towns, eradicating coca crops, and sufficiently stabilizing the zone to enable the U.S. Agency for International Development (USAID) to launch 538 "quick impact projects." For the 100,000 people living in La Macarena, there were noteworthy improvements in everyday life.[6] Schools were built, water systems patched up, roads regraded and sometimes paved, police stations constructed, and soccer fields got floodlights. It looked and felt good, as the cable traffic from the U.S. mission indicated.[7] But the transfer of liberated areas to civilian authorities, who trickled in only to trickle back out, never happened.[8]

Instead, La Macarena became a highly secured cluster of towns that served as a sort of counterinsurgency theme park for a steady stream of national security tourists from Washington during the Obama administration. CIA director Leon Panetta, multiple congressional delegations, several assistant and deputy secretaries of State and Defense, two Southern Command CinCs, and, perhaps most importantly, journalists from most major media outlets in the United States all took the 90-minute helicopter ride from Bogotá to the former FARC stronghold. For the Americans, La Macarena was not just emblematic of success in Colombia, it also supposedly proved that such stability operations could rescue other "failing states" such as Mexico and Afghanistan.[9] Democrats on Capitol Hill liked La Macarena because it emphasized social development over military aid and offered "peaceful solutions to consider in Afghanistan."[10] After his own tour of La Macarena in March 2009, Admiral Mike Mullen, chairman of the Joint Chiefs of Staff, agreed, vowing to apply "our learning in Colombia" to Pakistan and Afghanistan.[11] The Colombians understandably reveled in the idea that they were now a stellar showcase in America's "global war on terror."

Rhetorical escalation soon followed. No longer was Colombia just a "model." It was now a "miracle"—"the most successful nation-building exercise by the United States this century," Ambassador Bill Brownfield declared.[12] "President Uribe is heroic," said Defense Secretary Robert Gates on a visit to Bogotá in April 2010, describing Colombia as "a linchpin of security and prosperity in South America" and "a unique source of experience and expertise." Admiral Mike Mullen, back again for yet another visit in June 2010, thought Colombia's success was the key to stabilizing a host of "failing states." After being promoted by President Obama to director of the CIA, General David Petraeus's first foreign trip was—where else?—to Bogotá, where the press described Petraeus as "redesigning" the counterinsurgency war for the grateful Colombians.[13]

How did peace talks begin?

In August 2010, when Uribe's understudy Juan Manuel Santos Calderón donned the presidential sash, few thought that the stolid and colorless former defense minister would do much more than continue his predecessor's *machtpolitik*. But Santos surprised everyone. In his inaugural address, he told the country that "the door to dialogue [with the guerrillas] is not locked," assuring his listeners that it was "possible to have a Colombia at peace, a Colombia without guerrillas, and we're going to prove it! By reason or by force!" Shortly thereafter, he called President Obama to let him know how he intended to push the FARC toward the peace table. Obama gave him, in the words of a senior diplomat who staffed their phone conversation, his "unqualified support" along with his personal consent to turn over the American-controlled GPS precision-guided munitions (PGM) technology to the Colombian armed forces.

A month later, guided by a tracking device placed in the boot of the FARC's eastern bloc commander, Jorge Briceño Suárez ("Mono Jojoy"), the PGM sortie found its mark, killing Briceño and 20 of his associates in the La Macarena region. In spite of the death of its leading military commander—or maybe because of it—the FARC responded positively to President Santos's encouragement to meet secretly beginning in March 2011. The FARC even took a symbolic step toward peace thereafter by announcing that it would no longer engage in kidnapping. By that time, the two parties had jointly selected "guarantor countries" (Cuba and Norway) as well as "facilitator countries" (Venezuela and Chile) to fortify the peace process, choosing Havana as the permanent site for negotiations.

In August 2012, the parties initialed a roadmap for formal talks and five substantive areas for negotiations leading to a "durable peace": land reform and rural development; post-peace political participation of the rebels; resolution of drug cultivation and production, conflict termination (in terms of ceasefire and guerrilla disarmament and demobilization); and the procedural implementation of the peace agreement. Santos's objective, abhorrent to Uribe, who immediately denounced the negotiations as selling out to murderers, was to create the basis for a *political* solution to the war.[14]

Accordingly, the new president began calling for change in the drug war: "If the world decides to legalize [drugs] and thinks that is how we reduce violence and crime, I could go along with that." The Colombian government, after having decriminalized marijuana and cocaine, now proposed including methamphetamine and ecstasy in harm-reduction initiatives.[15] It was a tricky move to challenge the drug war superpower on its prized turf, especially since the United States was outsourcing counternarcotics warfare to Colombian police and military in Mexico and Central America as well as joint-venturing with a Colombian special anti-drug forces unit called the JUNGLA Commandos (*Compañía Jungla Antinarcóticos*).[16]

What was Espada de Honor?

The Santos administration's diplomatic offensive was paired with a new counter-guerrilla strategy called *Espada de Honor* (Sword of Honor). After taking office as president, Santos had ordered his leading military and police commanders to look more deeply into the nature of criminalized insurgency.[17] They found that 92.8 percent of the nexus between political and criminal violence was occurring in no more than 10 places in the country—that the FARC, the ELN, and the criminal bands derived from the former paramilitary blocs had networks, operational hubs, and local infrastructure that could be precisely targeted via "intelligence fusion."

A key element in the new plan was *Corazón Verde* (Green Heart), a police strategy to protect populations (roads, neighborhoods, small farmers, and the like) while taking down criminal networks in the wake of the military sweep. The results of the new strategy were dramatic. In the three years of the joint military and police offensives that followed, the FARC suffered losses totaling 13,521 (3,916 demobilized, 8,511 captured, and 1,094 killed), in which 53 of its ranking officers and six of its front commanders had fallen; every one of these losses were noted in Defense Minister Juan Carlos Pinzón's meticulously rendered Excel list.[18] As for the criminal bands, their forces were reduced by 4,423 operatives during that same period of 2012–2015.[19]

What peacebuilding initiatives accompanied the peace negotiations?

Critical to peacebuilding was Santos's determination to *desarmar la palabra* (to deescalate the war of words) between the government and human rights groups that had been vilified, and even targeted, by his predecessor.[20] The Santos administration formed "guarantee roundtables" on a national and local basis for dialogue with human rights organizations. In 2011, the government proposed and the Congress passed the Victims and Land Restitution Law, which gave Colombia's six million victims of land dispossession the right to get back their stolen or abandoned property, the total of which was estimated to be 16 million hectares—14 percent of the country's entire territory. Nearly half of those displaced were female heads of households. The victims of human rights crimes were also entitled to reparations, including financial compensation, from guerrilla, paramilitary, and government perpetrators.

Progress in implementing the restitution law was tragically slow, however.[21] By the end of 2016, the *Unidad de Restitución de Tierras* (or URT, the land restitution unit housed in Colombia's Ministry of Agriculture) had adjudicated only 2 percent of the 90,000 land claims that had been filed. Given the lax and often contradictory process of land titling, the great majority of claims required an investigation by special government land tribunals into the history of land use and the indicia of ownership.[22] In almost all areas in which the URT sought to investigate and adjudicate claims, there were reprisals, some resulting in the murder of land activists and claimants. [23]

Another area of slow-motion justice involved the prosecution of the Colombian armed forces for extrajudicial executions and other acts of terror and dispossession against civilians. As of June 2016, the Attorney General's Office was investigating more than 3,600 unlawful killings that took place from 2002 through 2008 and had convicted more than 800 state agents in 210 rulings. Most of those convicted were low-level soldiers, but 11 generals have been questioned or arraigned.[24] Former president Uribe publicly denounced these investigations and, at times, seemed intent on inciting sedition in the armed forces against their democratically elected government.[25] Uribe also did what he could to defeat Santos in his bid for reelection in 2014. Although Santos lost to the Democratic Center Party nominee, Óscar Iván Zuluaga, by more than 4 points in the first round, the Uribe-backed candidate was implicated in a hacking scandal in which military intelligence was used to expose the interworkings of the peace negotiations in Havana.[26] That—and some key endorsements—were enough for Santos to win comfortably in the second and final round of voting.

How did the Obama administration bring about the U.S.-Colombia free trade agreement?

Like other bilateral free trade agreements between North and South, the essential driver of a U.S.-Colombia commercial pact—beyond all the cheery blather about rising tides, level playing fields, and creation of hundreds of thousands of new jobs—was the prospect of a corporate windfall for both sides.[27] For the Colombian elite, the stakes were significant. The United States remained (and remains) Colombia's largest trading partner, accounting for 39.6 percent of total

Colombian exports in 2007. Petroleum, coal, coffee, manu-factures, gold, and cut flowers were the export leaders. The United States was also the largest supplier (26.5 percent) of Colombian imports, of which machinery, grains, chemi-cals, transportation equipment, and mineral and consumer products were the leading items, all subject to Colombian tariffs of between 5 and 20 percent. Several of Colombia's *multilatinas* (Latin American multinational companies), al-ready enjoying a cross-market symbiosis with the United States, were looking for significant earnings gains from a free trade agreement.[28]

Curiously enough, the legacy of the drug war was also a driver of the FTA agreement. As a condition for Colombia to receive the lion's share of the $2.2 billion "Andean Initiative" to combat drugs proposed by President George H. W. Bush in 1991, the Gaviria administration had agreed to privatize state-owned companies, float its exchange rate, and rad-ically reduce tariffs and nontariff barriers. The sweetener in that particular drug deal was that Colombia (as well as Peru, Ecuador, and Bolivia) would get hundreds of tariff reductions for their exports into the United States via the Andean Trade Preferences Act (ATPA). Under George W. Bush in 2002, the renamed Andean Trade Promotion and Drug Eradication Act (ATPDEA) was broadened to include over 6,000 Andean duty-free exports to the United States.

In the course of the following four years (2003–2007) under this codependent scheme, U.S.-Andean trade doubled (from $9.61 billion to $22.51 billion) but so did the U.S. trade deficit with those countries. Suddenly, U.S. copper and gold-mining companies, California asparagus growers, as well as U.S.-based clothes and cathode manufacturers all saw their market shares shrink given the rising Andean trade flow. And did any of this "denarcoticize" those drug-exporting countries as it was sup-posed to? The U.S. International Trade Commission dutifully reported, year in and year out, that ATPDEA had practically no impact at all on the drug trade.[29]

From the American standpoint, the corporate windfall, though limited given Colombia's economic size, was also enticing. The National Association of Manufacturers projected major export gains in excavating equipment, heavy machinery, aircraft, chemicals, and plastic resins.[30] The FTA would also give U.S. businesses competitive access to Colombia's $180 billion banking, financial services, and government procurement sector. The most promising export gains of all, according to the U.S. International Chamber of Commerce, were in agricultural products where U.S. industrial efficiencies underwritten by government subsidies stood to realize significant export increases in beef, cotton, wheat, rice, and chicken parts.[31]

In the late summer of 2011, the Obama administration began "slow-walking" the bill on Capitol Hill, electing to forgo executive branch testimony given the bitter atmosphere between the two parties. Instead, U.S. ambassador to Colombia Mike McKinley, a trade veteran who had quarterbacked the negotiation and ratification of the U.S.-Peru free trade agreement in 2007 while serving as America's emissary in Lima, came home to lead the low-key advance on the Hill. The Colombian diplomatic mission in Washington had meanwhile retained two lobbying firms (Peck Madigan and Elmendorf/Ryan) with deep ties to both Republican and Democratic congressional leaders. The trade bill also picked up two key union endorsements, from the United Auto Workers and the United Food and Commercial Workers.

By that time, the Obama administration had put together and formally launched a "Labor Action Plan" to address the rampant rate of homicides among Colombian union organizers. The newly formed Ministry of Labor in Bogotá began deploying inspectors, special prosecutors, and judicial police investigators in the field to oversee compliance with collective bargaining agreements, report on union busting, apply an expanded criminal code against violators, and end indirect employment practices in port, palm oil, sugar, and other sectors. With the Americans supplying training, logistics, and intelligence tracking, union murders declined from 53 in 2010 to 30 in 2011 to 22 the following year.[32] That decline removed a major sticking point for House Democrats who had opposed the bill.

At Obama's insistence, Senate Democrats, then in the majority, amended the three-country free trade bill (South Korea and Panamá were the two others) to include $1 billion of trade adjustment assistance for retraining displaced workers and compensating negatively affected small businesses, a move that led to a Republican boycott of the Senate Finance Committee deliberation.[33] A compromise was hammered out, however, cutting the adjustment assistance to $575 million for a period of two years. On October 3, 2011, the Obama administration submitted draft legislation to both houses of Congress for the FTA with Colombia as well as Panamá and South Korea. Nine days later, the U.S.-Colombia trade pact was passed.[34]

Have free trade and deregulated foreign investment worked in Colombia?

For the rich, unquestionably. For everyone else, not so much.

The global commodity boom, aided by an exponential increase in foreign investment, paved the way for Colombia's economic comeback from the dire 1990s. The so-called super cycle in the global demand for oil, coal, textiles, and palm oil almost tripled the country's exports from $11.9 billion in 2002 to $29.4 billion in 2006. GDP growth reached 6.8 percent growth rate in 2006—the highest in 28 years and 2 points above the Latin American average. From 2002 to 2005, foreign direct investment shot up by a factor of 500 percent as the security situation improved and bilateral trade agreements between Colombia and both the United States and the EU were placed on the negotiating table. In 2007, the ratings agency Standard & Poor's restored Colombia's investment grade for foreign debt rating, upgrading the country from BB+ to BBB–, a rating shared by only Chile and Mexico in Latin America.[35]

In the course of the commodity boom, Colombia's exports as well as its overall economy radically changed. Coffee and manufacturing—the two powerhouses of the 1970s and 1980s, then accounting for 70 percent of total exports—declined to 22 percent by 2012. Oil and mining, averaging 19 percent of total exports in the 1970s and 1980s, soared to 70 percent of that total by the same year. [36] The *locomotora minero-energética*, as President Santos proudly called the mining and energy bull market, pushed foreign investment and foreign exchange earnings to historic levels.

But along with those gains came the "Dutch Disease"—the syndrome in which rapidly rising commodity exports (tulips in the case of 17th-century Holland) push up the national currency and make noncommodity industries uncompetitive. The result was a massive manufacturing deficit.[37] Agriculture also stagnated. Public spending in agricultural extension, land titling, and plant and soil R&D plummeted. The fact that manufacturing and agriculture made up 30 percent of the country's employment (and mining and oil only 1 percent) exacerbated the losses in income in those traditionally important sectors. The export-intensive petroleum, coal, and palm oil industries were meanwhile gobbling up land at historically high levels, something that displaced and often physically threatened Afro-Colombian and indigenous communities.[38]

As long as the commodity boom continued, however, the economy generated sufficient cash and enough social investment to weather the harsh effects of Colombia's restructured economy. But with the advent of a commodity crash, most notably oil whose global barrel price fell by 50 percent in six months during 2014, Colombia began to come to terms with its resource curse. From 2014 to 2017, the peso plunged by almost 80 percent, igniting inflation and driving the public sector into paralyzing arrears. In the first quarter of 2015, the current account deficit as a percentage of GDP reached 7 percent. As for the first three years of the free trade agreement, U.S. exports to Colombia increased four times as fast as Colombian exports to the United States.[39] In agricultural products—especially corn, rice, dairy, fruit, and chicken quarters—the U.S. advance into the Colombian market has been even more dramatic.

A century earlier, in Colombia's coffee-fueled run-up to the Dance of the Millions, Colombian presidents such as Pedro Nel Ospina had carefully managed the influx of U.S. capital while strategically diversifying the country's agricultural and industrial portfolio. By the middle of the 20th century, the state rigorously intermediated import substitution industrialization by preferential bank credit, tax policy, trade protection, and subsidized energy. If production costs tended to be high and the goods themselves expensive and uncompetitive in global markets, Colombia enjoyed a higher and more stable growth rate during the pro-industrialization period (5.1 percent from 1950 to 1980) than the pro-liberalization period (3.7 percent from 1990 to 2012).[40] Labor union membership during the pro-industrialization period increased from 250,000 in 1959 to nearly 900,000 in 1990. By 2002, in the course of free-market liberalization, the rate of union membership had fallen to among the lowest in Latin America.[41] Despite noteworthy advances in poverty reduction, educational coverage, and health security during the first decade of the 21st century, Colombia's measurement of income inequality in 2016 was, with the exception of Honduras, the worst in the Southern Hemisphere.

12

IN SEARCH OF PEACE

What happened to the peace accord between the FARC and the Colombian government?

The national plebiscite to approve the peace treaty seemed like a shoo-in. On September 26, 2016, six days before the vote, in an atmosphere of national celebration, there was a theatrically-staged event in Cartagena covered by much of the world's media, to witness the treaty's signing. The celebrants, all clad in white and including the UN secretary-general, several heads of state, and Colombian notables, along with some 2,000 well-wishers, gathered near the port city's old slave market. After signing the treaty, President Santos handed the pen, fashioned out of a machine-gun shell, to FARC commander Timoleón Jiménez—also known as Timochenko—who, after initialing the document himself, addressed the assembly. In his remarks, Timochenko asked his fellow Colombians to forgive the FARC "for all the sorrow we have caused," a statement that led to loud cheers, standing applause, and even tearful affirmation by some of those looking on. Seconds later, however, a concussive blast shook the square as a Colombian air force jet-fighter, after swooping in low, turned on its afterburners and shot skyward. Stunned, mouth agape, Timochenko looked up to see two other jets make similar, ear-rending passes, drowning out the proceedings below.[1] As one journalist present reported, the bizarre interruption "lingered on forebodingly" even after the celebration went forward.[2]

Even more shocking, however, were the results of the plebiscite vote the following Sunday. By just 63,000 votes out of 13 million cast, Colombians rejected the peace accord in a stunning victory for former president Uribe and his followers. The *New York Times* attributed the upset to "deep scars" (namely, the bitter memories of the FARC's depredations) as well as the "complacency" of the pro-peace organizers in turning out no more than 37 percent of the electorate.[3] Among the ironies of the plebiscite was the fact that the urban and wealthier states, which had experienced low levels of violence during the previous decade, generally voted against the agreement, while the poorer and more rural states, many of which had suffered greatly, tended to support it. In Bojayá, Chocó, for example, where 118 civilians were killed in May 2002 by an exploding gas canister launched by the FARC, 96 percent of the largely Afro-Colombian population voted "yes."[4] Another unanticipated factor in the failed plebiscite was the rise of a right-wing *kulturkampf* in which Colombian Pentecostals, incensed by the legalization of same-sex marriage, medical marijuana, and gay adoption, rallied a reported two million "No" votes to vindicate "family values," thereby evening the score with the peace-loving secularists.[5]

Despite the failure to get the treaty approved in a popular vote, the government and the FARC announced that they would maintain the cease-fire and keep negotiating, something that the Nobel Peace Prize committee openly affirmed by making President Santos its 2016 laureate. Coming home from the ceremony, Santos stopped in Rome to visit Pope Francis, who prevailed on former president Uribe to join them for a meeting in the Vatican. After plying the two leaders in individual meetings with holy medals and copies of his three encyclicals, the pontiff sat down with both of them for a meeting in his private office. The unsmiling Uribe wanted none of it. "Your Holiness," he curtly told the pope, "you can't impose all this on us."[6]

In fact, Santos had already done so. Prior to his trip to Norway, the president had pushed a mildly-revised version of the treaty through the Colombian Congress while Uribe fulminated on Twitter. In one of his online volleys against the peace deal, the former president asserted that the treaty's land fund (giving 300,000 poor farming families up to 3 million hectares of mostly state land) would convert large landowners like himself into "assassins and displacers of peasants."[7] Paramilitary gangs, reclaiming drug lands left behind by demobilizing FARC forces, were already doing just that.[8] Between January 2016 and February 2017, a total of 134 political activists, indigenous and Afro-Colombian community leaders, and local land claimants were assassinated. Despite the wave of violence, thousands of FARC guerrillas continued following orders to stand down, filtering out of forests still wearing their rubber galoshes, walking down dusty dirt roads in the *llanos* (plains) with their families in tow, and boarding river boats in Chocó with burlap bags filled with grenades and AK-47 clips, all bound for the demobilization sites set aside by the government.[9]

What are the key elements of the revised peace plan—and where do things stand today?

The first element of the peace plan—and by far the most promising one to date—was the disarmament and demobilization of the FARC. By April 2017, roughly 9,000 FARC members had converged to the 26 disarmament camps, none of which had any of the promised housing structures ready for the demobilized fighters who, instead, camped out nearby with their families and followers. The government had also not fulfilled its commitment under the treaty to release all FARC POWs, 1,554 of whom were still being held in military jails. On the issue of FARC disarmament, the trend was nonetheless favorable, if far from complete. By June 2017, 7,000 weapons had been turned in to the UN monitoring mission, although an estimated 947 arms caches remained unrecovered in former FARC-held territories.[10]

The second key element of the peace plan involved the conversion of the FARC into a political movement. Under the terms of the treaty, the insurgency's successor party would be guaranteed 10 seats in Congress from 2018 to 2026 before being required to compete freely thereafter. As a form of reparation for areas that had suffered high levels of violence during the civil war, 16 special electoral districts will be reserved for candidates nominated by civil society organizations during that same eight-year period.

According to the former chief prosecutor of the International Criminal Court, Luis Moreno Ocampo, the greatest challenge in implementing the new peace treaty was and remains containing violence against former FARC fighters, thereby avoiding a reprise of what happened in the 1980s, when paramilitary and state security death squads murdered more than 3,500 members of *Unión Patriótica*.[11] In the first six months of 2017, with one social activist being killed every four days, the incidence of homicide was troubling. Seventy percent of those murders, according to the Peace and Reconciliation Foundation, were accomplished with "impunity."[12]

To protect social activists, ethnic and labor leaders, as well as the demobilized FARC members, the Colombian National Police are currently deploying 44 *carabinero* mobile strike units in violent zones. Given the professional transformation of the police—from an inept and corrupt force to a highly trained, well-armed cadre numbering a total of 183,471 today—the protection of targeted individuals seems achievable even if the example of the much-touted 2011 Labor Action Plan (LAP) is less than encouraging. Although the LAP, a government-wide campaign backed by the United States to halt the homicide of labor leaders and vindicate collective bargaining rights, did reduce the number of executed unionists per year from 53 in 2010 to 18 in 2015 (with union membership increasing by 150,000 during that five-year period), anti-union violence has stubbornly persisted.[13]

The "rural security deficit" as some have called it, may require a new, postconflict reconceptualization of "citizen security."[14] In the course of visiting France in January 2015, President Santos himself spoke of creating a rural police force (patterned possibly after the French *gendarmerie*) that would integrate demobilized guerrillas into its ranks, a sentiment that touched off a fierce reaction back in Colombia, even though it has worked well in post-conflict South Africa and El Salvador. In the thinking of María Victoria Llorente, head of the Ideas for Peace Foundation in Bogotá, postconflict policing must balance sophisticated criminal interdiction with stabilizing community-based governance that integrates diverse groups and populations. The alternative is the prospect of Colombia's return to a "war system" in which the political economy of violence eclipses peaceful stabilization.[15]

As it has in the past, Colombian geography could well undermine the best-laid plans of the peacebuilders. With less than 5 percent of the population residing in about half of the national territory, criminal enterprise or armed insurgency can still find easy sanctuary in the country's remote expanses. The peace accord admirably proposes programs to address rural economic sustainability, but research done by Paul Collier, the former director of development research at the World Bank, shows that poverty and inequality are statistically insignificant as factors causing conflict and civil war. Instead, the key correlations are primary products that are easily taxable by criminals and insurgents, a youthful and recruitable population that is relatively uneducated, a history of conflict, and a large territory with a dispersed settlement pattern. Colombia has all of these factors in spades.[16]

Coca and Eradication in Colombia

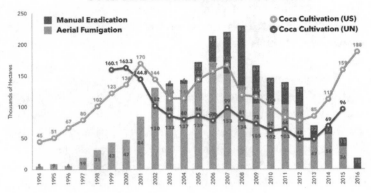

The dilemma is not just geographic; it is cultural. As Professor Tico Braun points out, "Since the arrival of the Spaniards, the historical dynamic of all Latin American nations has been urban, with aspirations of urbanity. In Colombia and elsewhere, we have not known what to do about the countryside, and we have few ideas and possibilities today, even though the peace agreement speaks to them."

A third element of the treaty concerns "comprehensive rural reform" in which a land fund, drawn principally from state lands or those seized from drug traffickers, will prospectively provide arable property for up to 300,000 landless families. In addition to a massive effort to properly delimit and title the land, the government has launched a series of private-public, all-party "community pacts for property renovation," targeting 170 of the country's poorest municipalities. If the snail's pace of previous land restitution efforts—bogged down by bureaucratic torpor, legal disputes, and a disturbing incidence of criminal vengeance against legitimate claimants—is any indication, rural reform faces a steep road. For one thing, the great pull of Colombian agriculture over the past 10 years in areas like the eastern plains has been massive agro-industrial consolidation, not public-sector investment in family farming.[17]

A fourth element of the peace treaty concerns transitional justice in which the so-called Special Peace Jurisdiction will try and punish war crimes that were ordered, planned, or committed by the FARC, the government, or private citizens. Provided the accused truthfully own up in "an early fashion" to their war crimes, however, they will face no more than "effective restraint of liberty for 5 to 8 years"—a concession opposed by many, but one that the government contends was the only way to get the FARC to disarm and demobilize. Even while serving sentences for grave abuses, former guerrillas can seek or hold public office, an aspect of the treaty that has been challenged and is under review by the Constitutional Court. A second issue under judicial review is the new law's standard for culpability in human rights crimes, one that establishes that to be indictable a commander must have had "effective control" along with "knowledge based on information at his disposal." As a 1998 signatory to the Rome statute that created the International Criminal Court, Colombia may be bound to a higher standard—namely, whether the accused commander "knew or, owing to the circumstances at the time, should have known" that a crime was committed.[18] If the looser "effective control" standard ultimately wins out, Colombian Army commanders will probably be excused from command responsibility for the 4,500 civilians murdered in the "false-positives" scandal.

The Special Peace Jurisdiction's flexible penal strictures have also led to an appeal by more than 1,500 former military officers and enlisted soldiers, currently serving time for human rights crimes, to be granted parole under the transitional justice system. With regard to civilians accused of aiding or abetting human rights crimes as in the "parapolitics" case of the Uribe era, they would remain immune from prosecution unless they consent "voluntarily" to be subject to the Special Peace Jurisdiction tribunals, or if compelling evidence, above and beyond any reports gathered by those tribunals, provides a prima facie case of guilt. This might be termed "transitional impunity."

The fifth objective of the peace plan is the promotion of crop substitution through voluntary eradication of coca and poppy plots. In exchange for subsidies, land titles, and technical assistance from the government, farmers would destroy coca bushes and poppy fields and cultivate legal produce. Popular knowledge across Colombia about this aspect of the peace plan may have perversely encouraged farmers to plant record levels of coca in 2016 in anticipation of the payouts the following year. The United Nations Office on Drugs and Crime (UNODC) reported a 52 percent increase from 2015 to 2016 in total area under coca cultivation (from 96,000 hectares to 146,000 hectares), along with an increase in U.S. consumption of cocaine, 90 percent of which comes from Colombia.[19]

For the moment, the cocaine scare in the United States seems to have fizzled, owing perhaps to the magnitude of the opioid crisis, which has been at least partially medicalized under the Affordable Care Act. With 22 U.S. states having legalized or decriminalized pot (and 46 having passed laws medicalizing marijuana), the trend toward addressing drug abuse in terms of harm reduction and common sense seems, at long last, to be irreversible. Even the Atlantic Council's bipartisan task force report about future engagement in Colombia conceded that "U.S. officials must acknowledge that the illicit drug trade is a shared responsibility, and one ultimately driven by demand."[20]

Of the $450 million approved by the U.S. Congress in May 2017 for "Peace Colombia," $187.3 million has been earmarked for USAID "Economic Support Funds" to assist the Colombian government in sustaining programs for the war's victims, minorities, the justice system, and human rights. These are laudable objectives, even if other parts of the package—narcotics control and Department of Defense counterdrug programs—get almost as much funding as USAID support for peacebuilding.[21] Finally, there is a major payout in the peace package to the Colombian armed forces of $39.9 million.

Given Colombia's continuing budget crisis, it is doubtful that Bogotá can sustain the level of road-building, agricultural extension, and land titling necessary to support a national program of crop substitution for coca. Moreover, some leaders, such as Colombian health minister Alejandro Gaviria, dismiss the multi-decade crop substitution program as "a complete failure" in any case.[22] Gaviria argues instead that "legal drugs" like medical marijuana could play an important role in stabilizing parts of rural Colombia. A Canadian multinational corporation, Pharmacielo, which is currently building huge greenhouses for cannabis production in the rolling hills outside of Medellín, is planning to export, as is legally permitted, marijuana-based oils and creams to the greatest drug emporium of all: the United States.

Is the Trump administration backing "Peace Colombia"?

On Good Friday in April 2017, former presidents Andrés Pastrana and Álvaro Uribe managed to steal their way into President Donald J. Trump's Mar-a-Lago resort and maneuvered themselves into a brief conversation with the new U.S. chief executive. The purpose of the encounter became evident two days later, when Uribe sent a blistering attack on the peace deal to every member of Congress and the Washington media, charging that the Colombian government had stopped aerial spraying to "please the terrorist FARC."

Although this and other claims did nothing to stop "Peace Colombia" funding by the U.S. Congress (and were thoroughly rebutted by the Washington Office on Latin America, the investigative journalism site *La Silla Vacia* in Colombia, and 50 members of the Colombian Congress), Uribe did succeed in pushing the drug debate back to the front burner in Washington.[23] President Trump pressed President Santos on the issue in their meeting in the Oval Office two weeks later and then launched into a discourse on "the terrible drug crimes" in their joint press conference.[24] To the extent that there is a discernible policy today, the Trump administration supported slashing aid to Colombia by $140 million in 2018 and

has decided to play hardball on drugs by ramping up senten-
cing in the United States, further militarizing interdiction at
"fleet-level" in the Caribbean, and prevailing upon Colombia
to resume aerial spraying.[25]

In September 2017, in a surprising rebuke of the White
House, however, the Senate Appropriations Committee unanimously marked up $391 million of funding for Colombia,
chiding the Trump administration for its "doctrine of retreat."

What are the challenges facing Colombia now and in the coming years?

If there is a reinvigorated drug war, the heft and penetration of
criminal enterprise will continue to be a cruel and inescapable
given in Colombia. It will likely subvert any real chance for
land justice and continue to corrupt institutions, effectively de-
grading improvements in the function of courts, elections, and
law enforcement. (Colombia is ranked 90th out of 176 countries in "corruption perceptions"—ahead of Argentina at 95th
but way behind Chile at 24th).[26] Although Santos and other
Colombian political leaders have rejected any return to aerial
spraying, Washington still brandishes other options such as
keeping the FARC on the State Department's list of terrorist
organizations or formally executing outstanding extradition
requests for some 60 FARC commanders.[27]

Will Washington, then, serve as a spoiler of Colombia's
hard-won peace accord? It is difficult to say. Despite the advent of peace, the so-called strategic partnership between
Colombia and the United States remains a militarized phenomenon. For the last 50 years, the Colombian political elite
has capitalized on "the Washington playbook," as Obama derisively called it—namely, the U.S. reflex of responding to security challenges by using military force. At least in the view of
senior American national security officials, the Plan Colombia
"model" confirms the utility of such force in counterdrug,
counterinsurgency, and counterterrorism operations. Even if

the breakthroughs in disarming and demobilizing, first, the paramilitaries and, then, the FARC were, in fact, cold-blooded political deals sustained by the Colombian state's enhanced military, intelligence, and diplomatic capacity, Washington still prefers to fixate on its military playbook.

Today, Colombia's proxy role as a "security exporter" in the U.S.-led drug war in Central America only reinforces that codependency, one marked by U.S.-Colombian success in accomplishing assassinations. From the hunt for Pablo Escobar to the targeted killings of the FARC leadership, "leadership decapitation" remains an inviting, if potentially double-edged, expedient. In 2016, a joint U.S.-Colombian Special Forces operation, using GPS-guided aerial munitions, killed 12 members of the paramilitary gang Clan Úsuga in northern Chocó.[28] Whether or not such "targeted hits" continue, the American role in training and supplying the regular Colombian military will probably decline, a trend that reflects the downsizing of the Colombian armed forces by as much as one-third over the coming years.[29] Perhaps at that point the United States will turn to real peacebuilding. But that remains to be seen.

The United States could look to its own history. A generation into a dozen bloody interventions by the United States in Latin America, President Franklin Roosevelt declared that Washington had had enough: America, he promised in his 1933 inaugural address, would become a good neighbor "who resolutely respects himself and, because he does so, respects the rights of others." (FDR used the word "respect" four times in that brief peroration.) Embracing a strategy of creative coexistence, the Roosevelt administration proposed a grand bargain based on accepting "nonintervention" in Latin American countries in exchange for building an inter-American system of collective security led by the United States. If Washington's effort to showcase Latin culture in the United States and to underwrite cross-cultural exchange with its southern neighbors fell short of the mark, its stellar diplomacy certainly didn't, producing an extraordinary strategic dividend—a united pan-American front against the Nazis. Today, Pax Americana again requires an end to militarized bungling and a new era of creative coexistence.[30]

Colombia's security gains are fragile, in the judgment of Adam Isacson.[31] The U.S. role in helping to stanch social decomposition as well as to fortify rural and urban security remains critical. Even if Colombia was able to net the *Economist's* coveted Country of the Year in 2016 (beating out Canada and China) because of the peace treaty, it was followed in 2017 by anemic GDP growth of only 1.8 percent, with unemployment increasing to 9.4 percent. The country is also struggling to absorb more than one million Venezuelan refugees who have poured into Colombia at a time when Bogotá's political establishment is deeply divided. "What kept it [the establishment] together was the guerrillas," Fernando Cepeda observes. "The consensus is now broken."[32]

For all of that, as I noted in the introduction, Colombia has never been as prosperous and safe as it is today. The gains in income (though still unequal) and health and physical security (though varying greatly by region) are such that Colombians have an index of "overall life satisfaction" equal to that of French citizens, according to the UN 2016 Human Development Report. For a country still counting and coming to terms with 420,000 murdered and eleven million of its citizens displaced over the last 70 years, that level of perceived well-being seems extraordinary.[33] In terms of gender development, Colombia vies with Brazil and Cuba in having the lowest fertility rate in Latin America, places second in the most years of female schooling (14.5), and, in terms of the ratio of male-to-female per capita earnings, is the best in the Southern Hemisphere.

With 74 percent of its 50 million citizens now urban dwellers, Colombia has become a nation of cities, with the rural residents continuing to stream into the burgeoning slums and shantytowns at the periphery of those metropolitan areas. Medellín, once regarded as one of the most dangerous cities in the world, has undergone an urban resurrection since the dark days of the late 1990s thanks to the mayoral leadership a decade ago of former university mathematics professor Sergio Fajardo. Under the slogan "Medellín: The Most Educated," Mayor Fajardo radically altered the accepted possibilities of public education, opening up 10 *parques bibliotecas* (library parks) in Medellín's lethal and poverty-stricken neighborhoods. Today, Santo Domingo, one of those violence-ridden slums, not only has an award-winning granite library with new public schools, soccer fields, and scrubbed-up homesteads nearby, but a breathtaking aerial gondola tram that moves people up and down the steep mountainside from Santo Domingo to Medellín's city center.[34]

In the 2018 presidential elections, Fajardo ran a close third in the first round of voting in May of that year. The two top vote-getters were former Bogotá mayor Gustavo Petro Urrego and Senator Iván Duque Márquez, a 42-year-old technocrat and protégé of fellow *antioqueño,* former president Álvaro Uribe. In the final round, Duque, criticizing the peace deal with the FARC and calling for tax cuts to spur economic growth, crushed Petro by a margin of almost 14 points. Since he took the oath of office in August 2018, however, the personable Duque has faced a worsening economy, an officer corps furious over being subjected to prosecution for human rights violations by the Special Peace Jurisdiction, and the entry of more than one million Venezuelans fleeing their failing country. Duque's decision to stick with the peace treaty, at least notionally, has meanwhile earned him few friends. Within six months of his inauguration, his approval rating dropped from 54 percent to 27 percent.

Where is Colombia culturally speaking?

Seventy years of human obliteration and social upheaval have only seemed to nourish what García Márquez once noted about his compatriots—their "insatiable creativity, full of sorrow and beauty." Given the breathing space provided by peace, Colombian literature and fine arts have zoomed off in vivid new directions, as writers, artists, and musicians "rediscover their cultural goods," as one journalist has put it.[35] At the street level, in the more than 1,000 *ferias* (fairs) and *fiestas patronales* (patron-saint festivals) each year, Colombians joyously continue to revisit folk arts and religious beliefs in days and nights of communal revelry. Even in the formulaic wasteland of television, Colombia brandishes a certain originality. *Yo soy Betty la fea* (I am ugly Betty), a soap opera that premiered in 1999 about an unsightly nerd equipped with a unibrow who uses her brilliance to find true love, has become one of the most popular dramas in television history with re-dramatized releases around the world in more than 80 languages. More recently, *Narcos*, a taut, matter-of-fact drama in the *Goodfellas* vein about the mayhemic rise and fall of Pablo Escobar, is now in its third successful season as a Netflix original series.

Outside of the realm of make-believe, however, Colombians have faltered in facing up to their country's bloody history. Two years ago, in calling for the "rescue of memory" from public denial and indifference, Colombian indigenous, political, and intellectual leaders broke ground in central Bogotá to build the *Museo Nacional de la Memoria* (National Museum of Memory).[36] The museum's new director, Martha Nubia Bello, describes the as-yet unfinished structure as one whose constantly changing space will serve to resurrect the victims of violence as well as their stories of resistance. To do anything else, observes Gonzalo Sánchez, the director-general of the Center for Historic Memory, would be "catastrophic": Colombia's future would simply become the past happening, over again.[37]

National and local efforts to bear witness to the past—"to name the unnamable and to forgive the unforgivable," as one victim of violence from Villavicencio put it—seem to be gaining force. In the *Museo Casa de Memoria* in Medellín, which opened in 2012, there are heart-rending exhibits of victims' personal effects; in Mampuján (Bolívar), villagers have woven tapestries that depict a massacre that took place in March 2000; and outside the city of Bucaramanga, school-children have turned a mass grave-mound into a flower garden. In the "heart of the world," as the indigenous *wiwa* call their mountain fastness in the Sierra Nevada de Santa Marta, *mamos* (shaman elders), who helped break ground for the new museum of memory, continue to pray to Serenkua, the ancient mother and god of all things, to "restore balance on the earth." On a visit to Colombia in 2017, Pope Francis flew to Meta province to bless ex-paramilitary soldiers and former FARC guerrillas while beatifying Bishop Jesús Emilio Jaramillo, who was murdered by the ELN in 1989. Again and again in the course of his visit, Pope Francis urged the faithful, "Ask for forgiveness and offer it."[38] The pontiff is right: if reconciliation is to work, it has to come from the ground up and not just the top down.

Beyond its history of savage capitalism and a stunted democracy, Colombia's nationhood remains rooted in the stoic resilience of its people. "In spite of oppression, plundering, and abandonment," García Márquez told the world in his Nobel laureate speech, "we respond with life." The days when my mother-in-law Zulma Moreno stood, six months pregnant, at the bottom of a gold mine in ankle-deep water with a pick and shovel in hand are long gone. Her miner's wages got her five children enough schooling for some of them to go on and get advanced degrees, others to start successful businesses (both in Chocó and Bogotá), and, in the case of one brother, to do what *chocoanos* have done for 500 years—buy and sell gold. In a video of her surprise 80th birthday party, she dances lightfooted through three generations of family, all serenading her by singing a *vallenato* at the top of their lungs. When I spoke with her recently about some bad news from Santander province regarding a *paro armado* (an armed shutdown) by a paramilitary gang, she listened but said nothing.

"Do you really have any hope about the future?" I asked her.

"What else is there?"

NOTES

Introduction

1. The conquest of the capital of the Aztec Empire took place from 1518 until 1521 although the pacification of the Yucatán continued for decades thereafter. In Peru, the Incan emperor was captured and killed in 1532, but the fighting to subdue the empire went on for another 60 years. By 1543, the Spanish had conquered the Muiscas, if not pacified them.

2. Fernando Díaz, "Estado, Iglesia, y Desamortización," in Jaramillo Uribe et al., eds., *Manual de Historia de Colombia, Tomo II* (Bogotá, 1982), 413.

3. Eliot Morrison, *The Oxford History of the American People* (New York, 1965), 38.

4. David Bushnell and Neill Macaulay, *The Emergence of Latin America in the Nineteenth Century*, 2nd ed. (New York, 1994), 8.

5. John Leddy Phelan, "Authority and Flexibility in the Spanish Bureaucracy," *Administrative Science Quarterly*, 5, no. 1 (June 1960), 47–65.

Chapter 1

1. See "Discoverer of the Pacific Ocean," *Bulletin of the American Geographical Society*, 45, no. 10 (1913), 757–59.

2. Juan Friede, "Antecedentes histórico-geográficos del descubrimeinto de la meseta Chibcha por el licenciado Jiménez de Quesada," *Revista de Indias*, 10, no. 40 (1950), 331–32.

3. See Juan Friede, "La conquista del territorio y el poblamiento," in Alvaro Tirado Mejía, Jaime Jaramillo Uribe, and Jorge Orlando Mejo, eds., *Nueva Historia de Colombia* (Bogotá, 1978), 79–80.

4. Frank Safford and Marco Palacios, *Colombia: Fragmented Land, Divided Society* (New York, 2002), 29.

5. Quoted in J. Michael Francis, *Invading Colombia: Spanish Accounts of the Gonzalo Jiménez de Quesada Expedition of Conquest* (University Park, PA, 2007), xi.

6. Excerpt from the anonymous "Relación de Santa María" (c. 1545), as quoted in Francis, *Invading Colombia*, 63–66.

7. Juan de Castellanos, *Elegías de varones ilustres de Indias*, 4 vols. (Bogotá, 1955), as quoted and cited in David Bushnell, *The Making of Colombia: A Nation in Spite of Itself* (Berkeley, 1993), 9.

8. Francis, *Invading Colombia*, 83.

9. Friede, "La conquista del territorio y el poblamiento," in Mejía, Uribe, and Mejo, eds., *Nueva Historia de Colombia*, 82.

10. Jorge Orlando Melo, prologue, "Las mujeres en la historia de Colombia," Vol. 1, *Mujeres, Historia y Política* (Bogotá, 1995), xiv.

11. Before the *conquistadores* could return to Santa Marta, they learned that two other European expeditions were converging on the Muisca highlands—the column of Belalcázar coming from Ecuador and the expeditionary force of Nikolaus Federmann, a German mercenary who had led 200 men from the Venezuelan coast across the eastern cordillera over a two-year period before reaching the verdant valley where Jiménez de Quesada held sway. Although the normal mode of contest among rival *conquistadores* was to annihilate each other, as they were then doing in Peru, Jiménez de Quesada successfully persuaded the two other men to refer their claims of conquest to Madrid for the crown's decision. Ultimately, the Council of the Indies awarded the new realm to none of the *conquistadores* and had Jiménez de Quesada arrested for having supposedly embezzled some of the gold destined for the king. Bailed out of jail by his uncle—and now charged with the murder of Sajipa—Jiménez fled Spain for France where he spent several years at the gaming tables before returning to Nueva Granada where he was awarded the honorific of "Mariscal (Marshal) of Santafé." At least initially, Belalcázar fared better, becoming the governor of gold-rich Popayán. But later, he was condemned to death in Madrid for the murder of another *conquistador*. As for Federmann, after failing to contest his rights and being charged with fraud, he lost everything. Suspected of being a Lutheran by the Inquisition,

he spent the balance of his life in prison, a status that at least afforded him time to rewrite his memoir. The erudite and irrepressible Jiménez de Quesada, however, was not done yet. Back in Santafé, he assumed command of the royal militia while authoring several books, one of which would survive—a wicked put-down of Italian Renaissance humanist Paolo Giovio. Incredibly, his decade-worth of appeals to the Spanish king to give him one more chance to find El Dorado finally netted him just that: King Philip II gave the elderly *conquistador* his blessing to mount a new search into the trackless Orinoco River Basin. It became a death march with a "trail of bones . . . was strewn across the *llanos* [plains]: animals, dead Indian bearers and Spaniards. Discarded saddles, abandoned suits of armor, trinkets intended for trade with the natives . . . [but] still Quesada marched on." Three years after the expedition was launched—with one chronicler now dead but another, Fray Pedro de Aguado, in his place—45 survivors of the original 400 expeditionaries made it back to Santafé led by the emaciated but unbowed man who had launched it all. Scholars would later venture that Jiménez de Quesada served as the model for another chivalric fool—Don Quijote de la Mancha who may have dreamed of golden cities but ended up jousting windmills. See Hugh Thomas, *The Golden Empire: Spain, Charles V and the Creation of America* (New York, 2015), 387–88. See also Nikolaus Federmann, *Indianische Historia. Ein schöne kurtzweilige Historia Niclaus Federmanns des Jüngern von Ulm erster raise.* Drafted prior to his imprisonment, this history was published in 1557. See also Juan Friede, *El adelantado don Gonzalo Jiménez de Quesada*, 2 vols. (Bogota, 1979). Also Robert Silverberg, *The Golden Dream: Seekers of El Dorado* (New York, 1967), 274–75; Germán Arciniegas, *El Caballero de el Dorado* (Mexico, 1978); José Martínez Ruiz, *La Ruta de don Quijote* (Madrid, 1948); and Eduardo Santa, "Jiménez de Quesada y Don Quijote de la Mancha," *Boletín de Historia y Antiguedades*, 92, no. 828 (March 2005), 24–41.

12. Selden Rodman, *Colombia Traveler* (New York, 1971), 13.
13. Bartolomé de las Casas. *Brevísima relación de la destrucción de las Indias* (Seville, 1552).
14. See Safford and Palacios, *Colombia*, p. 35, citing a survey by López de Velasco (circa 1570).

15. Estimates of the number of Native Americans living in greater Colombia vary from 850,000 to the probably more accurate number of 3 to 4 million. See Jorge Orlando Melo, *Historia de Colombia: La Dominación Española*, 2nd ed. (Bogotá, 1978), 63–69. Also Jaime Jaramillo Uribe, "Ensayos de historia sobre la historia colombiana" in *Nueva Historia de Colombia III* (Bogotá, 1968), 91.

16. See Bushnell, *Colombia*, 13–14, and Safford and Palacios, *Colombia*, 37–38.

17. Well before the decimation of the Indians took place around the middle of the 16th century, slaves from both Spain and Africa were being transported to the New World. Within the large retinue of human carriers in Quesada's expeditionary column in 1536, for example, there were black slaves. The conquistador Sebastian Belalcázar asked for royal authorization in 1543 to import 100 slaves to work in the mines near Popoyán. See Frederick Bowser, *El esclavo africano en el Perú colonial, 1524–1650* (México, 1977), 108.

18. Most materials on slavery can be found in the *ramo* (branch) named "*Negros y esclavos*"—some 58 volumes in total. *Archivo General de la Nación*, Bogotá.

19. Eduardo Posada, *La Esclavitud en Colombia* (Bogotá, 1933), 22–45.

20. Anthony McFarlane, *Colombia before Independence: Economy, Society, and Politics under Bourbon Rule* (Cambridge, 1993), 104–6.

21. The author toured the common graves in April 2015. See also Friede, "La conquista del territorio y el poblamiento," in *Nueva Historia*, 100–102.

22. Cited in Jorge Palacios Preciado, "La esclavitud and la sociedad esclavista," in Álvaro Tirado Mejía ed., Nueva Historia de Colombia II (Bogotá, 1989) 63–78.

23. George Reid Andrews, *Afro-Latin America, 1800–2000* (New York, 2004), 24–25. When slaves did marry other slaves, the tendency was to have stable relationships and produce children in wedlock, as one document from 1782 indicated. See William Frederick Sharp, *Slavery on the Spanish Frontier: The Colombian Choco, 1680–1810* (Norman, OK, 1976), 124–25.

24. Andrews, *Afro-Latin America*, 36.

25. Sharp, *Slavery on the Spanish Frontier*, 148–49.

26. Rates of manumission tended to be about 1.2 to 1.3 percent per annum. Compounded over 300 years, that number became significant. See Andrews, *Afro-Latin America*, 41–42.

27. Aquiles Escalante, *El Negro en Colombia* (Bogotá, 1964), 133–34.
28. Quoted in James F. King, "Negro Slavery in the Viceroyalty of New Granada," (Ph.D. dissertation, University of California, Berkeley, 1940) 192.
29. Michael Edward Stanfield, *Of Beasts and Beauty: Gender, Race and Identity in Colombia* (Austin, TX, 2013), 21.
30. Peter Wade, *Music, Race and Nation: Música Tropical in Colombia* (Chicago, 2000), 61.
31. Manuel Serrano y Sáenz, ed., *Cedulario de las provincias de Santa Marta y Cartagena de Indias* (Madrid, 1913).
32. Preciado, "La esclavitud y la sociedad esclavista," 168–69.
33. Nina S. de Friedemann, *Ma Ngombe: Guerreros y ganaderos en Palenque* (Bogotá, 1979). See also Friedemann's chapter, "Las mujeres negras en la historia de Colombia," in *Las mujeres en la historia de Colombia*, II.
34. King, "Slavery in New Granada," 311.
35. Quoted in Carlos Alberto Montaner, *Las raíces torcidas de América Latina* (Madrid, 2008), 11–12. The full title of the document was "El Requerimiento de Palacios Rubios." See Severo Martínez Peláez, "La pátria del criollo. Ensayo de interpretación de la realidad colonial guatemalteca."
36. For a full account of Church history in Nueva Granada (and later Colombia), see Juan Pablo Restrepo, *La Iglesia y el Estado en Colombia* (Bogotá, 1987). Also Germán Arciniegas, *Latin America: A Cultural History* (New York, 1966), 144.
37. See Fray Toribío de Benavente, *Historia de los Indios de Nueva Espana* (Madrid, 2014).
38. Bernadino de Sahagún, *Historia General de las Cosas de la Nueva Espana*, cited in Arciniegas, *Latin America: A Cultural History*, 146.
39. Arciniegas, *Latin America: A Cultural History*, 181.
40. Cited in Preciado, "La esclavitud y la sociedad esclavista," 167.
41. See Nicole von Germeten, ed. and trans., *Alonso de Sandoval, Treatise on Slavery* (New York, 2008).
42. J. Lloyd Mecham, "The Origins of 'Real Patronato de Indias,'" *Catholic Historical Review,* 14, no. 2 (July 1928), 205–27.
43. José Manuel Restrepo, *Historia de la Revolución de la República de Colombia* (Bogotá, 1826), 102. See also Bushnell, *Colombia,* 21–22.
44. See Germán Colmenares, *Las haciendas de los jesuítas en el Nuevo Reino de Granada* (Bogotá, 1969), 221–24.
45. Cited in Arciniegas, *Latin America: A Cultural History*, 157.
46. Rachel Kemper, *Costume* (New York, 1977), 11, 78.

47. Ibid., 182.
48. See Mariano Picón Salas, *De la conquista a la independencia: Tres siglos de historia cultural hispanoamericana* (Mexico, 1942), 84. The accounts of persecuted unruly members of the underclass in Cartagena can be found in its archives in the old city.
49. Henry Charles Lea, *The Inquisition in the Spanish Dependencies* (London, 1922), 464.
50. McFarlane, *Colombia before Independence*, 26–28.
51. The report by the two scientists was requested by the royal bureaucracy in Spain, the contents of which were provided to King and later published in 1826 as *Noticias secretas de América sobre el estado naval, militar, y político de los reinos de Perú y provincias de Quito, costas de Nueva Granada y Chile. Gobierno y régimen particular de los pueblos de indios. Cruel opresión y extorsión de sus corregidores y curas: abusos escandalosos introducidos entre estos habitantes por los misioneros. Causas de su origen y motivos de su continuación por espacio de tres siglos.*
52. Jaime E. Rodríguez, *The Independence of Spanish America* (Cambridge, 2013), 22–23.
53. The law authorizing Church property to be seized and auctioned was the Royal Law of Consolidation to America.
54. The vice-regency was first established by Spain in 1717, retracted in 1723, and then reestablished in 1738 when Spain went to war against Britain.
55. Safford and Palacios, *Colombia*, 55–56.
56. Restrepo, *Historia de la Revolución de la República de Colombia*, 108.
57. See John Lynch, *The Spanish American Revolutions, 1808–1826* (London, 1986), 8–17. The source for the transformation of the *colegios* is found in Safford and Palacios, *Colombia*, 57.
58. Mexican Jesuit Francisco Javier Clavijero published the four-volume *Storia ántica del Messico* (1780–81). Juan de Velasco, S.J., formerly of Ecuador, wrote *Historia del Reino de Quito* (1789). See Rodríguez, *The Independence of Spanish America*, 16–18.
59. See John Leddy Phelan, *The People and the King: The Comunero Revolution in Colombia, 1781* (Madison, WI, 1978). See also Safford and Palacios, *Colombia*, 65–69.
60. Francisco de Miranda to John Turnbull, January 12, 1798, *Archivo del General Miranda*, xv:207.

61. Lynch, *The Spanish American Revolutions, 1808–1826*, 21. The
    cédulas de gracias al sacar initially cost 1,500 *reales de vellón* but
    were later reduced in 1801 to 700 *reales*.
62. Simón Bolívar, *Cartas del Libertador*, 12 vols. (Caracas, 1929–1959).
    Letter from Bolívar to Páez, August 4, 1826, vi:32.

Chapter 2

1. François Antoine, Jean-Pierre Jessenne, Annie Jourdan, et al.,
   L'Empire Napoléonien: Une Expérience Européenne? (Paris, 2014),
   213–22.
2. Jaime E. Rodríguez, *The Independence of Spanish America*
   (Cambridge, 1998), 52.
3. Javier Ocampo López, "El proceso político, militar y social de la
   Independencia," in Tirado Mejía, ed., *Nueva Historia de Colombia*,
   Vol. 2, 19
4. Frank Safford and Marco Palacios, *Colombia: Fragmented Land,
   Divided Society* (New York, 2002), 88. The *virreina* was later
   rescued and escorted back to her residence by female members of
   the creole elite.
5. See table of elite male professions in late colonial Granada in
   Victor M. Uribe-Urán, *Honorable Lives: Lawyers, Family and Politics
   in Colombia, 1780–1850* (Pittsburgh, 2000), 25.
6. Bolívar thought Napoleon "a tyrant, a hypocrite, an enemy
   of freedom" for crowning himself emperor in 1804. Later,
   he expressed admiration for Napoleon's capacity to inspire
   adulation. See John Lynch, *Simón Bolívar: A Life* (New Haven, CT,
   2006), 24–25, 236.
7. This is the characterization of John Lynch in the preface to his
   book, *Simón Bolívar*. See also David Bushnell, *Simón Bolívar: Una
   síntesis del Libertador, Revista Credencial Historia* (Bogotá), April 16,
   1991, 6–11.
8. Known as the "Manifiesto de Cartagena," Bolívar composed this
   document in December 1812 in Cartagena. For the text, see www.
   ensayistas.org/antologia/XIXA/Bolívar/Bolívar4.htm.
9. Even after his triumphant reentry into Caracas where the
   salutation "Viva el Libertador" first rang in the streets, Bolívar,
   unable to conclude an exchange of prisoners with the defeated
   royalist leader, gave the order to execute 800 Spanish and
   Canarian prisoners.

10. *Times* (of London), September 4, 1817, 8.

11. Moisés Enrique Rodríguez, *Freedom's Mercenaries: British Volunteers in the Wars of Independence of Latin America* (Lanham, MD, 2006).

12. Quoted in Lynch, *Simón Bolívar*. 107. The explosive potential of the execution was evident the next day when Bolívar addressed his largely colored soldiers: "Have not our arms broken the chains of the slaves? Has not the odious distinction between classes and colors been abolished forever? Have I not ordered national property to be distributed among you? Are you not equal, free, independent, happy and respected? Could Piar give you more? No. No. No."

13. Charles Stuart Cochrane, *Journal of a Residence and Travels in Colombia during the Years 1823 and 1824*, Vol. I (Boston, 1832), 68. Cochrane, a captain in the Royal Navy, interviewed several of the veterans of Bolívar's cross-Andean campaign.

14. José Manuel Restrepo, *Historia de la Revolución de la República de Colombia* (Paris, 1827), 9.

15. Since it seemed foreordained that with Bolívar back at war to liberate the rest of royalist Spanish America, Santander, the new vice president, would be acting chief executive in the huge new state. Bolívar constantly sent messages and guidance to Santander. In these communications, he did not spare Santander his skeptical views of the likelihood of their success: "The Spaniards have inspired terror in our national spirit. The more I think of it the more I am convinced that neither liberty, nor laws, nor the most brilliant enlightenment will make us law-abiding people, much less republicans and true patriots. Friend, we do not have blood in our veins but vice mixed with fear and error. What civic virtues!" (Bolívar to Santander, June 1, 1820), in Carrer Dumas, *Simón Bolívar Fundamental I*, (Caracas, 1974) 170.

16. Cited in Safford and Palacios, *Colombia*, 111–12.

17. Margarita González, "Las rentas del Estado," in *Nueva Historia de Colombia* II, 192–93.

18. Bolívar to Santander, April 18, 1820, in *Cartas Santander-Bolívar*, II (Bogotá, 1988) 85. Jorge Palacios Preciado, "La esclavitud y la sociedad esclavista," in *Nueva Historica de Colombia II*, 169.

19. Harold A. Bierck Jr., *Selected Writings of Bolívar* (New York, 1951), 213.

20. Thomas Jefferson to John Adams, September 4, 1823. Library of Congress exhibitions online.

21. Jefferson to Adams, May 17, 1818, cited in Brian Steele, *Thomas Jefferson and American Nationhood* (Cambridge, 2012), 97–98. See also Jeremy Adelman, *Sovereignty and Revolution in the Iberian Atlantic* (Princeton, NJ, 2006), 4. As president in 1806, Jefferson had been embarrassed by the discovery of his administration's role in the arming and underwriting of a naval assault force (with 200 American volunteers) led by Venezuelan patriot and intimate friend of Alexander Hamilton, Francisco de Miranda. The Spanish, after intercepting and destroying the revolutionary sortie, had threatened the United States, demanding indemnity. Jefferson and Madison, his secretary of state, had done their best to deny and cover up the American role. See E. Taylor Parks, *Colombia and the United States, 1765–1934* (Durham, NC, 1935), 50–56.

22. Parks, *Colombia and the United States*, 132.

23. James E. Lewis Jr., *The American Union and the Problem of Neighborhood: The United States and the Collapse of the Spanish Empire* (Chapel Hill, NC, 1998), 14.

24. Monroe to Jefferson, October 17, 1823, and Jefferson to Monroe, October 24, 1823.

25. It is generally conceded that the decision not to respond to Great Britain's *démarche* for a joint declaration, but rather unilaterally to release the message, is attributable to Secretary of State John Quincy Adams, who stated in a cabinet meeting on November 7, 1823: "It would be more candid, as well as more dignified, to avow our principles explicitly to Russia and France, than to come in as a cockboat in the wake of the British man-of-war."

26. David Bushnell and Lester D. Langley, *Simón Bolívar: Essays on the Life and Legacy of the Liberator* (New York, 2008), 135.

27. Lewis, *The American Union and the Problem of Neighborhood*, 210–11.

28. Bolívar (his emphasis) to Santander, August 16, 1821, in *Cartas Santander-Bolívar* III, 132.

29. Fernando Díaz Díaz, "Estado Iglesia y desamortización," in *Nueva Historia de Colombia*, vol. 2, 204–5. See also Safford and Palacios, *Colombia*, 114–15.

30. *La Gaceta de la Ciudad de Bogotá*, March 12, 1820, quoted in David Bushnell, *The Santander Regime in Gran Colombia* (Newark, DE, 1954), 198.

31. See *Internet Encyclopedia of Philosophy* at http://www.iep. utm.edu/bentham/. Accessed June 11, 2015. For a detailed understanding of Santander's educational reforms, see Jaime Jaramillo Uribe, "El proceso de la educación del virreinato a la época contemporánea," in Jaime Jaramillo Uribe ed., *Manual de Historia de Colombia*, Vol. III, (Bogotá, 1982), 256–30.

32. See Bushnell, *The Santander Regime in Gran Colombia*, 113–14.

33. Frank Griffith Dawson, *The First Latin American Debt Crisis: The City of London and the 1822–25 Loan Bubble* (New Haven, CT, 1990), 19.

34. Restrepo, *Historia de la Revolución*, Vol. 6, 495.

35. José Miguel Groot, *Defensa del Doctor Miguel Peña* (Caracas, 1826), 327–37.

36. Adelman, *Sovereignty and Revolution in the Iberian Atlantic*, 396–97.

Chapter 3

1. John Lynch, *The Spanish American Revolutions, 1803–1826* (New York, 1986), 356.

2. Charles Stuart Cochrane, *Journal of a Residence and Travels in Colombia during the Years 1823 and 1824*, Vol. I (Boston, 1832), 88–89.

3. Isaac F. Holton, *New Granada: Twenty Months in the Andes* (Carbondale, IL, 1967), 17.

4. Magdala Velásquez Toro, "Condición juridical y social de la mujer," in *Nueva Historia de Colombia*, IV (Bogotá, 1989), 10.

5. David Bushnell and Neill Macaulay, *The Emergence of Latin America in the Nineteenth Century* (New York, 1988), 50.

6. Beatriz Castro Carvajal, "Policarpa Salavarrieta," in Jacqueline Barco Barco and Margarita Cárdenas, eds., *Las Mujeres en la historia de Colombia*, XII, no. 23, Universidad Militar, June 2009, 143–58.

7. See Jean-Baptiste Boussingault, *Memorias* (Caracas: Ediciones Centauro, 1974), 303, 306.

8. In the Constitutional Congress of 1831, lawyers (12) outnumbered the military (11), priests (7), and merchants (4). See Victor M. Uribe-Urán, *Honorable Lives: Lawyers, Family and Politics in Colombia, 1780–1850* (Pittsburgh, 2000), 93.

9. President Jackson had never replied to Santander's appeal from a dungeon in Cartagena after Santander had been imprisoned for supposedly conspiring against the life of the Liberator. See David Bushnell and David Sowell, "Santander y los Estados Unidos: la opinión pública norteamericana dividida entre Bolívarismo y Santanderismo," in *Revista Credencial Historia* (Bogotá, Ed. 28; April 1992), 17–31.

10. Frank Safford, "Social Aspects of Politics in Nineteenth-Century Spanish America: New Granada, 1825–1850," *Journal of Social History*, 5, no. 3 (Spring 1972). Neither economic class nor occupational differences adequately explain the two parties' differences, Safford argues. Family ties, social standing, and regional party preeminence may be better signifiers.

11. Javier Ocampo López, *Breve Historia de Colombia* (Caracas, 1989), 259. The reasons for the revolt varied a good deal: centralism versus federalism; the battle over the Church, the regions against Bogotá, the winner-take-all contest between the Liberals and Conservatives with regard to the subject of spoils, the violent factionalism within the parties, the struggle between free trade and protectionism, and the abolition of slavery.

12. David Bushnell, *The Making of Colombia: A Nation in Spite of Itself* (Berkeley, 1993), 76–77.

13. Malcolm Deas, "The Fiscal Problems of Nineteenth-Century Colombia," *Journal of Latin American Studies*, 14, no. 2 (November 1982), 116–42.

14. Thomas E. Skidmore and Peter H. Smith, *Modern Latin America* (New York, 2005), 231.

15. La Comisión Corográfica bajo la dirección de Agustin Codazzi, *Jeográfica física i política de las Provincias de la Nueva Granada*, 3 vols. (Bogotá, 1858–1859).

16. Michael J. LaRosa and Germán R. Mejía, *Colombia: A Concise Contemporary History* (New York, 2012), 164–65.

17. The other countries were Argentina, Uruguay, Peru, Venezuela, and Ecuador. Frank Safford and Marco Palacios, the authors of *Colombia: Fragmented Land, Divided Society* (New York, 2001), make the important point that the Conservative rebellion was not just about the abolition of slavery. In Antioquia, for example, armed protest was related to the defense of the Church and the Liberal effort to break up Antioquia as a province.

18. José María Samper, *Ensayo sobre las revoluciones políticas*, 68, 82, as quoted in Frank Safford, "Race, Integration, and Progress: Elite Attitudes and the Indian in Colombia, 1750–1870," *Hispanic American Historical Review*, 71, no. 1 (1991), 16, 22.

19. In 1953, for example, Miguel António Arroyo would write that "the black has not been able to free himself of the moral deficiency of improvidence." Cited in Peter Wade, *Blackness and Race Mixture: The Dynamics of Racial Identity in Colombia* (Baltimore, 1993), 17.

20. Cited in Safford and Palacios, *Colombia*, 173.

21. Quoted in Safford and Palacios, *Colombia*, 177.

22. See Catherine LeGrand, *Frontier Expansion and Peasant Protest in Colombia, 1830–1936* (Albuquerque, NM, 1986).

23. "The tensions generated from this process blossomed into a new form of land violence . . . by the end of the nineteenth century, land ownership and the conditions of work on the land became the two major causes of violent clashes among the Colombian people." LaRosa and Mejía, *Colombia*, 35–36. See also Marco Palacios, *Between Legitimacy and Violence: A History of Colombia, 1875–2002* (Durham, NC, 2006), 13.

24. See *El Neo-Granadino*, August 6, 1848. Claude Henri de Rouvroy, comte de Saint-Simon (1760–1825), the father of the concept of meritocratic industrialism and utopian socialism, is best analyzed in Amand Bazard, *Exposition de la doctrine de St. Simon* (Paris, 1828–1830), 2 vols.

25. David Bushnell, *Ensayos de Historia Política de Colombia, siglos XIX and XXX* (Medellín, 2005), 27.

26. See especially chapters 3 ("Origins of National Consciousness") and 4 ("Creole Pioneers") in Benedict Anderson, *Imagined Communities: Reflections on the Origin and Spread of Nationalism* (New York, 2006, rev. ed.).

27. Entrevista con Gabriel Gárcia Márquez por María Elvira Samper, "El Libro es Vengativo," *Semana*, April 10, 1989. Another Nobel laureate and contemporary of García Márquez, the Mexican poet and essayist Octavio Paz, summarized the consequences of liberal constitutionalism even more harshly: "The liberal and democratic ideology, far from expressing our concrete historical situation, obscured it. The political lie installed itself almost constitutionally among our countries. The moral damage has been incalculable and reaches into the deep layers of our

character. Lies are something we move in with ease. During more than a hundred years, we have suffered regimes of brute force which were at the service of feudal oligarchies, but utilized the language of liberty."

28. Sálvador Camacho Roldán wrote at the time, "The Indians were converted into day-laborers, with salaries of 10 cents a day; food became scarce, agricultural land was converted to pasture for cattle, and the rest of the indigenous race, the former owners of these regions for centuries, dispersed in search of better wages in the hot lowlands, where their sad conditions have not improved."

As quoted in Carlos Mario Londoño, *Economía agrária colombiana* (Madrid, 1965), 14. Other leading essayists of that period, like Hernán Jaramillo Ocampo and Jose María Samper, report similarly deplorable consequences. Modern scholarship, however, tends to indicate that the effects of *resguardo* elimination were mixed, with the Indians in areas like Pasto never selling off their lands.

29. Mariano Ospina to General Pedro Alcántara Herrán, March 26, 1855.

30. Nancy Otero Buitrago, "Tomás Cipriano De Mosquera: Análisis de su correspondencia como fuente historiográfica y mecanismo de poder. 1845–1878," unpublished thesis, Universidad del Valle, Departamento de Historia, 2013.

31. Frank Safford, "Race, Integration, and Progress: Elite Attitudes and the Indian in Colombia, 1750–1870," *Hispanic American Historical Review*, 71, no. 1 (1991), 30.

32. See Eduardo Rodríguez Piñeres, Academia Colombiana de Historia, *Historia exten*sa, Vol. XV, I, (Bogotá, 1964), 45.

33. Charles W. Bergquist, *Coffee and Conflict in Colombia, 1886–1910* (Durham, NC, 1978), 8–9.

34. Memoria de Hacienda, 1870–1874, cited in James William Park, *Rafael Núñez and the Politics of Colombian Regionalism, 1863–1886* (Baton Rouge, LA, 1985), 56. Import duties represented 71 percent of total public income in 1874.

35. Salvador Camacho Roldán, *Escritos varios* (Bogotá, 1892–1895), Vol. 2, 73.

36. Conservative Plan of 1849 cited in LaRosa and Mejía, *Colombia*, 85.

37. Fernando Díaz, "Estado, Iglesia, y desamortización," *Nueva Historia de Colombia*, (Bogotá, 1989) 215.

38. Quoted in James D. Henderson, *Modernization in Colombia: The Laureano Gomez Years, 1889–1965* (Gainesville, FL, 2001), 36.

39. Park, *Rafael Núñez and the Politics of Colombian Regionalism*, 149.

40. Conservative journalist and politician Sergio Arboleda wrote of the Liberals in 1872: "They despoiled the interests of the only ruling group with political experience, enlightenment, and a sense of direction on social issues: the clergy." Jaime Jaramillo Uribe, *El pensamiento colombiano en el siglo XIX* (Bogotá, 1964), 271.

41. Jesús A. Bejarano, "La herencia del siglo XIX," in *Manual de Historia,* 3 (Bogotá, 1982), 17–20.

42. Following President Roosevelt's impassioned defense of his behavior before his cabinet in the White House, Secretary of War Elihu Root told him: "You have shown that you were accused of seduction and you have conclusively proven that you were guilty of rape." The Nicaraguan poet, Rubén Darío, was struck by the moral pose in it all: "A wealthy country joining the cult of Mammon to the cult of Hercules; while Liberty, lighting the path to easy conquest, raises her torch in New York." Quoted in George C. Herring, *From Colony to Superpower: U.S. Foreign Relations since 1776* (Oxford, 2008), 366–68.

43. See Henderson, *Modernization in Colombia*, 49–50.

Chapter 4

1. Quoted in Charles W. Bergquist, *Coffee and Conflict in Colombia, 1886–1910* (Durham, NC, 1986), 221.

2. Ignacio Arizmendi Posada, *Presidentes de Colombia, 1810–1990* (Bogotá, 1989), 196.

3. See Vincent Baillie Dunlap, *Tragedy of a Colombian Martyr: Rafael Uribe Uribe and the Liberal Party, 1896–1914,* unpublished dissertation, University of North Carolina, Chapel Hill, 1979.

4. See Eduardo Lemaitre, *Rafael Reyes: Biografía de un gran colombiano* (Bogotá, 1967), 203–12.

5. E. Taylor Parks, *Colombia and the United States, 1765–1934* (Durham, NC, 1935), 432–36.

6. Marco Palacios, *Between Legitimacy and Violence: A History of Colombia, 1875–2002* (Durham, NC, 2006), 49.

7. Mark Pendergrast, *Uncommon Grounds: The History of Coffee and How It Transformed the World* (New York, 2010), 58.

8. Marco Palacios, *Coffee in Colombia, 1850–1970: An Economic, Political and Social History* (Cambridge, 1980).

9. Salomón Kalmanovitz and Enrique López Enciso, *La agricultura colombiana en el siglo XX* (Bogotá, 2006), 77.

10. The term is from Frank Safford and Marco Palacios, *Colombia: Fragmented Land, Divided Society* (New York, 2001), 272.

11. Quoted in Palacios, *Coffee in Colombia*, 206.

12. Bergquist, *Coffee and Conflict*, 262.

13. See José Ortega Torres, ed., "Respice Polum Estrella del Norte," in Marco Fidel Suárez, *Obras* (Bogotá, 1958), II, 167.

14. "An oil proposition has been pipelined into the Treaty." Quoted in Thomas A. Bailey, *A Diplomatic History of the American People* (New York, 1950), 543. See also Darío Mesa, "La vida política despúes de Panamá, 1903–1922," in Jaime Jaramillo Uribe ed., *Manual de Historia*, Vol. III, (Bogotá, 1982) 172.

15. See Pedro Nel Ospina, *Ficha Biográfica*, undated, Biblioteca Virtual, Biblioteca Luis Ángel Arango. Pedro Nel, who spoke German and French as well as English, was also a published poet and man of letters.

16. *New York Times*, May 4, 1922.

17. *New York Times*, May 5, 1922.

18. *New York Times*, June 2, 1922.

19. Paul W. Drake, *The Money Doctor in the Andes: The Kemmerer Missions, 1923–1933* (Durham, NC, 1989), 42–54.

20. E. W. Kemmerer's papers are in the Seeley G. Mudd Manuscript Library at Princeton University. Aside from a yearly retainer at Dillon, Read of $3,000, Kemmerer took no commissions or fees for his investment advice. Dillon, Read did fund his endowed chair in finance in the Department of Economics. See *Correspondence*, 1922–27.

21. Vernon Lee Fluharty, *Dance of the Millions: Military Rule and Social Revolution in Colombia, 1930–1956* (Pittsburgh, 1957), 32.

22. James D. Henderson, *Modernization of Colombia: The Laureano Gómez Years, 1889–1965* (Gainesville, FL, 2001), 117.

23. *El Tiempo*, September 19, 1927, quoted in Stephen J. Randall, *Colombia and the United States: Hegemony and Interdependence* (Athens, GA, 1992), 110.

24. Henderson, *Modernization of Colombia*, 155.

25. Palacios, *Between Legitimacy and Violence*, 84.

26. Ospina did support and sign legislation giving workers the legal right to a day off on Sunday and providing for hygiene and safety standards.

27. Malcolm Deas, "Colombia, Ecuador and Venezuela," in Leslie Bethell, ed., *Cambridge History of Latin America* (Cambridge, UK, 1986), vol. 5, 661. Cano's strict *paisa* parents were less concerned about their daughter's fiery rhetoric than about whether or not she was being properly chaperoned. It turned out that she was. Often carried on stage to shield her from assault or assassination, she would refer to herself before huge crowds as "a soldier of the world," a Catholic communist in love with Christ the revolutionary. Labor rights, she said, were women's rights; they were *los derechos de todos* [the rights of everyone]. In a society in which at least two out of three people were consigned by race or gender to invisibility, these were words of revolt and revolution. Antioquia's powerful cleric, Bishop Miguel Ángel Builes, while furiously denouncing Cano and the "socialist slave-drivers," sought to outflank radical labor by opening a seminary, *El Obrero Católico* (the Catholic Worker) in Medellín, to train both lay leaders and priests in social action and, of all things, labor organizing. See also Escuela Nacional Sindical, *María Cano: Una voz de mujer les grita, 1887–2007* (Medellín, 2007), 28. See *La Defensa* (the Catholic newspaper published in Medellín), September 3, 1925. Cano and Torres had their own newspaper called *Justicia* founded in 1927. Ivan Darío Osorio provides an excellent account of Colombian syndicalism. See "Historia del sindicalismo," in *Historia de Antioquia* (Medellín, 1988), 278–86.

28. See Jorge Ivan Marín Taborda, "María Cano, Su época, su historia," in *Las mujeres en la historia de Colombia* (Bogotá, 1995), 156–72. María Cano, 1887–2007, *Una voz de mujer les grita* (Medellín, 2007). Also, María Cano, *Escritos, Revista de la Escuela* (Medellín, 1989), 9.

29. J. Fred Rippy, *The Capitalists and Colombia* (New York, 1931), 181.

30. Cano, Torres, and Mahecha, among others, were all arrested and variously imprisoned after the massacre. The following year, other socialists attempted a bloody and unsuccessful takeover of El Líbano. Regarding Cano's life thereafter, see Velásquez, "Condición jurídical y social de la mujer," especially 42–44 in Tirado Mejía, ed., *Nueva Historia de Colombia* (Bogotá, 1989). In 1930, she was purged from the Communist Party; she died in

1967 in her native Medellín. Among Cano's writings are *El poeta maldito* (1921), *Vivir*, article published in *Lecturas para mujeres* (1923), *Casa de menores* (1923), *Los forzados* (1924), *Pan espiritual* (1924), and *Por los obreros* (1924). Gabriél García Márquez would later immortalize the 1928 massacre in his novel *One Hundred Years of Solitude*.

31. See Herbert Braun, *The Assassination of Gaitán: Political and Urban Violence in Colombia* (Madison, WI, 1985), 57–58. See also Jorge Eliécer Gaitán, *1928: La Masacre de las Bananeras* (Medellín, 1933), 115–19.

32. Mary Roldán, "La política de 1946 a 1958," in Jorge Orlando Melo, ed., *Historia de Antioquia* (Medellín, 1988), 165.

33. See Entrevista con Ofelia Uribe de Acosta: Una voz insurgente, published in *Colectivo ReXiste*, May 26, 2009. Interviewer: Anabel Torres. Date of interview: January 7, 1987. See *Ficha Biográfica: Ofelia Uribe de Acosta*, Bibioteca Virtual, Luis Ángel Arango, www.banrepcultural.org.

34. The states that fell to military rule in 1930–1931 were Argentina, Brazil, Chile, Peru, Guatemala, El Salvador, and Honduras. The military seized power as well in Cuba in 1933.

35. Olaya would later deny that there was any quid pro quo. "Olaya Tells of Talk with Mellon," *New York Times*, January 21, 1932.

36. It was that $20 million loan, Colombian president Guillermo León Valencia later told French president Charles de Gaulle, that conclusively put Colombia into the "natural orbit" of the United States. The price, however, was staggering. Colombia practically became an American neo-colony. The United States took control over rail lines and forced Bogotá to privatize irrigation infrastructure and give preferences to American companies for aviation, construction, banking, and telecommunications contracts issued by the government. Both United Fruit and a U.S. emerald company were given police protection. As if that were not enough, Kemmerer—who had been brought on to advise on servicing the $20 million loan—prescribed bitter financial medicine that included retention of the gold standard and a draconian debt service schedule to repay U.S. creditors. The Colombians did their best to swallow it, at least for a while. When National City Bank, in order to squeeze some more blood out of its Colombian partner, put a stop-order on the final tranche of the loan, President Olaya took the American

minister in Bogotá aside: "It breaks my heart to have Americans let me down in the end," he told him. Cited in Palacios, *Between Legitimacy and Violence*, 92. Colombia declared a debt repayment moratorium and abandoned the gold standard on November 26, 1932. *New York Times*, November 27, 1932.

President Hoover, who toured Latin America in 1928, was said to have raved about "the great differences between the Kemmerized countries and the non-Kemmerized countries." Paul W. Drake, *The Money Doctor of the Andes* (Durham, NC, 1989), 26.

37. Edward Santos, then governor of Santander, summed up the situation: "The Conservatives . . . feel menaced, persecuted, and abandoned though they exaggerate their plight. Liberals are in a permanent state of crisis. In spite of their overwhelming numerical superiority, they believe the slightest incident will cause their ruin." Quoted in Henderson, *Modernization in Colombia*, 223.

38. See U.S. Department of State, *Foreign Relations*, 1933, 245–54. The treaty was initialed on December 15, 1934, though not ratified until the following year. See also Stephen Meardon, "The (Far) Backstory of the U.S.-Colombia Free Trade Agreement," Economics Department Working Paper Series, 5, Bowdoin Digital Commons (2013).

39. CTC's strongest union, FEDENAL (river, air and maritime, and port transportation workers) remained communist. See Daniel Pécaut, *Política y sindicalismo* (Bogotá, 1973), 257.

40. "The idea of reforming the tax system," President López told the Congress, "was born here not of the necessity to punish a capitalist class of cruel and oppressive tendencies, but from that of creating a source of fiscal wealth different from, and more honest than the tax upon popular vices which obliges the State to become an importunate inn-keeper for its clients." *Mensajes del President López al Congreso*, 333.

41. Orlando Fals Borda, *Le hombre y la tierra en Boyacá* (Bogotá, 1957), 158.

42. Antonio García, *Problemas de la nación colombiana* (Bogotá, 1951), 273.

Chapter 5

1. Inaugural address of the president, March 4, 1933. The term "good neighbor" was actually coined by President Herbert Hoover on a goodwill trip to Latin America after his election in

1928. By the time FDR took office, the Hoover administration had also repealed the Roosevelt Corollary, which posited that only the United States could collect debts owed to foreigners in the Western Hemisphere.

2. Roosevelt, for example, had said in December 1933: "The definite policy of the United States from now on is one opposed to armed intervention" in Latin America. In 1934, the U.S. Congress nullified the 1903 Platt Amendment, which authorized U.S. occupation of Cuba. President Hoover had initiated a U.S. withdrawal from Nicaragua before leaving office in 1933.

3. Warren F. Kimball, *The Juggler: Franklin Roosevelt as Wartime Statesman* (New York, 1994), 107.

4. U.S., Department of State, Publication 1983, *Peace and War: United States Foreign Policy, 1931–1941* (Washington, DC, U.S. Government Printing Office, 1943), 438–39.

5. Peter H. Smith, *Talons of the Eagle: Dynamics of U.S.–Latin American Relations* (New York, 1996), 85, cited in George C. Herring, *From Colony to Superpower: U.S. Foreign Relations since 1776* (New York, 2008), 529.

6. Ladislas Farrago, *The Game of Foxes* (New York, 1971), 58–59.

7. Farrago, *The Game of Foxes*, 4.

8. FDR quoted in Max Paul Friedman, *Nazis and Good Neighbors: The United States Campaign against the Germans of Latin America in World War II* (Cambridge, 2005), 1. Secretary of State Cordell Hull called the Colombian ambassador to the United States S. Gabriel Turbay to personally apologize for the president's remark. In a cable back to his foreign ministry, Turbay noted "the marked tendency of the United States to exaggerate the dangers of Nazi penetration" in Latin America, whether "deliberately or unconsciously."

9. Eduardo Bushnell, *Eduardo Santos and the Good Neighbor, 1938–1942* (Gainesville, FL, 1967), 64.

10. James D. Henderson, *Modernization in Colombia: The Laureano Gomez Years, 1889–1965* (Gainesville, FL, 2001), 247.

11. These statistics are from Mary Roldán, *La Violencia in Antioquia, Colombia, 1946–1953* (Durham, NC, 2002), 53. The national cost-of-living index (1938 base year of 100) had risen to 235 by July 1946.

12. Charles W. Bergquist, "The Labor Movement (1930–1946)," in Bergquist et al., eds., *Violence in Colombia: The Contemporary Crisis in Historical Perspective* (Wilmington, DE, 1992), 66.

13. The Liberals, for example, controlled 437 municipalities in Colombia, and the Conservatives, 201. See Patricia Pinzón de Lewin, *Pueblos, Regiones y Partidos: La Regionalización Electoral* (Bogotá, 1989), 28. The Conservatives boycotted the 1942 national election.

14. Herbert Braun, *The Assassination of Gaitán: Public Life and Urban Violence in Colombia* (Madison, WI, 1985), 54–55.

15. Ospina Pérez's plan as well as his efforts to share power were, at least, impressive on paper. See Mariano Ospina Pérez, *La Política de Unión Nacional* (Bogotá, 1946).

16. George F. Kennan, Memorandum by the Counselor of the Department (Kennan) to the Secretary of State, March 29, 1950. Foreign Relations of the United States, 1950, Vol. II, 289–302.

17. Robert W. Drexler, *Colombia and the United States: Narcotics Traffic and a Failed Foreign Policy* (Jefferson, NC, 1997), 61.

18. See the still-classified CIA document, "Collaboration between the Communist Party and the Liberal Party," dated March 31, 1948, as referenced in the Basic Intelligence Directive index, National Archives, College Park, MD.

19. Braun, *The Assassination of Gaitán*, 128.

20. Braun, *The Assassination of Gaitán*, 130–31.

21. Among the many accounts of the assassination and the events surrounding it are these: Richard E. Sharpless, *Gaitán of Colombia* (Pittsburgh, 1978); Gonzalo Sánchez G., *Los días de la revolución: Gaitanismo y 9 de abril en provincia* (Bogotá, 1983); Arturo Alape, *El Bogotazo: Memorias del olvido* (Bogotá, 1987); and Braun, *The Assassination of Gaitán*.

22. Miguel Ojeda Rodríguez was then 13 years of age. Interview: Ojeda, Bogotá, April 3, 2015.

23. Carlos Franqui, *Diario de una revolución* (Paris, 1976), 21–22.

Chapter 6

1. The estimate of 1,000 dead was that of the Red Cross. Other accounts place the death toll as high as 3,000. See Vernon Lee Fluharty, *Dance of the Millions: Military Rule and the Social Revolution in Colombia, 1930–1956* (Pittsburgh, 1957), 103.

2. Willard L. Beaulac, *Career Ambassador* (New York, 1951), 249.

3. James D. Henderson, *Modernization in Colombia: The Laureano Gómez Years, 1889–1965* (Gainsville, FL, 2001), 313.

4. Germán Guzmán Campos, Orlando Fals Borda, and Eduardo
   Umaña Luna, *La Violencia en Colombia*, 2 vols. (Bogotá, 1962–
   1964), 2:37. The notion that the "Red Menace" was behind it all
   immediately resounded in the echo chamber of anticommunist
   fear and loathing in Washington. "The coup which has just
   occurred in Colombia is manifestly Communist," Secretary
   of State George C. Marshall stated, "and the Ninth Inter-
   American Conference should continue since the contrary would
   mean giving Communism the battle for Latin America." At
   Marshall's insistence, the conference resumed its deliberations
   in a schoolhouse on the northern outskirts of Bogotá. There,
   delegates from the United States and 20 Latin American countries
   ratified the resolution creating the Organization of American
   States (OAS) and also passed the 2,300-word Final Act of
   Bogota regarding the "preservation and defense of democracy
   in America" and the identification of communism as "a foreign
   agent incompatible with American liberty and the dignity of
   the individual." See *El Relator* (Cali), April 13, 1948. See also the
   New York Times, April 13, 1948: "Backing up the findings of the
   Colombian Government, Secretary of State Marshall and other
   delegates to the Inter-American Conference have now likewise
   accused Soviet Russia, and its tool, international communism,
   of instigating the riots that wrecked Bogota and cast a pall over
   the whole Western hemisphere." Walter Lippmann took issue
   with this position. The Americans, he wrote, were engaging in
   "the very human propensity to insist on making the facts fit
   one's stereotyped preconceptions—in this case to treat a South
   American revolution as a phase of the Russian revolution, and
   then to suppose that all revolutionary conditions in the world
   begin and end in Moscow." Months later, in July 1948, Secretary
   Marshall told a visiting Colombian delegation that he had been
   having further thoughts about the underlying causes of the
   Bogotá uprising and that "explosions in the future which were
   caused in the main by the tremendous gap between the top
   and bottom strata of society . . . that give rise to social unrest."
   Improving the education of youth and selecting promising young
   leaders from the poor classes to be future leaders, he thought,
   was the right way to go. *Foreign Relations of the United States, 1948*,
   Vol. IX, *The Western Hemisphere* (Washington, DC, 1975), 603.

5. Gonzalo Sánchez G., *Los días de la revolución: Gaitanismo y nueve de abril en provincia* (Bogotá, 1983), 26.

6. Sánchez G., *Los días de la revolución*, 34–36.

7. Colonel Rojas partnered with the leader of the *pájaros*, León María Lozano, known as "el condor." See "El Condor y el General," *Semana*, December 12, 1988. A widely distributed photograph from 1952 showed the two men standing together at a political event.

8. Gómez quoted in Henderson, *Modernization in Colombia*, 312.

9. *El Tiempo*, May 1, 1948.

10. Quoted in Richard E. Sharpless, *Gaitán of Colombia: A Political Biography* (Pittsburgh, 1978), 183.

11. Alexander W. Wilde analyzes this brilliantly. See "Conversations among Gentlemen: Oligarchical Democracy in Colombia," in Juan L. Linz and Alfred Stepan, eds., *The Breakdown of Democratic Regimes, Latin America* (Baltimore, 1978), 37.

12. Quoted in Gonzalo Sánchez G., "The Violence: An Interpretative Synthesis," in Charles W. Bergquist, Ricardo Peñaranda, and Gonzalo Sánchez G., eds., *Violence in Colombia: The Contemporary Crisis in Historical Perspective* (Wilmington, DE, 1992), 85.

13. Marco Palacios, *Between Legitimacy and Violence: A History of Colombia, 1875–2002* (Durham, NC, 2006), 147–48.

14. The United States, however, did suspend arms shipments, even though the training of Colombian military officers continued.

15. The president's request asked for an "in-depth study of the causes and present circumstances of the Violence." Guzmán, Fals Borda, and Umaña, *La Violencia en Colombia*, 10.

16. Tico Braun in written response to the author's questions, August 13, 2017.

17. Thanatomania has a somewhat different meaning in English: suicidal mania or the morbid belief that one must die.

18. Guzmán et al., *La Violencia en Colombia*, 233.

19. Guzmán et al., *La Violencia en Colombia*, 233.

20. Among the best accounts of the communist *ligas* is that of Gonzalo Sánchez G., *Ensayos de historia, social y política del siglo XX* (Bogotá, 1985).

21. Interview with Herbert Tico Braun, *Congreso colombiano de historia XVI* (Neiva, 2012). YouTube.

22. Paul Oquist, *Violencia, política y conflicto en Colombia* (Bogotá, 1978), is drawn from his doctoral thesis in 1975 at the University

of California–Berkeley: "Violence, Conflict, and Politics in Colombia." The term "rediscovery" is that of Gonzalo Sánchez. Thereafter, regional studies like Jaime Arocha, *La Violencia en el Quindío* (1979) and Carlos Miguel Ortiz Sarmiento, *Estado y subversión en Colombia* (1985) mapped the character of the *Violencia* more deeply, linking it to conflictual colonization patterns in the coffee zone. Gonzalo Sánchez and Donny Meertens published a pioneering study in 1983, *Bandoleros, gamonales y campesinos* (later published in English as *Bandits, Peasants and Politics*) regarding the period from 1958 to 1965 when the *Violencia* turned to savage banditry and the start of revolutionary insurgency. Perhaps the most important single volume of articles is the compilation by Sánchez and Ricardo Peñaranda, *Pasado y presente de la violencia en Colombia* (*Past and Present of the Violencia in Colombia*), first published in 1986 and now in its fourth edition (2007). From 1990 to the present, no fewer than 700 scholarly books and articles have been written about the *Violencia*. Among the most important is Mary Roldán's magisterial *A sangre y fuego. La Violencia en Antioquia, 1946–1953* [*Blood and Fire: The Violencia in Antioquia, 1946–1953*] (Bogotá, 2003). The book contrasts "developed Antioquia," with income growth, secure land ownership, and devout Catholic belief, as well as an idealized concept of itself as racially white (even though it wasn't) as largely sheltered from the terror. The majority of homicides, rapes, and robberies took place in the more peripheral areas of Antioquia, where floating populations of seasonal workers and landless migrants (whom traditional *Antioquenos* saw as nonwhite, degenerate, and "predisposed to fetishism and anarchy") struggled to find work in cattle ranching and extractive industries. See *Blood and Fire*, 38–39, 395. Another excellent global analysis of the *Violencia* can be found in Mauricio Rubio, *Crimen e Impunidad, Precisiones sobre la Violencia* (Bogotá, 1999).

23. See Ricardo Peñaranda, "Surveying the Literature," in Charles W. Bergquist, Ricardo Peñaranda, and Gonzalo Sánchez G., eds., *Violence in Colombia* (New York, 1992), 305.

24. Robert A. Karl, *Forgotten Peace: Reform, Violence and the Making of Contemporary Colombia* (Berkeley, 2017), 224.

25. Thomas E. Skidmore and Peter H. Smith, *Modern Latin America*, 6th ed. (New York, 2000), 55–56. Import substitution strategy

was hardly new in Latin America, having been implemented, inter alia, in Argentina, Brazil, and Mexico. The theory was straightforward: Latin America could break its dependency on the disruptive ups and downs of exported primary products (whose value had historically declined vis-à-vis imported manufactures from the United States and Europe) by sheltering home-grown industrialization from foreign competition via tariffs and other forms of protectionism. The result, at least ideally, would be industrial self-sufficiency, rising employment in the industrial sector, and the establishment of a new, moneyed bourgeoisie that could counterbalance the traditional landed elite. ISI's first wave of statist protection had, in fact, galvanized economic recovery in large Latin America countries such as Argentina, Brazil, and Mexico. As Skidmore and Smith later argued, ISI subsequently foundered because of Latin America's small and underdeveloped internal markets, inefficient and often corrupt state companies, and continued dependence on expensive capital goods such as machine tools to improve productivity and product quality for the "infant industries."

26. Medófilo Medina, "Violence and Economic Development, 1945–50, 1985–88," in Bergquist, Peñaranda and Sánchezeds., *Violence in Colombia*, 157.

27. In addition to the manufacturer's lobbying group, ANDI, there was its rival FENALCO, the National Merchants Association, and the Society of Colombian Agriculturalists (SAC). See Miguel Urrutia, "Gremios, política económica y democracia," a monograph cited in Henderson, *Modernization in Colombia*.

28. Jesús Antonio Bejarano Avila, "La economía colombiana entre 1946 y 1958," in *Nueva Historia de Colombia*, Vol. V, (Bogotá, 1989) 150–52.

29. Carlos Ortiz Sarmiento, " 'The Business of Violence,' The Quindío in the 1950s and 1960s," in *Violence in Colombia*, 141. Colombia, Marco Palacios writes, was caught in a symbiosis of clientelism and violence: "Coffee, civilian supremacy, and the two-party system were at the heart of the collective identity of the country which, in spite of everything, was climbing the ladder of capitalist modernization. But it was really a collection of halfway modernizations, weighed down by privileges, conformity, impunity, and dead bodies." See Palacios, *Between Legitimacy and Violence*, 259.

30. These five outcomes were "structural continuity" (as in Quindío where large landowners escaped the ravages of the *Violencia*); "regressive transformation" (as in the north of Tolima where the large estate system was restored); "progressive transformation" (as in Valle de Cauca where agroindustrial consolidation resulted from violence); "peasant consolidation" (as in Sumapaz where peasant self-defense leagues collectivized property); and "expansive transformation" (as in the south of Tolima where large cattle ranchers gained political power and property at the expense of the *colonos*). Gonzalo Sánchez G., *Guerra y Política en la Sociedad Colombiana* (Bogotá, 1991), 125–27.

31. In his first months in office, President Gómez announced he would increase the military's share of the national budget from 16 to 25 percent.

32. Álvaro Valencia Tovar, "Historia militar contemporánea," in *Nueva Historia de Colombia*, II (Bogotá, 1989), 295–340.

33. Bradley Lynn Coleman, "The Colombian Army in Korea, 1950–1954," *Journal of Military History*, 69, no. 4 (October, 2005) 1137–77.

34. The battalion's official history is covered in Alberto Ruíz Novoa's *El Batallón Colombia en Corea, 1951–1954* (Bogotá, 1956). See also Álvaro Valencia Tovar, *Corea: Resurgimiento de las cenizas* (Bogotá, 1977); *Testimonio de una época* (Bogotá, 1992); and Álvaro Valencia Tovar and Jairo Sandoval Franky, *Colombia en la Guerra de Corea: La historia secreta* (Bogotá, 2001).

35. General Rojas was a 1927 civil engineering graduate of Tri-State Normal College in Angola, Indiana.

36. Gustavo Rojas Pinilla, *Seis meses de gobierno* (Bogotá, 1954), 11.

37. Central Intelligence Agency, National Intelligence Estimate: NIE 88-65, "Prospect for Colombia," July 9, 1965. DDQS.

38. See "Lo Que el Odio Destruyo," *Semana*, February 21, 1955.

39. Álvaro Tirado Mejía, "Rojas Pinilla: del golpe de opinión al exilio," *Nueva Historia de Colombia*, II, 115.

40. ANAC stands for *Asamblea Nacional Constituyente*.

41. Eminent Argentine jurist Carlos Fayt referred to Peronism as the "Argentine implementation of fascism." Rojas also admired Generalissimo Francisco Franco, whom he called "a model for all Latin America."

42. Luis Carlos Gómez Díaz, "Esmeralda abrió el camino a la mujer," *El Tiempo*, April 20, 1997.

43. Memorandum of Conversation between the President and the Secretary of State, August 23, 1955. Dulles Papers, Eisenhower Presidential Library.

44. See Telex 385 from Ambassador Bonsal to Department of State, May 18, 1955. *Foreign Relations of the United States, 1955–57.*

45. James Henderson, *When Colombia Bled: A History of the Violencia in Tolima* (Tuscaloosa, 1985), 191–98.

Chapter 7

1. See Jonathan Hartlyn, *The Politics and Coalition Rule in Colombia* (New York, 1988).

2. Robert H. Dix, *Colombia: The Political Dimensions of Change* (New Haven, CT, 1967), 159.

3. "President's Trip to Venezuela and Colombia," December 1961, State Department Briefing Book, President's Office Files (POF), John F. Kennedy Presidential Library (JFKL).

4. Alberto Lleras Camargo, *Primer gobierno del Frente Nacional,* I (Bogotá, 1968), 60. "We have understood, and late but still in time, that our civilization and culture were deceptively skin deep, that our controversial and intransigent words were transformed as they fell upon the lower strata of a primitive society, becoming the sectarian cudgel, the murderous gunshot, the abuse and cruelty unleashed by nothing more than justification from on high."

5. Jonathan Hartlyn and John Dugas, "Colombia: The Politics of Violence and Democratic Transformation," in Larry Diamond, Jonathan Hartlyn, Juan J. Linz, and Seymour Martin Lipset, eds., *Democracy in Developing Countries: Latin America*, 2nd ed. (Boulder, CO, 1999), 266.

6. Bruce M. Bagley, "Colombia: National Front and Economic Development," in Robert Wesson, ed., *Politics, Policies and Economic Development in Latin America* (Stanford, CA, 1984), 125.

7. Marco Palacios, *El populismo en Colombia* (Bogotá, 1971), 89. The three presidents elected subsequent to Lleras—Guillermo León Valencia (1962), Carlos Lleras Camargo (1966), and Misael Pastrana Borrero (1970)—lost ground in terms of total vote count but also in turnout of those over 21. Pastrana, for example, got 40 percent of the vote as compared to Alberto Lleras's 80 percent.

8. Francisco Alba and Jose B. Morelos, "Población y grandes tendencias demográficas," in UNESCO, ed., *Historia General de América Latina* (Madrid, 2006), 56.

9. Quoted in John D. Martz, *The Politics of Clientelism, Democracy and the State in Colombia* (New Brunswick, NJ, 1997), 77.

10. The baseline in this estimate relates to cities over 100,000. See Economic Commission for Latin America, *Some Aspects of Population Growth in Colombia* (Santiago, 1960), 27.

11. Currie was appointed by Lleras to the National Planning Council of Colombia in 1960. See Roger J. Sandilands, *The Life and Political Economy of Lauchlin Currie* (Durham, NC, 1990), 194–200.

12. David Bushnell, *The Making of Colombia: A Nation in Spite of Itself* (Berkeley, 1993), 238.

13. Aline Helg, "La educación en Colombia, 1958–1980," *Nueva Historia de Colombia* IV, 135.

14. Stephen J. Randall, *Colombia and the United States: Hegemony and Interdependence* (Athens, GA, 1992), 226.

15. Michael Edward Stanfield, *Of Beasts and Beauty: Gender, Race, and Identity in Colombia* (Austin, TX, 2013), 135.

16. Marco Palacios, *Between Legitimacy and Violence: A History of Colombia, 1875–2002* (Durham, NC, 2006), 180.

17. James C. Williamson, *El Estudiante Colombiano* (1962 monograph published by the Universidad Nacional).

18. Ivon Lebot, *Educación e ideología en Colombia* (Medellín, 1979), 148. *Frente Unido* (United Front), for example, was a Catholic left-wing group led by charismatic National University chaplain Father Camilo Torres (until his dismissal from that post) that called for the legalization of divorce, birth control, and an end to counterinsurgent warfare. When American philanthropist John D. Rockefeller III joined Colombian president Carlos Lleras on a visit to Colombia's prestigious National University in October 1967 to inaugurate the newly U.S.-financed faculty buildings and a research laboratory, they were set upon by hundreds of rock-throwing students and forced to flee. As he had done before, Lleras promptly sent in the military to hunt down the protesters, garrison Colombia's most prestigious public campus, and help stanch protests elsewhere in the country. Repression by the state, however, did not eliminate would-be guerrillas. Among the revolutionary groups formed in Colombian universities during this period were the *Ejercito de Liberación Nacional* (Castrist),

the *Movimiento Obrero Independiente Revolucionario* (Maoist), and the *Juventud Comunista* (pro-Soviet). The Communist Party itself, divided by rival tendencies and subjected to official repression (and accordingly incapable of gaining control of either confederated labor unions or peasant movements) remained a negligible factor in Colombian politics.

19. Bushnell, *Colombia*, 236.

20. Christopher Abel and Marco Palacios, "Colombia since 1958," in Leslie Bethell, ed., *Cambridge History of Latin America*, vol. 8 (Cambridge, 1991), 647.

21. Álvaro Tirado Mejía, *Introducción a la historia económica de Colombia* (Bogotá, 1972), 100. Albert O. Hirschman, *Journeys toward Progress: Studies of Economic Policy-Making in Latin America* (New York, 1963), 100–102. James W. Wilkie, *Measuring Land Reform: Supplement to the Statistical Abstract of Latin America* (Los Angeles, 1974).

22. Hirschman, *Journeys toward Progress*, especially chapter 2. See also Albert O. Hirschman, *Tierra: 10 Ensayos sobre la Reforma Agraria en Colombia* (Bogotá, 1961).

23. A. Eugene Havens, William L. Flinn, and Susana Lastarria Cornhill, "Agrarian Reform and the National Front: A Class Analysis," in R. Albert Berry, Ronald G. Hellman, and Maurico Solaún, eds., *Politics of Compromise: Coalition Government in Colombia* (New Brunswick, NJ, 1980), 357.

24. Robert H. Dix, *Colombia: The Political Dimensions of Change* (New Haven, CT, 1967), 154.

25. Carlos Lleras Restrepo, *Hácia la restauración democrática y el cambio social: Nuevo testimonio sobre la política colombiana* (Bogotá, 1963), Vol. 2, 280.

26. Abel and Palacios, "Colombia since 1958," 630–31.

27. Magdalen León, ed., *La mujer y el desarrollo* (Bogotá, 1977). Also Ofelia Uribe de Acosta, *Una voz insurgente* (Bogotá, 1963). Velásquez Toro, "Condición juridical y social de la mujer," *Nueva Historia* IV: 35–38.

28. The initial mandate of *acción comunal* was rural pacification of banditry. See CARE, *Acción Comunal en Colombia* (Bogotá, 1962), 4. Orlando Fals Borda, "Acción Comunal en una Vereda Colombiana," *Monográficas Sociológicas*, no. 4 (1961).

29. Foreword by Miguel Fornaguera, in Virginia Gutiérrez de Pineda, *Familia y Cultura en Colombia: Tipologías, Funciones y*

dinámica de la familia. Manifestaciones Multiples a través del mosaic cultural y sus estructuras sociales (Bogotá, 1968), 3.

30. William Paul McGreevey, "Population Policy under the National Front," in Berry et al., eds., *Politics of Compromise*, 418.

31. McGreevey, "Population Policy," 416.

32. Carlos Uribe Celis, *La mentalidad del colombiano: Cultura y sociedad en el siglo veinte* (Bogotá, 1992), 101–2, cited in James D. Henderson, *Modernization in Colombia: The Laureano Gómez Years, 1889–1965* (Gainesville, FL, 2001), 414.

33. "Manuel Zapata Olivella, South America's Voice of Consciousness," interview by Ja. A. Johanes, Bogotá, published online in inmotionmagazine.com.

34. Federico Blodek, "Un vistazo a la música tropical colombiana," blog.revistacronopio.com.

35. Peter Wade writes: "If music in Colombia is a powerful mediator of the differences located in the sexualized cultural topography of the nation, this is mainly because of the historically constituted links between music—and particularly dance—sexuality and (racialized) region." He concludes that, however oversimplified the complexities of cultural hybridization may be, "the end result is the constant reiteration of the founding myth of Colombian nationality, spoken through the medium of La Costa, where the indigenous and African elements are said to have a strong impact. As is always the case in talking about *mestizaje*, the music is seen as a symbol of fusion, of the overcoming of difference, but the representation of that symbol involves the continual reiteration of difference." Peter Wade, *Music, Race and Nation: Musica Tropical in Colombia* (Chicago, 2000), 23.

36. Wade, *Music, Race, and Nation*, 19–21.

37. *El Tiempo*, April 8, 1997.

38. See Alexander Wilde, "The Contemporary Church: The Political and the Pastoral," in Berry et al., eds., *Politics of Compromise*, 211.

39. *El Tiempo*, August 10, 1972.

40. *Mujer*, January–February 1964, 8–13, as quoted in Stanfield, *Of Beasts and Beauty*, 147.

41. See *New York Times*, April 7, 1960.

42. Bradley Lynn Coleman, *Colombia and the United States: The Making of an Inter-American Alliance, 1939–1960* (Kent, OH, 2008), 192–95. The United States had already sent a CIAnArmy "Special Survey Team" to Colombia the previous year to assess

the security situation. Although the survey team's report found the "communist" insurgency was not posing any threat to the national government, it did note that criminal gangs totaling 800 or so *violentos* (armed bandits) were continuing their mayhem in the central and northern parts of Tolima state. The team recommended immediate U.S. military training and assistance to restore internal security in Colombia. Eisenhower allowed the Colombian plan to wend its way through the national security complex before finally signing the authorization order just days before he left office. The report stated that there was "no military solution" to the violence, only the "developing of a true democratic government, reflecting the will of the majority of its people." Quoted in *The Past as Prologue? A History of U.S. Counterinsurgency Policy in Colombia, 1958–66*, Strategic Studies Institute, March 2002, 43. Under the terms of the so-called Morse Amendment as imposed by the Democratic majority in the U.S. Senate in 1959, foreign military assistance could not extend to "internal security" absent a formal presidential order. See also Richard D. Mahoney, "Ike and War Powers," unpublished monograph presented at the Eisenhower Presidential Library, April 26, 2011.

43. Mark Gilderhus, *The Second Century: U.S.–Latin American Relations since 1889* (New York, 1999), 173. The Kennedy administration brought in a former Marshall Plan coordinator, Harvard professor Lincoln Gordon, to replicate the success of European recovery. Yale economic historian Walt W. Rostow, who had become deputy national security adviser in the new administration, also began doing detailed assessments of key Latin American countries like Colombia. According to Rostow's treatise, *Stages of Development: A Non-Communist Manifesto*, Third World countries could be catapulted into "self-sustaining economic growth," thereby achieving a stable polity supported by a rising middle class. The critical variable, according to Rostow, was to develop the "pre-conditions for take-off."

44. Cited in Jerome I. Levinson and Juan De Onís, *The Alliance That Lost Its Way: A Critical Report on the Alliance for Progress* (New York, 1970), 62.

45. In response to the Lleras initiative, U.S. secretary of state Dean Rusk sent word of his "personal gratification" to the Colombian president as well as the assurance that the United States

was preparing "a massive plan" to underwrite the Alliance. Sectel 3 (from Rusk), July 3, 1961, in National Security Files (NSF): Colombia, JFKL. See also Embtel 111 (from Bogotá), May 6, 1961, NSF, JFKL.

46. Quoted in Adelman, *Worldly Philosopher: The Odyssey of Albert O. Hirschman* (Princeton, NJ, 2013), 161.

47. Interview: Lincoln Gordon, Washington, DC, July 13, 1976. Gordon later served as U.S. ambassador to Brazil (1962–1965).

48. President Lleras declared a national state of siege and sent Colombian Army chief of staff General Alberto Ruiz to the Pentagon for emergency talks with the Americans. Department of State Memorandum of Conversation with Colombian ambassador Carlos Sanz de Santamaría, Subject: Colombian Request for Additional Internal Security Aid, October 6, 1961. Embtel (from Bogotá) to Secretary of State, October 12, 1961. National Security Files, "Colombia," JFKL.

49. Senator J. William Fulbright, chairman of the Senate Foreign Relations Committee, later investigated the Alliance in Colombia, concluding that it had failed. Despite expending America's $732 million in economic and financial assistance from 1963 to 1968, Colombia's GDP per capita only increased from $276 per person to $295 during that period. See *New York Times*, February 1, 1969. Where it scored high points, however, was in the competition for Latin American hearts and minds. In an American-funded poll in 1963, Colombia led the continent with 78 percent of those polled siding with the United States over the USSR. Another poll showed JFK to be twice as popular as Fidel Castro in Colombia. What these popularity contests had to do with real development would be anyone's guess. See Fajardo, "From the Alliance for Progress to the Plan Colombia: A Retrospective Look at U.S. Aid to Colombia," Working Paper no. 28, 13. See also Williamson, *El Estudiante Colombiano*, 24–25.

50. In her brilliant book, *More Horrible Than Death: Massacres, Drugs, and America's War in Colombia* (New York, 2003), Robin Kirk makes the dispositive case that Marquetalia was hardly a communist enclave, but rather a motley assemblage of Liberal, criminal, and assorted communist resisters. See especially 44–55.

51. Arturo Alape, *Diario de un guerrillero* (Bogotá, 1978), 71–74. Jacobo Arenas, *Diario de la Resistencia de Marquetalia* (Bogotá, 1972), 80–84.

52. Certain high-ranking Colombian officers like Generals Alberto Ruiz Novoa and Álvaro Valencia Tovar genuinely believed the armed forces should spearhead national economic and social development in the course of addressing the root causes of violent insurgency. As war minister during the presidential term of President León, General Ruiz called for greater land redistribution (beyond the modest measures of Law 135), provision of expanded labor rights, and use of the army for rural development. When he publicly sympathized with a national strike in 1965, General Ruiz was dismissed by León, who proceeded to crush the strike himself. As for General Valencia, another reform-minded flag officer who had served in Korea, his national reknown as an outstanding historian and author of a best-selling novel, *Uisheda* (1970), enabled him to run for president in 1978, though not successfully.

53. Michael McClintock, *Instruments of Statecraft: U.S. Guerrilla Warfare, Counter-Insurgency, and Counter-Terrorism, 1940–1990* (New York, 1992), 192–93, 222–24.

54. McClintock, *Instruments of Statecraft*, 424.

Chapter 8

1. Stephen R. Kandall, *Substance and Shadow: Women and Addiction in the United States* (Cambridge, 1996), 20–24.

2. W. A. Hammond, "Cocaine and the So-Called Cocaine Habit," *New York Medical Journal*, 44, 637–39. By the end of the 19th century, America's pharmaceutical corporations were marketing new "medicines" to replace coca-laced syrups, wines, and bromides: benzedrine (Smith Kline & French), refined cocaine (Merck), and cocaine kits with syringes (Parke-Davis).

3. Kandall, *Substance and Shadow*, 69–70.

4. *New York Times*, February 14, 1914.

5. *New York Times*, March 12, 1911, cited in Kandall, *Substance and Shadow*, 70. Blacks, a respected jurist told a House of Representatives committee during this period, "would just as leave rape a woman as anything else and a great many of the southern rape cases have been traced to cocaine."

6. Kandall, *Substance and Shadow*, 65.

7. David T. Courtwright, *Dark Paradise: A History of Opiate Addiction in America* (Cambridge, 2001), 108–9.

8. The Ku Klux Klan, whose numbers swelled to some 6 million members in the early 1920s, acted as a vigilante force in attacking bootleggers. Professor Leonard J. Moore argues that the revival of the Ku Klux Klan was, in many ways, a starting point in the history of the modern right. "The main forces that drove the Klan movement—the desire to uphold white Protestant cultural hegemony and an inflamed populist opposition to the growing power of political, economic, and cultural elites—have played a fundamental part in shaping conservative and right-wing movements from that time until the present. Leonard J. Moore, "Good Old-Fashioned New Social History and the Twentieth-Century American Right," *Reviews in American History*, 24, no. 4 (December 1996).

9. Kandall, *Substance and Shadow*, 111.

10. Courtwright, *Dark Paradise*, 150.

11. Ryan Grim, *This Is Your Country on Drugs: The Secret History of Getting High in America* (New York, 2009), 52–53.

12. Richard D. Mahoney, *Sons and Brothers: The Days of Jack and Bobby Kennedy* (New York, 1999), 141.

13. See Dan Baum's interview with former Nixon special assistant John Ehrlichman. It is quoted in *International Business Times*, March 23, 2016. Nixon felt that the drug war could "take down" the liberals whose "intellectual arrogance, obsession with style, fashion and class, and permissive attitude towards drugs" not only led to the drug epidemic in the United States but also caused America's defeat in Vietnam. "They went over to the other side." See Richard Nixon, *In the Arena* (New York, 1990), 133.

14. If marijuana became scarce, the Bureau of the Budget argued, harder drugs would be used as substitutes. "Even more seriously, the hard drugs lend themselves to manufacture and/or distribution by organized crime syndicates. It seems probable that the Mafia would be a strong supporter of a diversion of Federal resources to marihuana as opposed to hard drugs." White House cover memo from Tom Whitehead to Bud Krogh with Bureau of the Budget attachment, September 29, 1969. White House Special Files: Staff Members and Office Files, Egil M. Krogh files. Nixon Presidential Library. See Kate Doyle, "Operation Intercept: The Perils of Unilateralism," electronic briefing book, George Washington University, April 13, 2003.

15. Hernando José Gómez, "La economía illegal en Colombia: Tamaño, Evolución, Características e impacto económico," in Juan G. Tokatlian and Bruce M. Bagley, eds., *Economía y Política del Narcotráfico* (Bogotá, 1990), 58.

16. Robert Coram, "The Colombian Gold Rush of 1978," *Esquire,* September 12, 1978.

17. Coca paste is the first crude extracted product from coca leaves which are mashed with alkali, kerosene, and then sulfuric acid (and sometimes potassium permanganate). The result is an off-white paste containing 40 to 70 percent cocaine, as well as other alkaloids, benzoic acid, kerosene residue, and sulfuric acid. After the paste is converted to base, it is further processed by using acetone, ether, and then hydrochloric acid to bring it to 99 percent pure cocaine.

18. Patrick L. Clawson and Rensselaer W. Lee III, *The Andean Cocaine Industry* (London, 1996), 38.

19. *Frontline,* "Drug Wars: Part One," air date: October 9, 2000. Two Cali-based brothers, Miguel Ángel and Gilberto Rodríguez Orejuela, who had consolidated the processing of coca paste from Peru, were not far behind the traffickers in Medellín. When Washington brought pressure on the Bahamas to shut down Norman's Cay, the effort went nowhere because Bahamian prime minister Lynden O. Pindling was receiving $200,000 a month from Lehder to provide cover for the mammoth smuggling operation. Guy Gugliotta and Jeff Leen, "Kings of Cocaine: Inside the Medellin Cartel," in *Today's Best Nonfiction 1989, Reader's Digest* (New York, 1989), 39.

20. The Ford administration was notably neutral in the drug war. Retrenching after the debacle of Vietnam in the early 1970s, Washington had neither the will nor the means to bring the drug war to Colombia. Relations instead were marked by an interlude of repose in which an internal study done by the U.S. embassy in Bogotá concluded that "containment" of the various Colombian insurgencies was the "obtainable goal for both the Colombian and U.S. governments." Accordingly, the United States would limit military assistance and instead finance the Colombian government's "nation-building projects that contribute directly to national welfare." On the drug war, the United States seemed equally modest. The Colombian criminal element, Secretary of State Henry A. Kissinger noted, was "abundant and

sophisticated" and fully in control of judges and local officials. Kissinger, who visited Bogotá in February 1976, spending the night at Hato Grande, the Colombian equivalent of Camp David, may well have agreed with President López Michelsen: the drug problem was America's problem, not Colombia's. See "The Reasons for Discarding the Objective of Elimination of the Insurgency," Department of State, Supplementary Annex to FY 1972 Colombia CASP, NARA, NND969035. Also, Department of State Airgram No. 232, U.S. Embassy Bogota, May 22, 1970, NND969035, as cited in Nazih Richani, *Systems of Violence: The Political Economy of War and Peace in Colombia*, 2nd ed. (Albany, NY, 2013), 45–46, 197–99. See also Abraham F. Lowenthal, "Two Hundred Years of American Foreign Policy: The United States and Latin America: Ending the Hegemonic Presumption," *Foreign Affairs*, 55, no. 1 (October 1976), 64–81. See also Briefing Memorandum for the Secretary of State from ARA—William D. Rogers, "Your Breakfast with Colombian President Lopez," February 13, 1976.

21. Quoted in Richard Davenport-Hines, *The Pursuit of Oblivion: A Global History of Narcotics, 1500–2000* (London, 2001), 345.

22. Peter Bourne, Memorandum to the President, Meeting with President Lopez-Michelsen, June 24, 1977, Carter Presidential Library. Official visit to Bogota, Colombia, by Mrs. Rosalynn Carter, wife of president of the United States Jimmy Carter, June 9–10, 1977. Carter Presidential Library as cited in Eduardo Sáenz Rovner, "Estúdio de caos de la diplomácia antinarcóticos entre Colombia y los Estado Unidos," no. 13, Documentos FCE-CIA, Universidad Nacional de Colombia, July 2012.

23. Memorandum to the President from Peter Bourne, Meeting with President Lopez-Michelsen, June 24, 1977. JCPL. Pastor NSC files, NLC-126-8-10-2-0.

24. Jimmy Carter, Drug Abuse Message to the U.S. Congress, August 2, 1977. *The American Presidency Project.*

25. See Carter's written order on Bourne's memorandum dated June 2, 1977: "Do not send helicopters—Give me CIA info. J.C." Carter's authorization is reflected in "Policy Decisions by Country—Colombia" (Pastor), June 6, 1977, NLC-24-60—1-3-5, JCPL.

26. Robert W. Drexler, *Colombia and the United States: Narcotics Traffic and a Failed Foreign Policy* (Jefferson, NC, 1977), 104. Varón's

attendance at the ceremony is mentioned in U.S. Embassy Bogotá telex 1094, August 18, 1977.

27. See Memorandum to Robert Lipshutz from Peter Bourne, Subject: Memo to the President on Drug Trafficking in Colombia, February 21, 1978. NLC-43-1-22-1-8, JCPL. In the memo, Bourne explains how the Bourne Memorandum fell into the hands of CBS.

28. Juan Gabriel Tokatlian, "El asunto de las drogas y su lugar en las relaciones entre Bogotá y Washington," in Carlos Gustavo Arrieta, Luis Javier Orjuela, Eduardo Sarmiento Palacio, and Juan Gabriel Tokatlian, eds., *Narcotráfico en Colombia. Dimensiones políticas, juridícas e internacionales* (Bogotá, 1991), 294.

29. "López y Turbay rechazan cargos de la TV americana sobre drogas," *El Tiempo*, April 4, 1978, as cited in Eduardo Sáenz Rovner, "Estudio de caso de la diplomácia antinarcóticos entre Colombia y los Estados Unidos" (2012), 33. In the course of the *desmonte* (dismantling of the National Front) begun during Carlos Lleras's time in office, President López Michelsen had asserted a more independent role for Colombia by taking a nonaligned stance on international issues and restoring diplomatic ties with Cuba. Colombia had also joined the General Agreement on Tariffs and Trade (GATT), signed the UN draft convention banning torture, and enacted civil divorce into law. López had also taken action to soak up the massive influx of narco-dollars by opening a "side window" [*ventana siniestra*] in the central bank in which dollars were freely exchanged for pesos. Whether those initiatives could have socialized the drug business at the margin, leading to its gradual integration into the economy and society as a whole, is, of course, anybody's guess. But López's capacity to accomplish much of anything in his last year in office was hampered by civil unrest and military rebellion. After a wave of national strikes in 1977 (over wages devalued by inflation, which had reached 42 percent that year) led to a series of violent confrontations between police and protesters, 33 military commanders had tried but failed to impose a *diktat* on the president that would have granted them emergency powers to take over the country. Gabriel Murillo Castaño, for example, argues that "economic amnesty" gave the drug lords "legitimacy." See Gabriel Murillo Castaño, "Narcotráfico y

Política en la Década de los Ochenta," in Arrieta et al., eds., *Narcotráfico en Colombia*, 229.

30. *TIME*, January 29, 1979, 113, no. 5.

31. Guy Gugliotta and Jeff Leen, *Kings of Cocaine: Inside the Medellin Cartel* (New York, 1989), 47–48.

32. "Carter Aide Bourne Resigns over False Prescription," *Washington Post*, July 21, 1978.

33. Occasionally, in the flood of antinarcotics status reports and updates being generated by three different federal agencies in Washington, there were revealing asides about the total folly of what the government was attempting. One State Department memo found in the files of the National Security Council of the Carter White House, for example, reports that Colombians were asking why "the most powerful nation in the world can continue to permit itself to be 'invaded' by drug-smuggling planes and ships." Why indeed? Reporting to Carter that, "our present cocaine policy is a complete failure," Dr. Bourne alluded to "narcotics-related corruption" in *both* (author's italics) Colombia and the United States as one reason why. See Peter Bourne, Memorandum to the President, Cocaine Trafficking in Colombia, June 2, 1977, NLC-24-70-5-5-8, JCPL. The other assertion by Bourne regarding "narcotics-related corruption" is found in his 11-page "Bourne Memorandum" on page 2. NLC-63-2-7-3-0, JCPL.

34. Prices in 1982 in the United States were from $45,000 to $50,000. By the late 1980s, they were $10,000 to $20,000. Clawson and Lee, *The Andean Cocaine Industry*, 38. See also Kenneth E. Sharpe, "The Drug War: Going after Supply: A Commentary," *Journal of Interamerican Studies and World Affairs*, 30, no. 2/3 (Autumn 1988), 866–981.

35. *Frontline*, "Drug Wars, Part 1," air date: October 9, 2000.

36. Davenport-Hines, *Pursuit of Oblivion*, 353.

37. Juan Gabriel Tokatlian, "Política Exterior," in *Narcotráfico en Colombia*, Arrieta et al., eds., 296–97.

38. "La bonanza de marihuana en Colombia," *El Tiempo*, September 20, 2010.

39. Department of State Briefing Paper, "Narcotics Cooperation," undated, NLC-133-15-3-4-0. See also Memorandum for the President from Acting Secretary of State Warren Christopher, October 2, 1978, NLC-7-20-8-3-1. See also Mario Arango and

Jorge Child, *Coca-coca. Historia, manejo político y máfia de la cocaina* (Bogotá, 1986), 253.

40. The so-called Percy Amendment was repealed in 1981. *Chicago Tribune*, May 10, 1981.

41. Marco Palacios, *Between Legitimacy and Violence: A History of Colombia, 1875–2002* (Durham, NC, 2006), 197.

42. Hernando José Gómez, "La economía ilegal en Colombia: Tamaño, Evolución, Características e impacto económico," in Tokatlian and Bagley, eds., *Economía y Política del Narcotráfico*.

43. Eduardo Sarmiento Palacio, "Economía del Narcotrafico," in Arrieta et al., eds., *Narcotráfico en Colombia*, 77–93.

44. According to prominent economist and central bank board member Salomón Kalmanovitz, "Cocaine stopped the balance of payments from collapsing, which would have pushed us into the spiral of hyper-devaluation that shook most of the rest of continent, for which the 1980s was the lost decade." Quoted in Strong, *Whitewash*, 186. The cocaine boom of the late 1970s coincided with a coffee boom in which yearly coffee revenue went from $1.4 billion in 1974 to $3.9 billion in 1980.

45. U.S. Embassy from Bogotá telex 17710, Subject: Cocaine and the Colombian Economy, December 21, 1987, National Security Files, Reagan Presidential Library (RPL).

46. Sidney Zabludoff, "Colombian Narcotics Organizations as Business Enterprises," in Economics of the Narcotics Industry Conference Report, Central Intelligence Agency, 1994, as cited in Clawson and Lee, *The Andean Cocaine Industry*, 20. Below the narco elite of 500 or so executives were 5,000 specialists in money laundering, enforcement, and laboratory operations. Beneath that second echelon were another 1,000 or so "skilled freelancers" (pilots, chemists, financial advisers, professional assassins, lawyers, accountants, and paramilitary operators). The next cohort was composed of 10,000 physical and communications support personnel (guards, runners, surveillance teams, radio operators, and couriers). At the base of the industry were small coca cultivators, agricultural workers, and independent base processors numbering some 120,000 to 135,000.

47. Clawson and Lee, *The Andean Cocaine Industry*, 26.

48. In the 1982 elections, Betancur won by 3,155,000 votes to 2,749,000 for former president López and 751,000 for New Liberal challenger, Luis Carlos Galán.

49. Drexler, *Colombia and the United States*, 138–39.

Chapter 9

1. Memorandum for John M. Poindexter, From: Raymond F. Burghardt, Subject: Assassination of Colombian Minister of Justice: Proposed Presidential Messages, May 1, 1984, national security files, RPL.

2. *Frontline*, Craig Delaval, "Cocaine, Conspiracy Theories and the CIA in Central America," in Lowell Bergman, ed., *TheDrug Wars*.

3. Central Intelligence Agency Inspector General Report of Investigation, Allegations of Connections between CIA and the Contras in Cocaine Trafficking to the United States (96-0143-IG) Volume II: The Contra Story." https://www.cia.gov/library/reports/general-reports-1/cocaine/contra-story/contents.html. The final report from a two-year investigation by a subcommittee of the Senate Foreign Relations Committee concluded that "senior U.S. policy makers were not immune to the idea that drug money was a perfect solution to the Contras' funding problems." The chair of that subcommittee, Senator John Kerry of Massachusetts, told the *Washington Post* in 1986 that "there is no question in my mind that people affiliated with, on the payroll of, and carrying the credentials of the CIA were involved in drug trafficking while involved in support of the contras." See also "Drugs, Law Enforcement and Foreign Policy," Subcommittee on Terrorism, Narcotics and International Communications (Kerry Committee), Foreign Relations Committee, United States Senate (Washington, DC, 1987), Vol. I, 287.

4. In 1984, Seal's criminal adventure began to unravel when he was charged in Florida by the DEA for trafficking in Quaaludes. This time, his national security patrons in Washington refused to provide cover for him, so he cut a deal to become a DEA informant for the payment of $800,000 a year. He agreed to set up a sting operation against the Medellín cartel, one that would implicate the Sandinistas in drug trafficking. The CIA then rigged "Fat Lady" with cameras and Seal flew south, landing on his return trip at a Nicaraguan air base where the cameras took pictures of a Sandinista official helping Seal load 25-pound bags

of cocaine. When these photos reached the desk of Colonel Oliver North in the White House not long before a key congressional vote on military aid to the *contras*, North leaked the photos and the story to the *Washington Times*. With his cover as a DEA informant now blown, Seal was a marked man, not just for the Medellín cartel but for the Reagan administration, which had its own crimes to hide. Sentenced for an old drug charge to six months in a Salvation Army halfway house in Baton Rouge, Seal didn't last long. A hit crew dispatched from Medellín caught up with him in February 1986 while he was parking his white Cadillac outside the halfway house. The lead assassin emptied 12 rounds from his silenced MAC10 into Seal's head. President Reagan went on nationwide television thereafter, accusing the Sandinistas of drug running and showing Seal's surreptitious photo as proof of their involvement. See Roger Morris, *Partners in Power: The Clintons and Their America* (New York, 1996), 395.

5. Interview: Lewis A. Tambs, March 9, 1987, Tempe, Arizona.
6. Duane R. Clarridge (with Digby Diehl), *A Spy for All Seasons* (New York, 1997), 231.
7. The best account of the fate of *Unión Patriótica* is Steven Dudley, *Walking Ghosts: Murder and Guerrilla Politics in Colombia* (New York, 2006).
8. Bogotá U.S. Embassy telex 03997, March 2, 1987. Subject: Guerrillas: Looking Towards a Bigger War, National Security Files, RPL.
9. Pablo Escobar's son later testified to the role his father played in the siege, as did Virginia Vallejo, a TV anchorwoman romantically involved with the drug lord, in her memoir, *Amando a Pablo, Odiando a Escobar* (Bogotá, 2007), 230. See also Ana Carrigan's account, *El Palacio de Justicia: Una tragedia colombiana* (Bogotá, 1993). Carrigan later changed her view of Escobar's role: namely, that he collaborated in the attack. See *Cromos*, November 25, 2005. One of Escobar's lieutenants later confirmed to British journalist Simon Strong in writing that "the storming of the Palace of Justice was organized by Pablo Escobar, with [Jaime] Bateman, an M-19 leader, and [Andres] Almarales; the objective was to negotiate non-extradition, but, as there was not a dialogue, it was decided to burn the archives." Simon Strong, *Whitewash: Pablo Escobar and the Cocaine Wars* (London, UK, 1995), 146.

10. "Comisión de la Verdad citará al ex-presidente Belisario Betancur por toma del Palacio de Justicia," *El Tiempo*, November 10, 2005.

11. Colonel Alfonso Plazas Vega was later convicted and sentenced in 2010 to 30 years in prison for the disappearances.

12. See Andrés Dávila, *El juego del poder: Historia, armas y votos* (Bogotá, 1988), and Francisco Leal Buitrago, *El oficio de la Guerra* (Bogotá, 1994).

13. "8 Latin American Nations Agree to Revive Contadora Peace Initiative," *New York Times*, August 9, 1986. See also Juan G. Tokatlian, "National Security and Drugs: Their Impact on Colombian-US Relations," *Journal of Interamerican Studies and World Affairs*, 30, no. 1 (Spring 1988), 133–55.

14. Strong, *Whitewash*, 221–23.

15. Even if every study done in the United States during this period concluded that the drug war was a hopeless cause, 20 years of official mendacity had produced its desired effect on the American population. In a 1988 CBS News/*New York Times* poll, 48 percent of the American public considered drugs to be the principal *foreign policy* challenge facing the United States and 63 percent thought drugs should take precedence over the anticommunist struggle. Washington had long demanded and finally achieved a blank check. Drug czar William Bennett told Larry King that public beheadings of drug dealers were in order, and the White House targeted another vulnerable social group with the claim, as *Newsweek* headlined it: "POT CAN MAKE YOU GAY."

16. "El general Maza Márquez va a la carcel," *Semana*, November 20, 2013. U.S. ambassador Charles A. Gillespie Jr. had intervened at the start of the Barco regime to protect General Maza from being replaced. The CIA station chief in Bogota had insisted that Maza was "honest and upstanding." See interview with Charles Anthony Gillespie Jr. (by Charles Stuart Kennedy), Foreign Affairs Oral History Program, 418, the Association for Diplomatic Studies and Training.

17. Charles Krauthammer, "The Unipolar Moment, America and the World, 1990," *Foreign Affairs*, 70, no. 1 (1990–1991). According to Krauthammer, "The center of world power is an unchallenged superpower, the United States, attended by its Western allies." Mexican professor (and later Mexican foreign minister) Jorge G. Castañeda analyzes the strategic consequences of the eclipse

of the Cold War in Latin America in "Latin America and the End of the Cold War," *World Policy Journal*, 7, no. 3 (Summer 1991), 195–219.

18. The modification of Executive Order 12333, which prohibited assassination, gave the president the right to "employ clandestine, low visibility or over military force [which] would not constitute assassination if the U.S. military forces were employed against the combatant forces of another nation, a guerrilla force, or a terrorist or other organization whose actions pose a threat to the security of the United States."

19. Mark Bowden, *Killing Pablo: The Hunt for the World's Greatest Outlaw* (New York, 2001), 72–75.

20. Robin Kirk, *More Terrible Than Death: Drugs, Violence, and America's War in Colombia* (New York, 2003), 156–57.

21. "El Fin de El Mexicano," *Semana*, June 8, 1992.

22. Among those seized by Escobar's men were Diana Turbay, the former president's daughter; Francisco Santos, the editor of *El Tiempo*; Marina Montoya, the sister of Barco's secretary-general of the presidency; and Maruja Pachón, the sister-in-law of the slain Galán. Faced with this hostage situation, the Colombian government offered broad concessions to exonerate Escobar and his lieutenants from their crimes and to excuse them from being extradited to the United States. Two of the hostages were ultimately killed: Diana Turbay during a police raid and Marina Montoya, who was executed by orders from Escobar.

23. Bowden, *Killing Pablo*, 194.

24. This is the author's interpretation, not Mark Bowden's. On August 3, 1993, Ambassador Busby expressed his concerns in a secret cable entitled "Unraveling the Pepes Tangled Web," one in which he refers to himself in the third person and expressly requests that its contents not be shared with any other national security agency. The "crackdown" on *Los Pepes* did occasion their own announcement that they were disbanding their group. This was followed by the continuation of their savage work. See Bowden, *Killing Pablo*, 281–220.

25. Palacios, *Between Legitimacy and Violence*, 249–51. See also John Dugas, ed., *La Constitución política de 1991: ¿Un pacto político viable?* (Bogotá, 1993), especially 21–52.

26. Ana María Bejarano, "The Constitution of 1991: An Institutional Evaluation Seven Years Later," in Charles Bergquist, Ricardo

Peñaranda, and Gonzalo Sánchez G., eds., *Violence in Colombia, 1990–2000: Waging War and Negotiating Peace* (Wilmington, DE, 2001).

27. "The failure to successfully confront rural poverty through astute agrarian policy provided a basis of strength for the guerrilla groups, a fertile ground for the illicit drug industry, and (indirectly) a raison d'être for the paramilitary forces."

   See Albert Berry, "Agriculture, Rural Development and Attempts at Land Reform in Colombia," in Bruce M. Bagley and Jonathan D. Rosen, eds., *Colombia's Political Economy at the Outset of the Twenty-First Century: From Uribe to Santos and Beyond* (Lanham, MD, 2015).

28. José Antonio Ocampo, "Performance and Challenges of the Colombian Economy," in Bagley and Rosen, eds., *Colombia's Political Economy*, 3.

29. "La tercera fuerza: Con recursos internacionales y del sector privado colombiano las CONVIVIR lográn financiar su fortaleciemiento en la ilegalidad," *Semana*, March 22, 1999. See also Fernando Cubides C., "From Private to Public Violence: The Paramilitaries," in Bergquist, Peñaranda, and Sánchez, eds., *Violence in Colombia, 1990–2000*. See also Juan Diego Restrepo E., "Alvaro Uribe, entre las 'Convivir' y las AUC, *Semana*, September 19, 2013.

30. The amount of the campaign donation was later said to be $6 million.

31. Interview: Robert S. Gelbard (former assistant secretary of state for narcotics and international law enforcement), August 18, 2016 (by phone). Gelbard, based on his reading of the transcribed telephone intercepts between Cali cartel leaders and principals in the Samper presidential campaign, had repeatedly pressed President-elect Samper during Samper's visit to Washington to admit his guilt in the affair. See also Russell Crandall, *Driven by Drugs: U.S. Policy toward Colombia* (Boulder, CO, 2008), 84. DEA agent Joe Toft's motivations and actions are covered in Bowden, *Killing Pablo*, 270–72. See also Douglas Farah, "The Crack-up," *Washington Post*, July 21, 1996.

32. Washington continued to target President Samper.
   U.S. ambassador in Bogotá Myles R. R. Frechette argued (in a classified cable that was leaked to the *Washington Post*) that he should be isolated and debilitated. When the lower house of

the Colombian Congress let Samper off the hook for the alleged drug contributions to his campaign, Washington revoked his visa to the United States. When Samper failed to extradite four of the arrested leaders of the Cali cartel, the United States decertified Colombia in 1997, consigning America's oldest ally in Latin America to the ranks of criminal dictatorships like Afghanistan, Burma, Syria, and Iran. See *Washington Post*, June 30, 1996. Depending on the week, President Samper posed as either a persecuted patriot or a born-again drug warrior worthy of U.S. benediction. Sometimes it seemed like both. En route to the United Nations in September 1996 to unveil his "new global campaign against drugs," as the *New York Times* derisively reported it, Samper carried a capsule of cyanide with him just in case American officials seized him at the airport in New York for arriving with nothing more than his special UN entry chit. Shortly before he boarded the plane bound for the United States, Colombian police confiscated eight pounds of heroin that had been secreted aboard. See "Colombian President Speaks at U.N., Drugs Found on His Plane," *News Briefs*, November 1996.

33. Jim McGee, "Ex-Prosecutors Indicted in Cali Case," *Washington Post*, June 6, 1995.

34. "American Drug Aid Goes South," *New York Times*, November 25, 1996.

35. Although the army covered for Colonel Hiett by clearing him of any criminal wrongdoing, the U.S. Customs Service blew the whistle, and he was ultimately charged and convicted along with his cocaine-addicted wife. See Alan Feuer, "Drug War Ensnares an Army Colonel Who Fought It," *New York Times*, April 16, 2000. See also Bruce Shapiro, "The Corruption of Col. James Hiett," *Salon*, July 5, 2000.

36. Kirk, *More Terrible Than Death*, 243–45.

37. The author toured the area around Puerto Asís in September 2000 with a drug-dusting pilot contracted by Dyncorp.

38. Interview with María Clemencia Ramírez, "Una mirada comparative entre las marchas de campesinos cocaleros, de 1996 y las del Catumbo, 2013, y su representación mediática," *Agencia Prensa Rural*, February 21, 2014.

39. "Glysophate Fact Sheet," State Department, cited in Julia Buxton, *The Political Economy of Narcotics: Production, Consumption and Global Markets* (London, 2006), 180.

40. Jeremy Bigwood, "Monsanto and the 'Drug War,'" *Earth Island Journal*, Winter 2001–2002, 19–39.

41. See "Colombia: Momentum against Paramilitaries Lost (U)," Bureau of Intelligence and Research, Department of State, April 7, 1998. Also, "Colombia: Paramilitaries Assuming a Higher Profile," Central Intelligence Agency, August 31, 1998. National Security Archive.

42. See U.S. Embassy telex 13985, January 10, 1999, in which Ambassador Kamman details the complicity of Colombian generals. See also telex 9929, July 16, 1999, in which Kamman sets forth evidence of the armed forces' knowledge and facilitation of paramilitary massacres. National Security Archive.

43. Adam Isacson and Jorge Rojas Rodríguez, "Origins, Evolution, and Lessons of the Colombian Peace Movement," in Virginia M. Bouvier, ed., *Colombia: Building Peace in a Time of War* (Washington, DC, 2009), 19.

44. The FARC command later admitted to the killing of Terence Freitas, Ingrid Washinatok, and Lahe'ena'e Gay.

Chapter 10

1. Stephen M. Walt, "Two Cheers for Clinton's Foreign Policy," *Foreign Affairs*, March/April 2000, 65.

2. "Multilateral Invasion Force for Colombia?" *NACLA Report on the Americas*, May/June 1998, 46.

3. What the Americans were eagerly calling "the battle of Bogotá" was actually a series of probing, soft-target attacks by FARC urban irregulars. Among the most respected analysts about the balance and capacity or guerrilla forces at the time was Alfredo Rangel Suárez. See his chapter, "Las FARC-EP: una mirada actual," in Malcolm Deas and Maria Victoria Llorente, eds., *Reconocer la guerra para reconstruir la paz* (Bogotá, 1999), 46–47.

4. Rand Beers later told Winifred Tate in an interview that he surmised that Hastert and Goss had given him their plan because of his military background—"everybody thought I was a Republican." See Winifred Tate, *Drugs, Thugs, and Diplomats: U.S. Policymaking in Colombia* (Stanford, CA, 2015), 141.

5. Thomas R. Pickering, "Anatomy of Plan Colombia," *American Interest*, 5, no. 2 (November 1, 2009), 2–21.

6. Russell Crandall, *Driven by Drugs: U.S. Policy toward Colombia* (Boulder, CO, 2002), 123.

7. Winifred Tate's lucid exegesis about the "origin stories" of Plan Colombia reflects my analysis to some extent, but it goes far deeper. See *Drugs, Thugs, and Diplomats*, 137–63.

8. In an interview with the author, Jon Stivers, senior legislative assistant to Representative Pelosi in her capacity as the ranking minority member of the Foreign Operations Subcommittee, noted that Pelosi had consistently staked out her own positions on human rights in China, global AIDS action, and so forth, independent of the Clinton administration. Interview: Stivers (by telephone), December 15, 2016.

9. Former Marine colonel John "Jack" Murtha, a Democratic congressman from Johnstown, Pennsylvania, added that the same report provided the conclusion that no amount of militarization in sealing borders or engaging in combat would stop the drug flow. See Peter H. Reuter, Gordon Crawford, Jonathan Cave, Patrick Murphy, Don Henry, William Lisowski, and Eleanor Sullivan Wainstein, "Sealing the Borders: The Effects of Increased Military Participations in Drug Interdiction" (RAND, 1988). In an interview with the author, Murtha recounted his contention that if Plan Colombia was really a counterinsurgency plan, "you couldn't fight it with drug-fighting assets like helicopters and anti-narcotics units much less methods like mass fumigation. It had to be population-centric, building better lives and winning hearts and minds." Plan Colombia, he concluded, was "flying under false colors." Interview: Congressman John P. Murtha, June 22, 2004, Washington, DC.

10. This account is based on Ingrid Vacius and Adam Isacson, "'Plan Colombia': The Debate in Congress," Center for International Policy, December 4, 2000. For a fuller archive on key documents, committee votes and statements, and the floor debate in both House and Senate, see https://web.archive.org/web/20070710215959/http://ciponline.org/colombia/aid0001.htm.

11. Quoted in Francisco Ramírez Cuellar, *The Profits of Extermination: How U.S. Corporate Power Is Destroying Colombia* (Monroe, ME, 2005), 32.

12. Liberal Democrats in the Senate like Dick Durbin (D-IL) and John Kerry (D-MA) were at least minimally satisfied by social spending commitments as well as the promise of rule of law reforms in Colombia and, thus, ultimately backed the bill. Senators Ted Kennedy (D-MA) and Patrick Leahy (D-VT) fought

successfully to keep stringent human rights conditions on the
proposed aid to the Colombia military, but efforts to gut Plan
Colombia's funding in favor of domestic drug treatment (by
Senators Wellstone [D-MN] and Barbara Boxer [D-CA]) failed by
a wide margin in the floor debate. Ultimately, 18 Black Hawks
(and 42 Super Hueys) were authorized in Plan Colombia.

13. "What is the basic plan? Is it a peace strategy with a military
component? A counterinsurgency drive? A bulwark to salvage
the Pastrana administration? A Marshall Plan for South America?
And what will define its success?" See Christopher Marquis,
"America Gets Candid about What Colombia Needs," *New York
Times*, February 25, 2001.

14. Paul Krugman, "Vision of Power," *New York Times*, April 27, 2004.

15. T. Christian Miller, "U.S. Troops Answered Oil Firm's Pleas," *Los
Angeles Times*, December 30, 2004.

16. "Sí, apoyamos candidatos: 'Paras,'" *El Tiempo*, February 12, 2002.
AUC chief Salvatore Mancuso was quoted as saying, "We're
telling people for whom they should vote. Thirty percent of
the congressional aspirants represent people from our zones."
Quoted in James Jones, "U.S. Policy and Peace in Colombia,"
in Virginia Marie Bouvier, ed., *Colombia: Building Peace in a Time
of War* (Washington, D.C., 2009), 360. In his autobiography,
Uribe quotes the *Washington Post* in December 2000 as asserting
that "Uribe has been tied in the Colombian media to the
paramilitaries." See Álvaro Uribe Vélez, *No hay causa perdida*,
(New York, 2012), 175–76.

17. National Security Archive, "U.S. Intelligence Listed President
Uribe among 'Important Colombian Narco-traffickers' in
1991," August 2, 2004, http://nsarchive.gwu.edu/NSAEBB/
NSAEBB131. The DIA report, although not "finally evaluated,"
is an interagency document cross-checked "via interfaces with
other agencies." See "Entrevista con Michael Evans," *Semana*,
August 8, 2004. In a communiqué from the presidential office,
Casa de Nariño, dated July 30, 2004, the Uribe government
contested and clarified several controversial aspects of the
president's record, although not the allegation that the president
was associated with the Medellín cartel or that his father was
a friend of Pablo Escobar. See National Security Archive, "U.S.
Intelligence Listed President Uribe." In his memoir, Uribe
explains why he used Pablo Escobar's helicopter to fly to

Yolumbo, the Antioquian town near where his father was killed, contending that it was registered, in fact, to "a serious entity." See *No hay causa perdida*, 71.

18. Fernando Cubides, "Los paramilitares y su estratégia," in María Victoria Llorente and Malcolm D. Deas, eds., *Reconocer la guerra para construir la paz* (Bogotá, 1999), 54–71.

19. Interview with the author: Adam Isacson, August 10, 2016, Washington, DC. See also Ben Wallace-Wells, "How America Lost the Drug War," *Rolling Stone*, March 24, 2011, 72. Regarding the pacification of Medellín, Winfred Tate cites human rights reports from the International Crisis Group, Amnesty International, and the Inter-American Commission on Human Rights, all of which described the role of paramilitary terror and neighborhood cleansing schemes in securing the Antioquian capital city. See Tate, "From Greed to Grievance," in Bouvier, ed., *Colombia: Building Peace in a Time of War*, 123. Tate's book *Counting the Dead: The Culture and Politics of Human Rights Activism in Colombia* (Berkeley, 2007), is the dispositive account of Colombia's tormented human rights odyssey.

20. By the time Plan Colombia took the fight to the FARC in the south in 2004, the paramilitaries had created a mafia-like parastate in Barrancabermeja. They controlled the police, local elections, municipal government, and city contracting. In addition to operating legitimate businesses, the paramilitaries monopolized cocaine trafficking, robbed large amounts of gasoline from the state oil company, and targeted leftist sympathizers and anyone associated with them for intimidation or execution. See Lesley Gill, "The Parastate in Colombia: Political Violence and the Restructuring of Barrancabermeja," *Anthropologica*, 51, no. 2 (2009), 324.

21. "Colombia's Capitulation," *New York Times*, July 4, 2005.

22. Interview with the author: Maria McFarland Sánchez-Moreno, November 17, 2016, by phone. McFarland is currently the co-director of the U.S. program at Human Rights Watch and previously worked for HRW in Colombia.

23. "Tras la muerte de Yolanda Izquierdo gobierno intenta frenar cacería a victimas de los paramilitares," *Semana,* February 2, 2007. See also the open letter to U.S. ambassador William B. Wood from Human Rights First, Subject: Recent Serious Attacks on Human Rights Defenders, February 12, 2007. By 2014, of the

31,849 demobilized paramilitary fighters, 4,237 faced human rights charges. Of those, 19 had been convicted and 268 released from prison pending their final verdicts; 30 had been extradited to the United States. See Adam Isacson, "Ending 50 Years of Conflict in Colombia: A New Report from WOLA," *Occasional Publication*, April 14, 2014.

24. "Senador Mario Uribe, primo del president, vinculado al proceso de la 'parapolítica,' " *El Tiempo*, July 11, 2007.

25. When Jorge Noguera, Uribe's chief of state intelligence (a bureau roughly comparable to the FBI) was indicted for funneling intelligence to paramilitary enforcers to murder or otherwise terrorize human rights defenders, Uribe rallied to defend him. Uribe spirited the accused Noguera to a consular post in Milan, Italy, but Colombian justice, for once, prevailed. Noguera was indicted as an accessory to murder and sentenced to 25 years in prison. Uribe had better luck helping Noguera's successor, María del Pilar Hurtado, escape to Panamá where she was given asylum before she could be arrested on multiple charges for illegally spying. Chief Justice Jaime Arrubla, one of the main targets of the spying campaign, dryly noted that asylum should preferably be provided for "people facing political persecution, not for the persecutors themselves." See "Jorge Noguera condenó a 25 años de cárcel," *Semana*, September 14, 2011; and John Otis, "Colombia: Uribe's Legacy Haunted by Scandals," *TIME*, December 10, 2010. Hurtado later returned to Colombia and was convicted and sentenced to 14 years in prison along with Uribe aide Bernardo Moreno. See Sentencia 36784—CSJ: María del Pilar Hurtado Afanador—Bernardo Moreno Villegas. Corte Suprema de Justicia, May 7, 2015.

26. President Uribe, who had publicly proposed a law in April 2007 to provide amnesty for all politicians implicated in colluding with the paramilitaries, had called Supreme Court justice César Julio Valencia the day of his cousin's arrest and later sued Valencia for defamation and slander. See "Álvaro Uribe denunciará por injúria al presidente de la Corte Suprema, César Julio Valencia," *El Tiempo*, January 18, 2008. Uribe conceded that Don Berna's representatives—including attorney Diego Álvarez and Antonio López ("Job")—had indeed been interviewed at Casa de Nariño. See "El Complot de los Paras," *Semana*, April 23, 2008, and "El Coletazo," *Semana*, August 30, 2008.

27. Deborah Sontag, "The Secret History of Colombia's Paramilitaries and the U.S. War on Drugs," *New York Times*, September 10, 2016. By mid-2007, the Uribe administration had extradited over 500 Colombians to the United States on drug-related charges.

28. "Colombia General Sentenced in US for Paramilitary Links," BBC, December 14, 2012. See also "Reducen en EE.UU. la pena de prisión a Mauricio Santoyo, exjefe de seguridad de Uribe," *Agencia EFE*, September 1, 2016.

29. According to Ambassador Gillespie, it was the CIA station chief in Bogotá who had insisted that Maza be retained. See interview by Charles Stuart Kennedy with Charles Anthony Gillespie Jr., Foreign Affairs Oral History Program, 418, Association for Diplomatic Studies and Training.

30. Included in the eight agencies were the CIA, the FBI, the DEA, and the IRS. Brownfield's diplomatic cable is dated September 9, 2009. A week later, he reported telling Francisco Santos, Uribe's vice president, that "if another DAS scandal erupted, our Plan B was to terminate all association with DAS. Immediately." The U.S.-DAS relationship, however, continued for another seven months, at which point Brownfield pulled U.S. funding. "U.S. Aid Implicated in Abuses in Power in Colombia," *Washington Post*, August 20, 2011.

31. Myles R. R. Frechette, "Colombia and the United States—The Partnership: But What Is the Endgame?" The Letort Papers, Strategic Studies Institute, March 2007.

32. John M. Walsh, "Are We There Yet? Measuring Progress in the U.S. War on Drugs in Latin America," *Drug War Monitor*, WOLA, December 2004, 4.

33. Southcom CinC General James T. Hill, for example, told an audience at the Heritage Foundation that 19,000 Americans killed annually by drugs "constitutes, in my mind, the equivalent of a weapon of mass destruction."

34. William Neuman, "Defying U.S., Colombia Halts Aerial Spraying of Crops Used to Make Cocaine," *New York Times*, May 14, 2015. See also United States, Department of State, International Narcotics Control Strategy Reports, cited in Adam Isacson, Lisa Haugaard, Abigail Poe, Sarah Kinosian, and George Withers, "Time to Listen: Trends in U.S. Security Assistance to Latin America and the Caribbean," Latin American Working

Group Education Fund and Center for International Policy, September 2013.

35. Luisa Fernanda Solarte graduated in 1998 along with Julio Otálora, her then-boyfriend and future husband, from the Thunderbird School of Global Management where I was a professor. See Juan Forero, "Blast at Social Club Strikes at Colombia's Elite," *New York Times*, February 3, 2003. See also Guido Hoyos, "Beca en memoria de Luisa Solarte," *Semana*, July 7, 2003. Solarte's father, Alfredo Solarte Lindo, later backed the peace proposal between the government and the FARC. "Es hora darnos la oportunidad de la paz," *El Tiempo*, July 26, 2016.

36. Peter DeShazo, Tanya Primiani, and Phillip McLean, "Back from the Brink: Evaluating Progress in Colombia, 1999–2007," Center for Strategic and International Studies, November 2007.

37. Adam Isacson, "The Role of the United States and the Military in Colombia," in Bruce M. Bagley and Jonathan D. Rosen, eds., *Colombia's Political Economy at the Outset of the Twenty-First Century, From Uribe to Santo and Beyond* (Lanham, MD, 2015).

38. Invamer Gallup Colombia, "Gallup Poll 57," Medellín, February 2007.

39. Confidential Interview: SEAL Team 6 operative. In February 2003, the FARC captured three American contractors after their plane crashed in rebel-held territory. For the next two years, U.S. Special Forces searched but failed to find and rescue those contractors. In 2006, the United States began using Scaneagle drones to surveille the FARC. See Karen DeYoung, "Wikileaks: Colombia Began Using U.S. Drones for Counterterrorism in Colombia in 2006," *Washington Post*, March 23, 2011.

40. President George H. W. Bush's 1989 modification of Reagan's Executive Order 12333 permitted the United States "to employ clandestine, low visibility or overt military force [which] would not constitute assassination if the U.S. military forces were employed against the combatant forces of another nation, a guerrilla force, or a terrorist or other organization whose actions pose a threat to the security of the United States." Dana Priest cites the White House's Office of Legal Counsel as deciding that "the same legal analysis they applied to al-Qaeda could be applied to the FARC. Killing a FARC leader would not be an assassination because the organization posed an ongoing

threat to Colombia. Also, none of the FARC commanders
could be expected to surrender." See also Elizabeth B. Bazan,
"Assassination Ban and E.O. 12333: A Brief Summary," *CRS
Report for Congress*, January 4, 2002.

41. Dana Priest, "Covert Action in Colombia," *Washington Post*,
December 21, 2013.

42. Confidential interview with the author: CIA officer then serving
in the U.S. mission in Colombia.

43. Human Rights Watch reported that the number of murdered
trade unionists was 72 in 2006. The *New York Times* reported
the number to be 58. See Simon Romero, "Colombian Seeks to
Persuade Congress to Continue Aid," *New York Times*, April
30, 2007.

44. Paul Richter and Greg Miller, "Colombia Army Chief Linked to
Outlaw Militias," *Los Angeles Times*, March 25, 2007.

45. U.S. Congress, House Armed Services Committee, "Posture
Statement by Gen. James T. Hill, commander, U.S. Southern
Command," Washington, DC, March 12, 2003. Regarding
U.S. knowledge of "false positives," see National Security
Archive, "Body Count Mentalities: Colombia's False Positive
Scandal," NSA briefing book 266, January 7, 2009.

46. See "Pelosi Floor Statement on Colombia FTA," April 10,
2010, http://www.democraticleader.gov/newsroom/
pelosi-floor-statement-colombia-free-trade-agreement.

47. Tom Hamburger, Rosalind S. Helderman, and Anu
Narayanswamy, "The Clintons, a Luxury Jet and Their $100
Million Donor from Canada," *Washington Post*, May 3, 2015.
See also Sam Stein, "Bill Clinton's Ties to Colombia Trade Deal
Stronger Than Even Penn's," *Huffington Post*, April 16, 2008.
Anu Naraynaswamy, "Travels with Frank and Bill: A Look at the
Clinton-Giustra Friendship," *Washington Post*, May 3, 2015.

48. Colombian president León Valencia had used this metaphor to
describe Colombia's dependence on U.S. capital beginning in the
late 1920s.

Chapter 11

1. Kevin J. Fandl, "Bilateral Agreements and Fair Trade Practices: A
Policy Analysis of the Colombia-U.S. Free Trade Agreement," *Yale
Human Rights and Development Journal*, 10, no. 1 (2007), 71.

2. "President Bush Welcomes Colombian President Uribe to the White House," Office of the Press Secretary, The White House, February 16, 2006.

3. Peter Hakim, "Is Washington Losing Latin America?" *Foreign Affairs*, 85, no. 1 (January–February 2006), 51–68.

4. Thomas A. Marks, "Sustainability of Colombian Military/ Strategic Support for 'Democratic Security,'" Strategic Studies Institute, Army War College, July 2005.

5. Annual U.S. military expenditures from 2008 through 2010 remained steady at over $400 million. The nonmilitary portion did as well. The total amounts expended for consolidation were a fraction of the $1 billion earmarked.

6. See Peter DeShazo, Phillip McLean, and Johanna Mendelson Forman, "Colombia's Plan de Consolidación de la Macarena: An Assessment," June 2009, Center for Strategic and International Studies.

7. See "September Colombia Strategic Development Initiative Update," telex 09BOGOTA3262, October 16, 2009. See also BOGOTA000715 telex, March 2, 2009. Wikileaks.

8. "GOC Faces Challenges in Expanding State Presence in Macarena," telex 08BOGOTA3582, September 24, 2008. Wikileaks. See also Adam Isacson, "Consolidating 'Consolidation': Colombia's 'Security and Development' Zones Await a Civilian Handoff, While Washington Backs Away from the Concept," Washington Office on Latin America, December 2012.

9. U.S. Embassy cable from Bogotá, "Consolidation Progress in Former FARC Stronghold Impressive," January 26, 2010.

10. Juan Forero, "Colombian Farmers Get Broad Incentives to Forgo Coca Crops," *Washington Post*, May 22, 2009.

11. Sara Miller Llana, "U.S. Applies Colombia Antidrug Lessons to Afghanistan," *Christian Science Monitor*, August 27, 2009.

12. Quoted in Max Boot and Richard Bennet, "The Colombian Miracle," *Weekly Standard*, December 14, 2009.

13. Petraeus visited Bogotá in the last week of January 2012. See "Colombia rediseña plan de combate contra las guerrillas," *América Economia*, February 17, 2002.

14. Uribe had made secret but unsuccessful approaches for peace talks with the FARC. "Los encuentros secretos de paz de Álvaro Uribe," *El Tiempo*, August 26, 2012.

15. Adam Isacson, Lisa Haugaard, Abigail Poe, Sarah Kinosian, and George Withers, "Time to Listen: Trends in U.S Security Assistance to Latin America and the Caribbean," Latin American Working Group Education Fund and Center for International Policy, September 2013, 6.

16. Nic Jenzen-Jones, "Run through the Jungle: Colombia's JUNGLA Commandos," *Small Wars Journal*, blog post, November 22, 2011.

17. The strategic revision group was called the *Comite de Revisión Estratégica e Innovación* and began meeting in the first months of 2012. See *Memorias al Congreso*, 2012–2013, Annual Report of the Colombian Department of Defense, 16.

18. Jorge Quintero, "Juan Carlos Pinzón: guerra y paz, El ahora Embajador de Colombia en Estados Unidos habló de su vida con la revista BOCAS," *El Tiempo*, June 22, 2015.

19. Quintero, "Juan Carlos Pinzón, " 45–47. See also "Examen al Plan 'Espada de Honor,'" ColombiaVanguardia.com, May 14, 2014.

20. Lisa Haugaard, "Human Rights Abuses in Colombia," in Bruce M. Bagley and Jonathan D. Rosen, eds., *Colombia's Political Economy at the Outset of the 21st Century* (Lanham, MD, 2015), 269.

21. Amnesty International charged in November 2014 that the government was "defrauding victims." Victoria McKenzie, "Colombia's Restitution Law Defrauding Victims: Amnesty International," Amnesty International, November 27, 2014.

22. In many cases, large companies like Argos S.A., a Colombian multinational cement company, or the Colombian subsidiary of the multinational mining firm Anglogold Ashanti, had bought stolen land and set forth a "good faith" defense regarding their acquisition, defenses the Constitutional Court did not accept. It was not enough, the court ruled, to aver good faith; what was required was "good faith free of guilt." See Elizabeth Dickinson, "5 Things to Know about Colombia's Land Restitution," July 26, 2016. www.devex.com/news.

23. Cassava farmer Miguel Serna, for example, who had fled his farm in El Toco (César) at paramilitary gunpoint in 1997, became a land restitution leader for 80 families in a cassava-farming area of northern Colombia after passage of the law. Serna survived two assassination attempts in 2013 by paramilitary criminals. See Chris Kraul, "Colombia Fails to Put Land Back in Farmers' Hands," *Los Angeles Times*, January 5, 2014.

24. Human Rights Watch reported that "the Attorney General's Office had summoned a total of 11 active or retired generals for questioning on their alleged role in false-positive cases. In August, retired general Henry William Torres Escalante was indicted, but no meaningful progress has been achieved in other cases against generals allegedly responsible for "false-positive" killings. In March 2016, prosecutors summoned the former head of the army, retired general Mario Montoya Uribe, for a hearing in which he was to be charged. The hearing had yet to take place as of November 2016. "Country Report: Colombia, Events of 2016," Human Rights Watch, https://www.hrw.org/world-report/2017/country-chapters/colombia.

25. When a Colombian officer leaked the top-secret location of the spot where rebel negotiators were to be picked up for their Red Cross–chaperoned flight from Colombia to the negotiations in Havana to Uribe, the former president posted the coordinates of the pickup on his Twitter account. Quoted in Stephanie Le Saux-Famer, "The Security Sector Dimension in Colombia's Peace Talks, Centre for Security Governance," June 5, 2015, http://secgovcentre.org/2015/06/backgrounder-the-security-sector-dimension-of-colombias-peace-talks.

26. "Escándalo: El video del 'hacker' y Zuluaga," *Semana*, May 17, 2014.

27. President Santos estimated Colombian job gains to range from 300,000 to 500,000. Obama spoke of "hundreds of thousands" of U.S. jobs. See Remarks by President Obama and President Santos of Colombia in Joint Press Conference, Cartagena, Colombia, White House Press Office, April 15, 2012.

28. "Time to Branch Out," Special Report: Colombia, *Economist*, October 29, 2015.

29. Office of the United States Trade Representative, Third Report to the Congress on the Operation of the Andean Trade Preference Act, Executive Office of the President, September 2006.

30. Written Statement by the National Association of Manufacturers, Hearing on President Obama's Trade Policy, February 9, 2011. The NAM stated that 10,000 small and medium-sized U.S. enterprises were already exporting to Colombia in 2009.

31. Upon enactment of the proposed agreement, 77 percent of Colombia's tariff lines affecting U.S. farm exports would go to zero, accounting for 52 percent of total U.S. exports. Most other

tariffs would be zeroed out within 15 years, including many that would be eliminated within five years. See Juan Carlos Hidalgo and Daniel Griswold, "Trade Agreement Would Promote U.S. Exports and Colombian Civil Society," *Free Trade Bulletin No. 44*, February 15, 2011, 6–17.

32. Union murders, at least for a while, did decline. What did not change were targeted killings and terrorist threats against human rights defenders and land rights advocates. "Labor in the U.S.-Colombia Trade Promotion Agreement," Office of the U.S. Special Trade Representative, https://ustr.gov/uscolombiatpa/labor. Accessed 9/16/2018. See also Lisa Haugaard, "A Plan Still on Paper: Three Years of the U.S.-Colombia Labor Action Plan," *Huffington Post*, April 9, 2014.

33. Stewart Doan, "GOP Senators Just Say 'No' to TAA on Free Trade Agreements," *Agri-Pulse Communications*, June 30, 2011.

34. Zachary A. Goldfarb and Lori Montgomery, "Obama Gets Win as Congress Passes Free-Trade Agreements," October 12, 2011, *Washington Post*. In the House vote, 31 Democrats voted for the U.S.–Colombia FTA (with 158 Democratic members voting "no"). In the Senate, 11 Democrats voted for the bill.

35. World Bank, *Colombia 2006–2010: A Window of Opportunity* (Washington, DC, 2007), 7.

36. José Antonio Ocampo, "Performance and Challenges of the Colombian Economy," in Bagley and Rosen, eds., *Colombia's Political Economy at the Outset of the 21st Century*, 7–11.

37. Ocampo, "Performance and Challenges of the Colombian Economy," 24.

38. Programa de las Naciones Unidas para el Desarrollo, *Informe Nacional de Desarrollo Colombia*, 315, as cited in Albert Berry, "Agriculture, Rural Development and Attempts at Land Reform in Colombia," in Bagley and Rosen, eds., *Colombia's Political Economy at the Outset of the 21st Century*, 43. See also Ulrich Oslender, "Fleshing Out the Geographies of Social Movements: Colombia's Pacific Coast Black Communities and the 'Aquatic Space,'" *Political Geography*, 23, 957–85.

39. "The U.S.-Colombia Free Trade Agreement at Three Years," U.S. Chamber of Commerce, September 14, 2015.

40. Ocampo, "Performance and Challenges of the Colombian Economy," 10.

41. Frank Safford and Marco Palacios, *Colombia: Fragmented Land, Divided Society* (New York, 2001), 327.

Chapter 12

1. YouTube video: "Discursos de Timochenko y Santos al firmar el acuerdo de paz," https://video.search.yahoo.com/yhs/search;_ylt=A0LEVvurBHFZLgkAHUwnnIlQ?p=Santos+Cartagena+acuerdo+de+paz+2016&fr=yhs-mozilla-003&fr2=piv-web&hspart=mozilla&hsimp=yhs-003#id=35&vid=21847c625af73eecc93971167f31fd3b&action=view.

2. Jon Lee Anderson, "How Colombia's Voters Rejected Peace," *New Yorker*, October 4, 2016.

3. Kirk Semple and Nicholas Casey, "Deep Scars and Complacency Defeated Colombia's Peace Deal," *New York Times*, October 3, 2016. Certain features of the proposed treaty, such as granting the FARC status as a political party along with a guaranteed number of seats for its successor movement in the Congress, were a hard-sell. Uribe called the excusing of FARC leaders who had committed war crimes from serving jail time a "veiled amnesty," with Amnesty International labeling it "impunity." See "Los 10 Duros Dardos de Uribe a la Firma de la Paz," *Semana*, August 17, 2016. Amnesty International is quoted in Human Rights Watch, "Colombia: Agreeing to Impunity," December 22, 2015.

4. FARC commanders had personally visited the *chocoano* village a year earlier to make a formal apology to the survivors of the atrocity.

5. Two days after the vote, President Santos and his peace negotiators met with a large group of evangelical Christian pastors to discuss their concerns. Nicholas Casey, "Colombian Opposition to Peace Deal Feeds Off Gay Rights Backlash," *New York Times*, October 8, 2016.

6. "No Progress as Colombia's President, Rival Meet with Pope," *Reuters*, December 16, 2016. See also, "Pope Francis' Pressure on Colombia, and Legitimate Resistance," *Destaque International*, January 10, 2017.

7. Uribe is quoted in *El Nuevo Siglo*, "Fondo de tierras: 300,000 familias beneficiadas," August 26, 2016. http://www.elnuevosiglo.com.co/articulos/08-2016-300-mil-familias-beneficiadas-con-el-fondo-de-tierras.

8. Interview with the author: Bruce M. Bagley (by telephone), November 10, 2017.

9. By April 2017, it was estimated that 5 to 6 percent of the FARC force had refused to disarm and demobilize.

10. Not counting the cached arms, FARC fighters have turned in 1.02 weapons per capita. The national homicide rate had fallen from about 16,000 in 2015 to 12,000 in 2016. These figures are from the *Fundación Paz y Reconciliación* as set forth in León Valencia, "'Aumento de cultivos ilícitos en Colombia está como hace 20 años': Informa Cómo va la paz," *Semana*, July 18, 2017.

11. José de Córdoba, "Hurdles Remain for New Colombia Peace Deal with FARC Guerrillas," *Wall Street Journal*, December 1, 2016.

12. Research by Eduardo Álvarez of the Bogotá-based Ideas for Peace Foundation indicates that half the perpetrators of these assassinations could not be identified, with the rest dividing between criminal bands and local members of the rural underworld. As Princeton professor Robert A. Karl commented, "The dead include a near-perfect distillation of all of the small, individual conflicts that have added up to Colombia's war." See Greg Grandin, "Will Last Year's Peace Treaty Survive, or Is the Past Prologue in Colombia? An Interview with Historian Robert Karl on the Country's Violent Demobilization," *Nation*, June 22, 2017. Interview with the author: Robert A. Karl (by phone), July 24, 2017.

13. "The Colombian Labor Action Plan: A Five-Year Update," U.S. Department of Labor and U.S. Special Trade Representative, April 11, 2016. According to U.S. congressmen George Miller (D-CA) and Jim McGovern (D-MA), who toured Colombia and whose committee staff did extensive research into the question, "murders and threats against union members and harmful subcontracting persist in Colombia largely unabated. At a minimum, 413 threats were documented and 22 trade unionists were murdered for their union involvement in 2012." See "'The U.S. Labor Action Plan in Colombia: Failing on the Ground,' A Staff Report on Behalf of U.S. Representatives George Miller and Jim McGovern to the Congressional Monitoring Groups on Labor Rights in Colombia," October 2013, 4.

14. María Victoria Llorente, Patricia Bulla, and Claudia Gómez, "De la seguridad para la guerra a la seguridad para la paz: Para un

debate de las opciones institucionales," Fundación Ideas para la
Paz, Friedrich-Ebert-Stiftung, January 2016.

15. Interview with the author: Dr. Nazih Richani (by phone),
July 14, 2017. See also Nazih Richani, "Colombia's
Peace Accord and the Prospects of the War System,"
June 27, 2017, https://aulablog.net/2017/06/27/
colombias-peace-accord-and-the-prospects-of-the-war-system

16. Malcolm Deas, "Plan Colombia," *London Review of Books*, 23, no. 7
(April 5, 2001).

17. Ironically enough, despite marginal public-sector spending on
extension, R&D, and agricultural credits, family farmers in the
1990s outproduced agroindustrial firms in terms of total area
under crop cultivation. See Jaime Forero Álvarez, Juan Andrés
Galarza, Luz Elba Torres, and José Luis Forero, "La Economía
Campesina Colombiana 1990–2001," 27–29, cited in Albert Berry,
"Agriculture, Rural Development, and Attempts at Land Reform
in Colombia," in Bruce M. Bagley and Jonathan D. Rosen, eds.,
*Colombia's Political Economy at the Outset of the Twenty-First
Century* (Lanham, MD, 2015), 42.

18. "Colombia: Chance to Fix Flawed Transitional Justice Law,"
Human Rights Watch, July 6, 2017.

19. The numbers of the U.S. Office on National Drug Policy—as
always—are different than those of UNODC. The increase from
2015 to 2016, according to the White House Office of National
Drug Control Policy, is 18 percent, amounting to a total of 188,000
hectares. See "ONDCP Releases Data on Cocaine Production
and Cultivation in Colombia," March 14, 2017. Among the most
discerning analysts of the illegal drug business is Hernando
Zuleta at the Universidad de los Andes. See his interview,
"¿Qué hay detrás del aumento de cultivos ilícitos en el país?" *El
Espectador*, July 14, 2017.

20. Independent Task Force Report, "A Roadmap for U.S.
Engagement with Colombia," Atlantic Council, May 2017.

21. Congressional Research Service analyst Marian Leonardo
Lawson has reported that State Department security assistance
remains "largely unevaluated." The Center for Global
Development titled its report about the imperative of requiring
independent project and program evaluations *When Will We
Ever Learn? Improving Lives through Impact Evaluation*, Report of

the Evaluation Working Group, Center for Global Development, May 2006.

22. Nicholas Casey, "With Rebels Gone, Colombia Jumps into the Pot Industry," *New York Times*, March 9, 2017.

23. See Updates from WOLA, "The Past Week in Colombia's Peace Process," April 21, 2017. http://colombiapeace.org/2017/04/21/the-past-week-in-colombias-peace-process.

24. Joint press conference of President Trump and President Santos of Colombia, May 18, 2017, The White House. https://www.whitehouse.gov/the-press-office/2017/05/18/remarks-president-trump-and-president-santos-colombia-joint-press. Two weeks after Santos's visit, the Trump administration's proposed foreign aid budget left no doubts that Washington's priorities were rapidly moving away from Latin America. Overall aid was cut by 35 percent to Latin America and the Caribbean with aid to Colombia cut by $140 million and foreign military financing reduced to zero for Colombia and all of Latin America.

25. On June 13, 2017, before the Senate Foreign Relations Committee, Secretary of State Rex Tillerson, in response to a question advocating a return to aerial spraying, replied: "We have told them, though, we've got to get back to the spraying; we've got to get back to destroying these fields. [We've told them] that they're in a very bad place now in cocaine supply to the United States, and the president talked to President Santos directly about that." President Santos, Environment Minister Luis Gilberto Murillo, eradication chief Eduardo Díaz, and Vice President Gen. Oscar Naranjo, a longtime former National Police chief who supervised the spraying program near its height, all responded that aerial spraying was a failed program. The State Department later walked back Tillerson's endorsement of a return to aerial spraying. See Adam Isacson, "Colombia and Drugs: Rex Tillerson's 'Coca Confusion,'" *The Crime Report*, June 27, 2017, https://thecrimereport.org/2017/06/27/colombia-and-drugs-washingtons-coca-confusion/. See also Statement of John F. Kelly, United States Marine Corps (Ret.), Former Combatant Commander, United States Southern Command Before the Committee on Homeland Security and Governmental Affairs, April 13, 2016. In his testimony before the Senate Foreign Relations Subcommittee on the Western Hemisphere, Transnational Crime, Civilian Security, Democracy and Human

Rights and Global Women's Issues, Assistant Secretary William R. Brownfield references General Kelly's claim that the United States has "eyes on" 90 percent of the cross-Caribbean, seaborne drug traffic. On average, approximately 2–3 percent of this total is, in fact, interdicted and seized.

26. See Transparency International 2016, https://www.transparency.org/news/feature/corruption_perceptions_index_2016.

27. The Colombian government bases noncompliance with the United States on the extradition treaty to its nonratification by Colombia in 1980. Even Uribe, who claims to have extradited over 1,000 Colombians to the United States, has recently admitted that extradition is illegal. In a written statement sent to the Miami judge regarding the case of Agriculture Minister Andrés Felipe Árias, due to be extradited to Colombia for embezzlement, Uribe said "Colombia does not recognize the treaty as valid or in effect because it was not properly ratified." Adriaan Alsema, "What Do You Mean Colombia's Extradition Treaty with the US Was Never Legal?" *Colombia Reports*, December 22, 2016.

28. Confidential interview with the author: CIA officer who served in the U.S. embassy in Bogotá from 2013 to 2015. See also "Bombardean campamento del 'Clan Úsuga' en Chocó," *Semana*, accessed March 3, 2015, at http://www.semana.com/nacion/articulo/miembros-del-clan-usuga-fueron-bombardeados-en-unguia/448488-3.

29. Adam Isacson, "El ejército colombiano enfrenta incertidumbre después del conflicto," WOLA, accessed March 24, 2016, at https://www.wola.org/es/analisis/el-ejercito-colombiano-enfrenta-incertidumbre-despues-del-conflicto. Given the political prominence of the officer corps and the controversy surrounding its legal accountability for human rights crimes, reduction in force will clearly stress civil-military relations. See also Jon Lee Anderson, "Can Colombia Solve Its Drug Problem through Peace?" *New Yorker*, May 22, 2015.

30. In the 18th century, the hyperactive Spanish Bourbons tried to revitalize their hegemony in the New World by militarizing clientelism as well. They too launched a costly and harebrained program of interdiction to stop smuggling by their imperial tributaries. It went nowhere. Upgrading Nueva Granada to a vice-regency (first in 1717 and again in 1738), the Bourbons

conscripted troops, built up coastal defenses, and poured on taxes while preparing for war against Great Britain. The first war began in 1739, ending a decade later in a gruesome stalemate. Renewed warfare between Britain and Spain (1762–1763 and 1779–1783) eviscerated Bourbon fiscal and commercial reforms and set the stage for colonial rebellion and Spain's loss of its imperium in the New World. Raúl Alameda, *Virreyes y funcionarios neogranadinos ante las reformas borbónicas, 1729–1818* (Bogotá: Academia Colombiana de Ciencias Económicas, 2014), 90–91. See also Frank Safford and Marco Palacios, *Colombia: Fragmented Land, Divided Society* (New York, 2001), 54–62.

31. Adam Isacson, "Why Continued U.S. Support Is Critical for Colombia's Peace Process," *Christian Science Monitor*, January 30, 2017.
32. Bello, "Can the Centre Hold?" *Economist*, May 4, 2017.
33. United Nations Development Programme, Human Development Report 2016, accessed at http://hdr.undp.org/sites/default/files/2016_human_development_report.pdf.
34. Joseph Stiglitz, "Medellin's Metamorphosis Provides a Beacon for Cities around the Globe," *Guardian*, May 8, 2014. In 2014, Medellín was awarded Harvard University's international green prize and hosted the World Urban Forum attended by 22,000 architects, city planners, and elected officials in the same year.
35. " 'En Colombia se cree que la cultura es un lujo y no un derecho': Germán Rey," *Semana*, May 28, 2016.
36. María Paula Rubiano, "Así se puso la primera piedra del Museo de la Memoria," *El Espectador*, April 9, 2016.
37. Gloria Castrillón, "El reto de crear un museo de la memoria," *Semana*, March 18, 2015. Sánchez's comment is in the documentary, "No hubo tiempo para la tristeza," at 31:45.
38. Reuters, "Pope Urges Skeptical Colombians to Accept Peace with Guerrillas," reprinted in *Colombia Reports*, September 9, 2017.

INDEX